Praise for

QUEENS OF A FALLEN WORLD

"What an invigorating book! Cooper asks a haunting question: How different would our world be had this man married either his concubine—who was the loyal mother of his child—or the young heiress he was betrothed to, instead of withdrawing from sexual relationships altogether?"

—Sarah Ruden, translator of Augustine's *Confessions*

"Fascinating and well-written, *Queens of a Fallen World* raises vital questions about the role of women in the founding centuries of Christianity, piecing together a rich backdrop to Augustine's life that has rarely emerged before. Cooper convinces us these women can be recovered, and that through his words and thoughts, their lives shaped the future of a fledgling religion. A brilliant new take."

—Janina Ramirez, author of
Femina: A New History of the Middle Ages,
Through the Women Written Out of It

"A marvelous achievement. Cooper shines her historian's spotlight on an Augustine so vivid in his *Confessions*, but so often overlooked: a man who loved and appreciated women. But *Queens of a Fallen World* does far more. Through her portraits of the four women who mattered most during Augustine's formative years, Cooper sketches an evocative landscape of the late Roman world in Milan and North Africa—from its courts to its churches, from military encampments to rural villas, from empresses to the enslaved. Above all, hers is a world of human beings suffering heartache and loneliness while trying to reconcile the pull of the heart with the lure of ambition."

—Susanna Elm, Sidney H. Ehrman
Professor of European History,
University of California, Berkeley

QUEENS
OF A
FALLEN
WORLD

QUEENS
OF A
FALLEN
WORLD

The Lost Women of
Augustine's *Confessions*

Kate Cooper

BASIC BOOKS
NEW YORK

Basic Books
Hachette Book Group
1290 Avenue of the Americas, New York, NY 10104
www.basicbooks.com

Printed in the United States of America
First Edition: April 2023

Published by Basic Books, an imprint of Perseus Books, LLC, a subsidiary of
Hachette Book Group, Inc. The Basic Books name and logo is a trademark
of the Hachette Book Group.

The Hachette Speakers Bureau provides a wide range of authors for speaking
events. To find out more, go to hachettespeakersbureau.com or email
HachetteSpeakers@hbgusa.com.

Basic Books may be purchased in bulk for business, educational, or promotional
use. For more information, please contact your local bookseller or the Hachette
Book Group Special Markets Department at special.markets@hbgusa.com.

The publisher is not responsible for websites (or their content) that are not
owned by the publisher.

Print book interior design by Linda Mark.

Library of Congress Cataloging-in-Publication Data

Names: Cooper, Kate, 1960– author.
Title: Queens of a fallen world : the lost women of Augustine's Confessions /
    Kate Cooper.
Description: First edition. | New York : Basic Books, 2023. | Includes
    bibliographical references and index. |
Identifiers: LCCN 2022035349 | ISBN 9781541646018 (hardcover) |
    ISBN 9781541646001 (ebook)
Subjects: LCSH: Augustine, of Hippo, Saint, 354–430—Family. | Augustine,
    of Hippo, Saint, 354–430—Relations with women. |
    Women—Rome—Social conditions.
Classification: LCC BR65.A9 C595 2023 | DDC 189/.2—dc23/eng/20221228
LC record available at https://lccn.loc.gov/2022035349

ISBNs: 9781541646018 (hardcover), 9781541646001 (ebook)

LSC-C

Printing 1, 2023

For Hildie, with love and admiration

Contents

Contents

PART 3: THE AFTERMATH

Illustrations

PROLOGUE:
A CHILD WITHOUT
A NAME

IN ROMAN AFRICA, DURING THE LAST YEARS OF EMPEROR Constantine the Great's long reign, a slave spoke up to criticize her master's daughter. The speaker was not the kind of person who is normally noticed by history, since she had neither wealth, nor power, nor legendary beauty. We know very little about her, only that she was a child. We do not know whether she survived to adulthood.

She may have been one of the many Roman children who did not live to see their tenth birthday. This was common in the Roman world, especially, but not only, among slaves and the poor. In the normal way of things, Illa would have been one of the forgotten people of history. But another child noticed her defiant act of truth telling and grew up to speak of what she learned from her.

We do not know what she was called. The one source that remembers her does so only as *ancilla*—the Latin for a handmaid or female slave—or *illa*, which simply means "she." We will meet her more than once in what follows, and we will speak of her as "Illa," letting the unfamiliar Latin form become something like a name.

In the Roman world, people living in slavery did not have legal names. They had informal nicknames, used perhaps by the people who cared for them as children or by those who exploited them when they were old enough to work. A slave's nickname might change with his or her circumstances. A handmaid might be addressed simply as *puella* ("girl") in the same demeaning way that men of color in the Jim Crow South were called "boy." A name was a sign of standing, something a slave did not have. But if Illa had no standing, she had a voice. And, perhaps remarkably, she was not afraid to let herself be heard.

Illa would sometimes run errands with the master's free daughter, and in later life the young mistress remembered her as a fierce little person. From Illa she learned a lesson she would carry with her all her life: that sometimes God's voice speaks through unexpected people. A person's earthly standing does not determine the value of what she or he has to say.

As the daughter of a provincial landowner of modest fortune, the young mistress was also a person who did not expect to be remembered in the historical record. But in the way of things, she grew up to become a mother, and one of her children grew up to become the most influential thinker of Latin Christianity: St. Augustine, bishop of Hippo. The young mistress would find a place in history as St. Monnica, one of the heroines of the early church.

Illa and Monnica grew up together in Roman Numidia, probably in the Tell, the countryside of fertile valleys just south of the coast, in what is now the northeastern corner of Algeria. It was a vast agricultural landscape dotted with rural estates and small communities that, even if they had municipal status, only counted a few thousand souls among their inhabitants. It was not the kind of place where one expected history to be made.

Yet long after she left Africa, Monnica told stories of her childhood to her children and grandchildren, and through her son Augustine, her stories passed into the historical record. They became part of the teachings of Christianity, along with the morals she drew from them. Monnica's childhood companion could not have known that the story of how she challenged her little mistress would be told again and again, across the centuries, to illustrate the idea that we live in a fallen world where the people in power are not always right. This simple insight was central to Augustine's mature thought, and it is in many ways Illa's legacy.

Illa, Monnica, and the other women in our narrative lived and died well over a thousand years ago, and it is surprising how well we know some of them given the passage of time. They were remarkable women. But in the ancient world, remarkable women routinely lived and died without leaving a trace. Only a very few received more than a line or two in the historical sources—one thinks of Mary, mother of Jesus; of Livia, wife of the emperor Augustus; or perhaps of Cleopatra, who was queen of Egypt in her own right. In each case they are remembered for their role in the supporting cast around an important man. Rarely does a source record the woman's inner thoughts.

But with Monnica of Thagaste, this changes. Alone among the women of the ancient Mediterranean world, Monnica raised a son who not only noticed women but explored in depth what he learned from them and broadcast what he learned to the wider world.

Monnica's son Augustine, it has long been acknowledged, was the first ancient writer to produce an autobiography. His *Confessions* tells the story of his early life and the people he knew, and in them he tries to make sense of his thoughts and experiences. In reflecting on his life, he explored wider ideas about the relationship between men and women, forged by years of listening to and even arguing with the women in his life.

Other men had experimented with sharing their private thoughts. Marcus Aurelius had composed his *Meditations* more than two centuries earlier. But Augustine had the instincts of a novelist. He was interested in how the seemingly insignificant facts of daily life, and the seemingly insignificant people in a household—the women and children—contributed to the process in which his character and destiny had taken shape.

Augustine was a man who noticed women. Among the influential figures he captures in his narrative, his mother, Monnica, stands out. He returns again and again to her actions, to the stories she told, to the emotions that colored her life. Historians have long recognized her profound influence on her son, but they have paid less attention to what his writings can tell us about Monnica herself. If we listen closely, in her son's words we can sometimes hear Monnica's voice.

Augustine had been living in an all-male monastic community for some time when he wrote his *Confessions*, so the fact that his reflections on his past are so rich with female characters comes as something of a surprise. As he remembers them, the women he writes about are bright and sharp—even spiteful at times. They are people who have agendas of their own. Not all of them are people he knew personally or cared for, but always, without exception, he shares details about them that we would not otherwise know. In all but two cases, the women of the *Confessions* are figures who would otherwise be lost to history. The two exceptions are the Roman empress Justina and Monnica, Augustine's own mother. In Monnica's case the only other marker of her life that remains is the epitaph inscribed on her tomb—the wide canvas of her life distilled into brief lines about how a virtuous mother is made fortunate by her offspring.

Because he is our only source, the women in this book are in some sense Augustine's women: they are characters in his narrative. We have no way of knowing what they were like aside from what he tells us, what uncomfortable facts he may have buried, or what he may have missed. As grateful as we may be for what he tells us about them in his *Confessions*, they are not the primary focus of the story he is trying to tell, and one can only imagine how the women themselves would have told their own stories. Augustine looms large, and seeing past him requires effort. His own thoughts and feelings keep intruding into the story in a way that is both revealing and distracting. So if we want to be able to imagine what it was like for these women to be alive, we have to be resourceful in reading between the lines.

Augustine and his women lived at a turning point in history, the closing decades of the Roman Empire. The whole Mediterranean was still under Roman rule in those days, and it had long been taken for granted that Rome's power reached to the end of the known world, from the Western Ocean to the desert of the East. But that was changing. Pressure on the northeastern frontier had been building; in Augustine's lifetime barbarian warlords would begin to chisel away whole regions, refashioning them as autonomous kingdoms.

Within living memory, a religious revolution had taken place: in the time of Augustine's grandparents, the emperor Constantine had prayed to the God of the Christians before a battle and pledged himself to their God when his armies proved victorious. It is almost impossible to capture the sense of uncertainty experienced by Roman citizens as the empire was beginning its long decline and by Christians in the brave new world where Christians were no longer a persecuted minority. The possibilities were endless, and the stakes were high.

Augustine's long life spanned from the reign of Constantine's son Constantius (AD 337–362) to the barbarian invasions of the first decades of the fifth century. His mature adulthood fell during the years when the groundwork for the social and cultural world of medieval Latin Christendom was being laid—and as things turned out, he would play a significant part in laying this groundwork. The beliefs he came to hold about love and marriage, about human disappointment and human hope, would have a far-reaching influence on how medieval people saw the world. So, whether they knew it or not, the people in Augustine's life—the *women* in his life—had a profound impact on the lives of Christians for centuries to come.

One of the central tenets of Augustine's mature thought is that as human beings, we can never know the consequences of our actions ahead of time; only God can know the future. We humans are trapped in time, and this compromises us morally: unintended consequences are the stuff of human experience. We have no way of knowing how our actions will intersect with unfolding events or the actions of other human beings, so we can never adequately judge the possible effects of our actions or be sure what is the right thing to do.

This was particularly true where relationships between men and women were concerned. Augustine might have appreciated the irony that one of the things that made the world unpredictable for Roman men was the immense energy Roman women put into seeming biddable. Roman women were full of surprises: as children, they learned to erase the traces of their own efforts wherever possible, even as they passionately pursued their own agendas and goals. This led Roman men to find them baffling. It also makes them worth watching, from a modern historian's perspective: sometimes keeping an eye out for what women were doing behind the scenes can shed a surprising light on the course of events.

Despite his own status as a privileged male, Augustine's writings open a window onto the lives of women from all walks of life. He writes about ordinary housewives, about women living in slavery, and even at times about the women of the imperial family. Often, he gives us surprising and unexpected glimpses into the challenges women faced and the space they were sometimes able to carve out for themselves. The story Augustine tells of the women in his life offers a glimpse of their struggle to maintain their dignity in difficult circumstances and to leave a trace of their lives.

We are used to thinking of the women of the past as silent, since few sources have survived to preserve their voices. But Augustine is not a writer who expects women to be silent. He often found them memorable precisely for what they said. He recalls, for example, his concubine's desperate vow when he ended their relationship and sent her away. Equally unforgettable are his mother's prayers, her cajoling, and her conversations with bishops in her quest for advice on how to shape her errant son into a good Christian. Even the slaves and children in the house where Monnica grew up played a part: one thinks of the elderly nurse who took care of Monnica when she was a child and of Illa, the playmate who challenged her and changed the way she thought about herself.

It should not be surprising, then, that in the *Confessions* enslaved women consistently come across as honest and reliable people capable of speaking truth to power. Augustine was fascinated by the idea that God distributes the ability to do good in the world evenhandedly and that human beings are just as likely to hear his voice speaking through women, slaves, and children as through powerful men. If the *Confessions* is partly a story about women struggling to make a difference, it is also a story about Augustine's own effort to understand those women. He needs to make sense of his relationships with them partly because he knows that those relationships are part of his path toward God.

Four women stand at the center of Augustine's story: an empress testing the limits of her power, an heiress preparing for an arranged marriage, a mother devoted to her son's career, and a woman of humble origins who became the love of Augustine's life. Two shared Augustine's origins in Roman Numidia; two, whom he knew less well, lived out their lives at the imperial court in Italy, where he played a small role during a few heady years in the 380s. Each of the women contributed to shaping Augustine's world and his worldview, along with the legacy he left to history.

We will meet the four women in descending order of their social standing, beginning with an empress and ending with a woman who may have been a slave. In this way, we will spiral in from the wider frame of late Roman society toward a more intimate story about the personal and private struggles of a group of women whose lives intersected more than a thousand years ago, with consequences that perhaps changed history.

Their stories converge in the imperial city of Milan during the pivotal years between 383 and 387, at a time when the Roman Empire was convulsed by civil war. A few years later, in 395, the empire was split permanently into two parts: a strong Eastern Empire centered on Byzantium, which would last for a further thousand years, and a weaker Western Empire with first Milan and then Ravenna as its capital, which was soon broken up into smaller barbarian kingdoms.

Empress Justina, mother of the child emperor Valentinian II and the first of our women, was a figure of unparalleled importance in the Western Empire during these years. History has dismissed her because she lost a propaganda war with a voluble bishop of Milan, Augustine's mentor Ambrose. As with many such conflicts between powerful women and the men who oppose them, it was Ambrose's side of the story that came to be handed down as historical truth. (Indeed, as we will see, Augustine himself played a role in amplifying Ambrose's narrative.)

In cases where historical sources vilify an ambitious woman, there is almost always more to the story. So it is useful to look at the world from Justina's point of view. In doing so, we begin to see that the culture war between empress and bishop was not, strictly speaking, about theological differences, as the sources suggest. It was about the emergence of a new kind of populist leadership in the church, which Justina understandably opposed. Like more than one female leader in more recent history, Justina found herself singled out by a master of misogynist rhetoric, who used stirring up indignation against her as a tool to steer the minds of their contemporaries. Remarkably, Justina was able to hold her ground in spite of the onslaught.

If Justina's ambitions involved the fate of the empire, other women pursued smaller dreams with equal passion. Social mobility in ancient Rome was a game of fortune hunting and marrying well, and shrewd players of the game knew how to play the card of beauty or talent in exchange for social status and wealth. Even at the lower end of the social scale, being attractive to the right people could be a meal ticket to survival and perhaps even security.

The spark that sent Augustine's life up in flames was a dowry, one belonging to a ten-year-old Milanese heiress whom he barely knew. It is unlikely that the child ever recognized the role their short-lived betrothal played in Augustine's story or what mark the catastrophic mess he made of it left on his thought. But through this young woman, a pawn in the marriage game, we can begin to grasp the paradox that wealth and social standing sometimes meant very little to women and girls; often what they wanted was simply to stay close to their families.

Of our four women, we know Monnica most intimately, thanks to the many stories she told her children about her own childhood in the plains of Roman Numidia and her early married life in Thagaste. Her story, as Augustine remembers it, is the saga of a woman who lived for her children, did her best to manage an abusive husband, and found in widowhood a kind of freedom that she had not known as a daughter or wife.

Monnica's influence on Augustine was profound, especially in her moral reasoning. He returns again and again to emphasize the lessons she taught him: to always look below the surface of a situation, to listen for what is going unsaid and to recognize the role that unexpected or unrecognized people might play in the course of events. Through her influence on her son's way of thinking, Monnica contributed an element of moral depth to the history of Christian thought. And at the center of her story there is something unique in ancient literature: the account of an unusually close friendship between a woman and her son.

Yet of all the women in Augustine's life, the one who perhaps came closest to knowing the truth of Augustine is the woman who lived with him as his star began to ascend, the mother of his illegitimate son. She crossed the Mediterranean with Augustine and stayed by his side for over fifteen years. His mishandling of the end of their relationship and her dignified reaction to his cruel treatment permanently damaged his sense of himself.

Augustine's concubine is the most elusive of our heroines because he skates over her story in the *Confessions* very swiftly. It is difficult to say whether he veils her identity to protect her or because it pains him to confront his memory of her more clearly; perhaps both things are true. One imagines Augustine mid-dictation, opening an old wound and finding the feelings too fresh, too intimate, and perhaps too human to confess to his God. A review of his later writings suggests that he agonized for the rest of his life over the circumstances of their parting.

Whatever Augustine may have wished or allowed her to believe, he could never have seriously intended to stay with her or marry her. Marriage was a carefully calculated game of advantage, and Augustine had long ago accepted that he would marry the richest woman who would have him. But when he and Monnica finally found their heiress and arranged the betrothal, he could not bring himself to go through with the marriage. His handling of the episode was a disaster that had far-reaching consequences. On the evidence of Augustine's writings, both the *Confessions* and his later work, the episode shook the foundation of his self-understanding. It was the catalyst that started him on the path away from being a self-involved thirty-something and toward becoming an ethical thinker whose writings would endure long after his death.

What, if anything, did these four women have in common? Augustine's narrative offers a rare opportunity to explore how women of different social backgrounds navigated the pressures and constraints of family and ambition in fourth-century Roman society and how much they had in common despite the vast differences of social class.

Theirs was a world where women were generally treated by their menfolk as pawns. In this game the single best opportunity for a woman lay in her ability to manage her sexual attractiveness. This involved a balancing act familiar to women across the centuries: being attractive but not too available—or available only on very specific terms. If she came from a respectable family, this meant refusing sex outside marriage. She would wed early, in her early to mid-teens, usually in an arranged marriage to a man who might well be twice her age, perhaps the owner of neighboring land or a business partner of her father. For a woman lower down the social scale, whether slave or free, things were more complicated. Controlling who had sexual access to her body was even more difficult. Avoiding sex altogether was often unrealistic, so the goal was to find someone who would shield her from the predatory attention of other men.

In a society that afforded few opportunities to act independently of men, women's energy was largely channeled into trying to manage and mitigate the intentions and impact of the men around them. A woman who was both lucky and skillful could hope to capture the eye of a man above her on the social ladder and be lifted by him into opportunity. But it was a risky game, and even apparent success might come with unpleasant or dangerous consequences. Most women simply tried to make the best of their situation, be it an arranged marriage or, for those of low status, a more exploitative arrangement.

If women needed the help and protection men could offer, they also knew that husbands and lovers could not be counted on. The one man a woman could love without reservation was her son. Women with sons knew themselves to be paragons of good fortune. Bearing a son gave a woman status in the eyes of her community, and it gave her an unparalleled opportunity to cultivate a genuinely devoted male ally. A son was the man with whom she had the best chance of creating a relationship of trust and for whom she would reserve her fiercest loyalty. Three of our four women had sons, and it was their devotion to these sons that informed their actions.

In what follows we will begin by exploring the hopes and intentions of each of our heroines, trying to understand her aims, the constraints she faced—and, where possible, her blind spots. Next, we will examine the crisis that erupted when their lives intersected—a crisis that would have far-reaching consequences for the women themselves, for Augustine, and for the future of Christianity. In the final part of the book, we will look at Augustine's later efforts to make sense of what happened and what he had learned.

What primed Augustine to notice the quiet struggles of women was a childhood spent listening to his mother's stories. His narrative gifts clearly owed a great deal to Monnica: she was a born storyteller and a thoughtful observer, someone who noticed things other people missed. She had grown up in a household where both enslaved and free women tested the boundaries of the domestic social order and looked for opportunities to speak up for themselves, and she had paid close attention to how their efforts played out.

Through Monnica's stories, as Augustine remembered and retold them, we gain a sense of what one ancient woman was able to make of the world around her, of the wisdom she was able to pass onto her children. But we will also have to reckon with the limits of that wisdom: during the heady and dangerous years in Milan, both Augustine and Monnica faced difficult choices.

Some of the choices they made are well known to historians: for example, Augustine's decision not to marry, which opened his path to an unexpected and influential future as a Christian bishop. But what has been less well understood is that the choice was part of a wider web of consequence. It was taken in the threatening atmosphere of civil war, in a city that was soon to face invasion by a hostile army.

Historical distance has a way of ironing away the specific texture of a place and time, and for this reason modern readers of the *Confessions* have tended to miss the fact that in the Milan of the mid-380s, things were not always what they seemed. In making their private and personal decisions, Augustine and those around him had to take into account the consequences that might follow from trusting the wrong person or betting on the wrong faction.

In this context, matters of the heart could also be a matter of life and death. Things could quickly spiral out of control, and decisions had to be made without knowing which seemingly insignificant choice might bring disaster. Even afterward, it was impossible to be sure of why things played out as they did.

Of course it is even more difficult for historians to make such judgments long after the fact. But we should recognize that the forces of history may be steered by a person whom others overlook or fail to notice: someone who would never dream of herself as a person of consequence but who nonetheless hopes to leave her mark on the world.

PART 1

∞

FOUR WOMEN

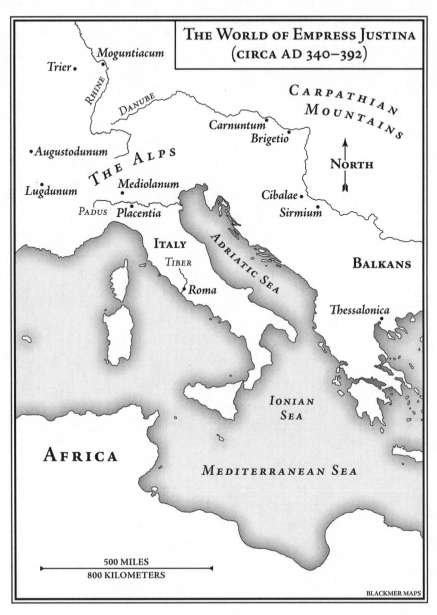

MAP 1. A daughter of the House of Constantine, the empress Justina was the wife of two emperors, mother of a third, and mother-in-law to a fourth. The life of an empress was in many ways luxurious, but it involved hardships, including travel across vast distances to be close to a husband who was often at the frontier. *Credit: Kate Blackmer.*

Chapter One

JUSTINA

I N THE CIVIC MUSEUM AT COMO, ITALY, A MARBLE POR-
trait survives of a fourth-century Roman empress whom many
scholars identify as Justina. This may be wishful thinking: no
other likeness of the empress survives. Vivid and controversial, Justina
has been sidelined by history, largely because she found herself on the
losing side of the great theological dispute of the fourth century, the
Trinitarian controversy.

Still, the Como portrait captures something of what we know of
the empress from other sources: her large, deep eyes and strong brow
convey intelligence, charisma, and a certain ferocity. The most striking thing about the portrait is the empress's gaze, which is lifted up
toward heaven. The marble has been drilled deeply so that the irises
and pupils of her eyes are arresting. Large, almost oversized eyes are
a hallmark of portraits of members of the House of Constantine;
this was a way of signaling the spiritual power of the God-favored

dynasty. It may also have reflected a physical characteristic shared by Constantine's relatives.

Framing her face is a mane of hair that has been brought under firm control in braided tresses. The hairstyle, one that was in vogue in the last quarter of the fourth century, is designed to create a setting for the distinctive jeweled diadem of the era. To begin with, the hair is divided at the crown of the head, with the tresses plaited and wound down around the head and looped below the ears. The diadem itself takes the shape known as the "stephane," the crested headband worn by ancient goddesses. A row of precious jewels in coffered settings runs along the band, with a finer row of pearls just above the hairline. A large jewel takes pride of place at the central point above the empress's brow.

Splendor of this type was required of an empress, who was meant to project a blazing vision of the imperial family's power and charisma. But the luxury and splendor of her person could also make her a target. The Roman tradition had always treated glamorous women ambivalently, as a source of fascination but also, by the same token, as a focus of resentment or scorn. In her early thirties, Justina was the dazzlingly beautiful trophy wife of the emperor Valentinian I, and in her late thirties and forties, after her husband's death in 375, she played a difficult and dangerous role as the advisor and protector of her son Valentinian II. Like many powerful women, she had many enemies—but if her enemies expected to sideline her, they had not anticipated her indomitable will.

Our sources for Justina's life concentrate on a brief period when she was in her mid-forties. This period began in August 383, when her stepson Gratian was murdered, leaving her twelve-year-old son Valentinian II as sole sovereign of the Western Roman Empire. The sources carry on through Easter of 385, when she was involved in a passionate face-off with the imperial capital's bishop, Ambrose of Milan, and begin to fade after the autumn of 387, by which time she had found a way to secure Valentinian's safety despite the fact that the man who had caused Gratian's death, the usurper Maximus, had invaded Italy and captured Milan.

The sources are almost uniformly unreliable, and it is often difficult to be sure where Justina was living at a given moment in time, even during her years as an empress. Like other women, empresses were expected to be seen and not heard, and when an empress was noticed at all, it was often as a target for criticism.

This is particularly true of Justina, because much of what we know about her comes from writers who took the side of Bishop Ambrose during the conflict that emerged between the two of them. One of these writers was Augustine, and we will see in a later chapter that his mother, Monnica, played a small part in the conflict herself.

Ambrose would become one of the heroes of medieval Latin Christendom, and it is for this reason that the surviving sources view Justina unfavorably. The operative word here is "surviving": almost certainly, other sources of the period presented Justina as a heroine in her own right or documented the phases of collaboration between the empress and the bishop rather than focusing on what seems to have been a short-lived conflict. But Ambrose's first biographer wanted to paint his hero as courageous in defying the imperial family, and so he depicted Justina—wrongly—as a committed heretic and the bishop's sworn enemy. Afterward, medieval librarians, who had an unfortunate tendency to purge their libraries of works believed to encourage unorthodox views, took care to eliminate any positive accounts of the empress. So Justina passed into history as a holy bishop's nemesis.

Reading between the lines of the surviving sources, we can see that the central conflict between Ambrose and Justina turned on whether the Christian Church should fall under the authority of the Roman state. At precisely the same time, in the Eastern Roman Empire, the groundwork was being laid for a very different theology, one that encouraged both church and state to obey the authority of an emperor chosen by God. But Ambrose championed the idea that the church should challenge earthly authority in God's name. To the extent that there was a genuine conflict between Ambrose and Justina, this was its source: like many fourth-century Christians, Justina believed that the emperor was responsible for the flourishing of the church and that the church in turn should obey the emperor. She would not have been surprised to learn that it was the Eastern Empire, placing its trust in a divinely appointed ruler, that flourished for a millennium after her death, even as the Western Empire spun into a chaos from which it would never recover.

Justina was one of a dying breed, among the last daughters of the House of Constantine. Constantine the Great, the dynasty's namesake, was the scion of a military family from the Balkans, warriors who rode beneath the standards of the Invincible Sun. But in the autumn of 312—so the story goes—a voice from heaven spoke to him, directing him to place his armies under the protection of an obscure Eastern divinity, the Christ. The next day, at the Battle of the Milvian Bridge, he destroyed his rival Maxentius and captured Rome. The God of the Christians had delivered a decisive victory: while the city was no longer the imperial residence, it was still the empire's greatest prize. After his victory at the Milvian Bridge, Constantine began to shower the Christian churches with favors, and Christianity began a new chapter as an imperial faith.

The women of Constantine's family were already known for their fierce character; now they became famous for their outstanding piety. Constantine's mother, the empress Helena, traveled to the Holy

Land and returned with an incomparable treasure, wood from the very cross on which Jesus had been crucified. His daughter Constantina proved both a political power broker and a patron of the church. The newly powerful Christian bishops were a mixed blessing for the imperial women. With their appreciation of female piety, the bishops were often valuable allies, but in their sermons they sometimes railed against women as sirens who would lure even the chastest of men away from God. Inflammatory rhetoric was always popular, and few bishops could resist the temptation to play to the crowd.

After Constantine died in 337, his sons divided the empire into three parts, which soon became two when one brother died. With one emperor in the East and another in the West, for the rest of the century Milan—not Rome—was the beating heart of the Western Empire. This was a sensible choice. The city was the all-important gateway between Italy and the frontier provinces, where the imperial armies were struggling against increasingly confident barbarian raiding parties. From 340 to 402, the Western court was more often in Milan than any other city, though other imperial palaces at Trier (Augusta Treverorum), Vienne, Sirmium, and Aquileia stood at the ready. In the 380s the poet Ausonius praised the "abundant wealth and innumerable stately homes" of the city, with its double walls, its circus and theater—"the people's delight"—and the sprawling imperial palace.[1] At the Baths of Hercules, the city's elite could take exercise—it was also a place to see each other and be seen. Milan was now a city not only of gleaming marble and glittering mosaic but of new money and new men.

Justina was well placed to understand the opportunities and dangers of such an environment. Her mother is believed to have been a niece or granddaughter of Constantine the Great himself, while her father, Justus, was governor of Picenum on the Adriatic coast of Italy.

As a daughter of the House of Constantine, she was a political player from her earliest years, witnessing the deadly games played by rival emperors from close range.

In the 340s, when Justina was a child, she was already a valuable political pawn. The Western Empire was ruled by Constans, the youngest of Constantine's sons, and her father, Justus, was close to Magnentius, the commander of the Imperial Guard. Both Justus and Magnentius were ambitious men. In January 350, when Justina was around ten, Magnentius moved against Constans, allowing an army at Autun in Gaul to proclaim him emperor in his own right. Soon afterward the usurper's supporters killed the unfortunate Constans, and as his popularity increased, Magnentius set his sights on the emperor of the East, Constantius II. Now Justina came into play. Despite the disparity in their ages—Magnentius was nearly fifty at the time—she was a female member of the reigning dynasty who could crown the usurper with a laurel of legitimacy. And so a marriage between Magnentius and Justina was arranged.

Justina's betrothal is almost certainly a sign that her father had cast his lot with the usurper, who seems to have attracted support from well-connected civilians as well as generals. Technically, the marriage in 350 was only a betrothal given the bride's age. Marriage could not take place under Roman law before she was twelve, but it was not uncommon for girls to be sent to live with a future husband's family to secure a promised union. We don't know whether this happened in Justina's case, but the ancient sources state that she remained a virgin throughout her marriage to Magnentius and for many years afterward.

After a three-year civil war with Constantius II, Magnentius accepted the failure of his cause, and in 353 he committed suicide. In the reshuffle after his death, Justina's family understandably came under suspicion. According to the fifth-century writer Socrates of Constantinople, Constantius turned against Justina's father because of a dream. "Justus...had a dream in which he seemed to himself to bring forth the imperial purple out of his right side. When this dream had been told to many persons, it at length came to the knowledge of Constantius, who conjecturing it to be a presage that a descendant of Justus would become emperor, caused him to be assassinated."[2] But as it turned out, Socrates reasons, the dream had been misunderstood. The purple had been a premonition not that one of the sons of Justus would be a usurper but that his daughter Justina would be the mother and grandmother of rulers long after the death of her father.

Later, as a widow, Justina caught the attention of another, more successful self-proclaimed Roman emperor, Valentinian I, who divorced his first wife in order to claim her. Justina's legendary beauty may have been one reason for this, but the other was again her bloodline. As it had for Magnentius, marriage to Justina opened the door for Valentinian to claim continuity with the God-favored dynasty of Constantine.

We do not know what happened to Justina immediately after her first husband's death. She may have remained in Milan, which was a favored seat of the Western emperors. We have no trace of the fate of her mother, and Justina herself disappears from the historical record until around 370, when she was nearly thirty. By the late 360s her brothers Constantianus and Cerealis were in Valentinian's service; Valentinian's father had also been a supporter of Magnentius, so the connection between the two families may have had deeper roots. The brothers succeeded one another as tribune of the stables (*tribunus stabuli*), the key procurement officer for the cavalry, first Constantianus, and when he died in 369, Cerealis. No ancient source records whether Cerealis had a hand in Justina's elevation as empress in 370, but it seems likely.

Still, the ancient sources record that it was through Severa, the first wife of Valentinian I, that Justina met her second husband. Severa and Valentinian initially had their home base in the imperial city of Sirmium in the Balkans, not far from Cibalae, the emperor's birthplace. This is where their son Gratian was born in 359. When Valentinian became emperor in 364, they moved west—first to Milan and then, a few years later, to the imperial palace at Trier in Gaul, close to the Rhine frontier. (The imperial court would not return to Milan until 381.) It was possible that Justina became attached to Severa's entourage while the court was in Milan.

Socrates records that Severa and Justina were close friends. "Eventually, their intimacy grew to such an extent that they were accustomed to bathe together."[3] Accompanying the empress at the baths was a very public sign of favor, since the baths were a venue for sociability and people watching. This almost certainly took place at Trier, where the massive imperial baths built in Constantine's day still stand.

As is the custom in a modern hammam, times were set aside for women to bathe together without the presence of men. This allowed them to bathe unclothed, and Socrates observes that when Severa saw Justina's perfect body, she could not contain her admiration. He writes, "She spoke of her to the Emperor, saying that the daughter of Justus was so lovely a creature, and possessed of such symmetry of form, that she herself, though a woman, was altogether charmed with her."[4] This seemingly innocent comment led to a change of fortunes for both women.

According to Socrates, the mere description of the radiant Justina led the emperor to decide to claim her for himself. "The Emperor, treasuring this description by his wife in his own mind, considered with himself how he could marry Justina."[5] Yet, perhaps to his credit, he did not want to set aside Severa, whose son Gratian had only recently been proclaimed as his co-emperor. According to Socrates, Valentinian took advantage of his position as lawgiver to resolve the problem: "He framed a law and caused it to be published throughout all the cities, by which any man was permitted to have two lawful wives."[6]

Polygamy was not unknown to the Romans. The imperial armies had been at war with neighboring Persia on and off for centuries, and within living memory the Persian emperor's wives, sisters, and children had been captured and presented to the emperor Diocletian as a spoil of war by one of his generals. But no trace survives of a fourth-century law of the type mentioned by Socrates. It is also possible that Valentinian intended not to institute bigamy but to assert the traditional right of a Roman citizen to divorce and remarry, which had been challenged by Christian churchmen.

Yet later historians looked for other explanations. Some suggested that Severa had been brought down by her own wrongdoing. In one version of the story, the empress had bought a garden from a woman who ran a nursery business, and when the surveyor came to make the valuation, he had undervalued the property in order to gain the empress's favor. As a result, Severa had paid the woman only a fraction of the property's true worth. When the emperor heard what had happened, he sent his own surveyors to value the property, "god-fearing men, and he bound them by a solemn oath to value it justly and equitably."[7] When a far higher valuation came back and the dishonesty of the original valuer was revealed, the emperor was livid. Holding the empress responsible, Valentinian "drove her from the palace and took to wife a woman named Justina, with whom he lived all the rest of his days."[8] The seventh-century chronicler who remembers this version of the story wanted to underscore the fair-mindedness of Valentinian, a man so concerned for his subjects that he was willing to cast aside even the mother of his son to ensure their fair treatment. But whatever the truth of how Justina came to replace her friend as empress, the moral of the story was the same: a place at the top of the imperial pyramid was never safe, and even one's closest friends could not always be trusted. Justina's rise understandably caused a rupture between the two women, but Severa could not have been surprised that Justina took her chance when it came.

The new empress quickly made the most of her elevation, bearing four children in rapid succession. First came a son, Valentinian, in 371, and then three sisters: Galla, Grata, and Justa. If beauty was highly valued, bearing children was even more important as a path to gaining what security an empress might reasonably hope for.

When Valentinian left for the northeastern frontier, Justina and her children settled at an imperial villa, Murocincta, near the military camp in Carnuntum. This was roughly three days' journey west of where the emperor and his armies were campaigning against the Quadi, in what is now northern Hungary. Although imperial women were by no means entirely protected from the rigors of the military lives their husbands led, on this occasion her accommodation was luxurious. Standing between Bruckneudorf and Parndorf in eastern Austria, the thirty-four-room villa was first excavated in the 1930s. The quality of its decoration—including splendid mosaic floors and richly frescoed walls—is such that more recent scholarship has asked whether the site should be understood as an imperial palace rather than a villa belonging to the imperial family.[9] The challenge of life at Murocincta was not in the standard of living but in its remoteness from the great courts where Justina had spent most of her life. But Valentinian's future depended on his father, and his father was at the frontier.

Justina's stepson Gratian, who had been proclaimed co-emperor with his father, was far away in the imperial city of Trier in the

Rhineland, watching over the northern frontier and making an effort to establish his own dynasty. In 374, the year before his father's death, he married the imperial princess Flavia Maxima Constantia, the daughter of Constantius II, who may have been Justina's cousin. The story of Constantia's journey to meet Gratian for their wedding illustrates both the toughness and the vulnerability of imperial women, who might be left in comparative isolation while their menfolk were on campaign, then expected to travel long distances to appear at their husbands' side when needed. These journeys were often dangerous, as wealthy women were targeted by brigands as prizes to be captured for ransom. Constantia's wedding journey offers a memorable example. En route from Constantinople to meet Gratian in Trier, she passed through Pannonia, where Valentinian's armies were attempting to drive back the Quadi, who were raiding villages and taking captives of either sex to be sold as slaves.

Constantia's entourage had stopped at a public inn, Ammianus tells us, when a raiding party arrived.[10] It was a close call: the raiders very nearly captured the princess, but fortunately for Constantia, the governor of the province was monitoring her journey very carefully, knowing that he would be held responsible for any harm she came to while in the territory under his control. He surprised the brigands and, making use of the state carriage, conveyed her to safety in the provincial capital at Sirmium. Ammianus drops the story there; the travels of a princess were not of interest to a military historian. But her capture would have been an incident to reckon with, and even a near miss was important enough to record.

Ammianus does not say how long Constantia remained at Sirmium or whether she visited Justina during her sojourn in the region. But we catch a glimpse of them being commemorated together in June of the same year, when Constantia made her first surviving appearance as empress on a public inscription. This is the dedication of a bath complex made by the emperors Valentinian and Gratian to their queens (*regnis suis*) on June 24, 374.[11] The inscription records the expectation of a harmonious future for the two emperors and their consorts, marking the hope that the stability of these marriages—and the resulting sons—would keep the empire safe.

Sadly, this was not to be. Constantia would die childless nine years later, in 383. Even in death, an empress was a prize to be protected and displayed; the ancient sources record that her body arrived in Constantinople for burial in the imperial mausoleum on August 31, 383. By then, the two emperors had died as well. Valentinian I died in 375, and Gratian died shortly after his wife in 383. Justina outlived them all.

Valentinian was at the legionary base at Brigetio on the Danube when he died in November 375, and though Justina was absent, her brother Cerealis, Valentinian's tribune of the stables, was on the scene and took swift action. Cerealis made the three-day journey to retrieve Justina's son, who was with his mother at Murocincta. The army agreed unanimously that the four-year-old should be proclaimed emperor in his father's stead, to rule the Western Empire jointly with his older brother Gratian. "When this had been approved by unanimous consent, the boy's uncle Cerealis was immediately sent to the place; he put him in a sedan chair, and brought him to the camp."[12] It all happened very quickly. "On the sixth day after the passing of his father, he was in due form declared emperor and after the customary manner hailed as Augustus."[13] The four-year-old Valentinian the Younger was now co-emperor with his older half brother Gratian.

The rub was that he had been proclaimed without waiting for his brother Gratian or his uncle Valens, the emperor of the East, to be consulted. Ammianus records that Gratian, who was ruling the

Western Empire jointly with their father, was far away at Trier when the proclamation was made. Gratian's reaction was to take the boy into custody, ostensibly in order to educate him. Ammianus insists that his motive was generous: "Besides being a kindly and righteous man, Gratian loved his kinsman with great affection and saw to his education."[14] But in practical terms, he may have wanted to control his newly powerful younger brother. The evidence suggests that the boy was whisked away to Gratian's court at Trier. But Justina may not have been welcome there, at least initially, due to strained relations with the dowager empress, Gratian's mother Severa.

There is some evidence to suggest that Justina and her daughters moved to the imperial city of Sirmium after her husband's death and that she was a patron of the church there, though she was a partisan of what would become the losing faction. Like most members of her family, Justina was a follower of the teachings of Eusebius of Nicomedia, the bishop who had baptized Constantine the Great. Under Eusebius's instruction, Constantine had rejected the creed of the Council of Nicaea, which taught that Jesus, the Son of God, was "begotten, not made, of one being with the Father." This view was later called "Arian" by the Nicene faction in an attempt to discredit it by linking it to Arius, a priest who had been condemned at Nicaea, but it was in fact the "orthodox" Christians from the point of view of most of the imperial family for most of Justina's lifetime.

In any case, Justina may not have been an entrenched supporter of the Eusebian cause. For example, one of her associates, whose headquarters was at Sirmium up to 375, was a fierce backer of the Nicene party. This was Sextus Petronius Probus, the senior civil officer of the Western Empire under her husband Valentinian. From 368 to 375, he served as praetorian prefect of Italy, Illyricum, and Africa, the imperial magistrate to whom the governors of the region reported. Perhaps thanks to his connections in this role, Probus seems to have been pivotal in securing the younger Valentinian's position at his father's death; one source indicates that it was Probus, as prefect, who gave the order for the boy to be crowned without waiting for the assent of his uncle and older brother.[15]

While at Sirmium, Probus had a brilliant protégé, Aurelius Ambrosius, also a member of the Nicene party. Given their shared connection to Probus, it is not surprising that Ambrose and Justina initially became allies when they both found themselves in Milan a few years later. But differences between them emerged, with far-reaching repercussions. Ambrose would become the great champion of the Nicene cause in the Western Empire.

Though her movements in this period are uncertain, by 378 Justina seems to have followed her son to Trier, a move characterized by one ancient writer as a reluctant return from exile. Gratian's mother, Severa, may have died around this time. (The date of her death is unknown, but it must have taken place during Gratian's reign, since it is Severa, not Justina, who is buried next to their husband Valentinian.)

Alternatively, the military events of that year may have led Justina to want to be closer to her son and her surviving brother. In August 378, only three years after the senior Valentinian's death, catastrophe struck the Eastern Empire. The Gothic armies won an astonishing victory at Hadrianople, well south of the Danube frontier and dangerously close to the Eastern capital at Constantinople. At Hadrianople the emperor Valens was killed, and Gratian, who arrived on the scene only after the fact, was left in command of a dispirited army. As he was now the senior emperor, Gratian's first task was to find someone to replace his uncle as emperor of the East; we will see in a later chapter that his choice, the Spanish general Theodosius, swiftly became a force to reckon with. It has been suggested that on the accession of Theodosius, Justina left Sirmium, which would now be subject to him rather than to a member of Valentinian's family.[16]

Justina's whereabouts are next firmly attested in Milan in the early 380s. Concern for the Danube frontier led Gratian to move his court from Trier in the Rhineland to Milan in 381, in order to be able to reach the frontier more swiftly than he could from Gaul. In Milan, the forces that would test Justina were brought into alignment.

To begin with, Milan was the city where Ambrose—now bishop— was building his power base. Initially, relations were cordial between Ambrose and Justina, and this was lucky for them both, because they soon faced another catastrophe. In the summer of 383, the usurper Magnus Maximus challenged Gratian for the purple, and on August 25, at Lugdunum (modern Lyons), Gratian was killed. Maximus was now in a position to make a play for the whole Western Empire. His logical next step was to eliminate Gratian's co-emperor, Valentinian, who was now twelve.

When news arrived that her stepson had been murdered, Justina faced the greatest challenge of what had already been an alarmingly eventful life. She knew that the consequences for Valentinian would be a matter of life or death. As the mother of the boy who was now sole Western emperor, she was the most powerful woman—by some accounts the most powerful person—in the Western Empire. If she could protect her son until he reached maturity, the future would belong to him. But for now, Valentinian was in danger.

Initially, Maximus moved slowly and deliberately. He took up residence in Gratian's former capital at Trier, and in the autumn of 383 he sent an ambassador, Count Victor, south to Milan with a curious offer addressed to Valentinian. Come to Trier with your mother, ran the message, and I will treat you as my own son. Of course, once the young emperor was in Maximus's keeping, there was no guarantee that the usurper would be true to his word.

But the court at Milan was ahead of Maximus. War, they felt, was inevitable, and Bishop Ambrose was sent on the twenty-five-day journey across the Alps to dissuade Maximus from an immediate invasion. He had already reached Moguntiacum (now Mainz), four days' journey from Trier, when he met the envoy Count Victor on his way south. When he reached Trier, Ambrose let it be understood that Valentinian might be receptive to the usurper's offer, even though this presumably involved letting Maximus act as senior emperor of the West.

Valentinian could not possibly travel without his mother at such a young age, Ambrose suggested, and his mother could not possibly cross the Alps in winter. Ambrose was highly skilled in the arts of persuasion, and Maximus accepted his reasoning. Still, as a precaution, he insisted that Ambrose remain in Trier until Victor had returned safely from Milan. Ambrose was finally on his way home, months later, when he crossed paths with another embassy from Milan, this time carrying the news that Valentinian had decisively rejected Maximus's offer. The Alpine passes were now garrisoned against an invasion. The question now was not whether Maximus would move against Valentinian but when the move would take place.

Ambrose, it seems, had bought time for Valentinian's preparations. He was an ally worth having, and in the crisis he showed courage as well as skill in service of the young emperor. In all likelihood it was his former mentor Petronius Probus who had recommended him for the role, certainly for his outstanding skill as a negotiator and perhaps also for his willingness—in service of a good cause—to make free with the truth.

From early 384 to the spring of 387, relations between Maximus and Valentinian settled into a tense holding pattern. Maximus built up his forces in Gaul, while the less experienced Valentinian tried to do the same in Italy. It was an open secret that when Gratian had begun to falter, his armies had deserted him for Maximus. Given his lack of battlefield experience, there was every danger that the same might happen to Valentinian.

Justina's task in these tense months was to bolster a network of loyal supporters. Maximus was almost certainly counting on the fact that he and the Eastern emperor Theodosius were old brothers in arms; they had served in Valentinian the Elder's army together. Maximus had lost valuable time due to the blandishments of Ambrose, but there was a danger that if Maximus led a successful invasion, Ambrose would swing behind him. During his long stay at Trier, Ambrose had been posing as a friendly ambassador, and it would not be surprising if he had developed a bond of trust with men in the usurper's entourage. There was also the dangerous fact that Ambrose and Maximus were both adherents of the Nicene Creed, while Justina accepted the creed approved at the Council of Rimini in 359. An intractable conflict had emerged between the Nicene bishops and those who subscribed to Rimini. So despite his many gifts, Ambrose could not be trusted; only Justina herself was committed to Valentinian above all else.

Ultimately Valentinian's fate was going to depend on whom the Eastern emperor Theodosius preferred as a colleague: a general or an inexperienced child. Theodosius and Maximus had served together during the African rebellion of the 360s; this, and their shared Nicene affiliation, gave Maximus an advantage. But there was a case to be made that Theodosius might prefer working with a malleable protégé instead of an independent-minded equal; here lay Justina's chance. With luck, her keen intelligence and long years of experience might prove the usurper's undoing. But in the end, people make their own luck. Somehow, Justina was going to have to gain the ear of the Eastern emperor.

Justina's ferocity in defending Valentinian went beyond a mother's love for her son. Having witnessed more than one regime change at close quarters, she knew that thousands of lives depended on the safety of this one person. When a ruler is deposed by violence, a period of chaos follows. The usurper's followers vie with one another for dominance, and ruthlessly destroying anyone who stands in the way of the new regime becomes a way to prove their loyalty. This had already happened in Gaul after the death of Gratian, and she would not allow it to happen in Italy. It would not be long before Valentinian was old enough to command an army. In the meantime, it fell to Justina to keep her son safe—or die trying.

~ CHAPTER TWO ~

TACITA

I N THE SUMMER OF 386, RUMORS OF A COMING INVASION
were spreading through Milan, but in the airy villas of the
wealthy, an effort was made to avoid discussing such matters in
front of the children. And so the child whose part in our story we
will now consider may not have known about her parents' fears or
the plans they were laying in case things began to spin out of control.
She would have known, however, that her own small life had reached
a crisis: she was engaged to be married to a man not much younger
than her father, a husband whose homeland was far away in Africa.
This last fact may have been kept from her, since he was settled in
Milan for the foreseeable future, and the idea of traveling so far from
her parents would have been a shock. She was still small; her fiancé,
Augustine, was in his early thirties, but she herself was only ten. We
don't know her name, but I have always thought of her as Tacita, a
Roman name that means "the silent one."

If Tacita was witty and clearheaded and able to stand up for herself like the other women in his life, Augustine did not notice. Or at least, he doesn't tell us what he noticed: even if her entry on the scene was the catalyst of his spiritual awakening, he seems to see her as a minor player on the stage of his life story. As he looks back through his past in the *Confessions*, his attention tends to remain focused on his mother and the woman he was in love with—the two figures who represented the forces at war in his mind and heart. Tacita, by contrast, was someone he hardly knew.

So it falls to us to try to conjure her. What kind of person was Tacita? What kind of life did she look forward to? What was it like to be a young heiress, practicing for a life in which vast quantities of land and gold could ride on a young woman's suitability as an ornament for a prospective husband's home?

Augustine gives us very little to work with. He skims over the details of his engagement, noting only that "the pressure [to find a bride] was put on, and I paid court to a girl, whose age was almost two years young for marrying, but because she was pleasing, I waited for her."[1] In the years before his religious conversion, one ambitious courtier in the imperial city of Milan found her pleasing; this is Tacita's entire biography as history records it.

And yet, if Augustine was not interested in her story, why does he tell us about her at all? Of course, the heroines of Roman stories were naturally understood to be attractive, and a bride—even a somewhat neglected one—is always a kind of heroine. But there are other reasons. These are his *Confessions*, and the way he broke the engagement is a sin to scrub from his conscience. This is also, of course, why he doesn't name his fiancée. Shielding her from the kind of speculation that inevitably follows such a rupture is a parting gesture, whether an exercise in damage limitation or a way of salvaging some sense of his own good intentions. He paid her the courtesy of signaling that it was through no fault of her own that she received the greatest insult that anyone could give to a Roman woman: repudiation as a bride. It is an awkward gesture, and frankly one that reveals how very out of his depth Augustine had been during his time at court.

We know that Tacita was ten because Augustine confesses that he was frustrated, when the betrothal was settled, by the fact that he would have to wait for two years until she came of age. The age difference itself raised no eyebrows. Twenty-five was the age of legal majority, and so it tended to be the age after which men of property expected to marry. But Roman girls normally married as soon as Roman medicine considered them able to bear children, generally between the ages of twelve and twenty. And perhaps unsurprisingly, it was the girls with the largest dowries who were usually spoken for first.

We can only imagine what Tacita felt about her engagement, before she knew how badly it would end. Roman girlhood was a long course of preparation for life as a wife and mother. This was a privilege of citizen women. Other women might bear children, but not as wives. The question of class also made a huge difference to motherhood itself; for example, women of Tacita's class did not engage directly in childcare.

The first year of life was the most dangerous, and as a result babies were often sent to the countryside, which was correctly seen as a healthier environment than cities, which were even then recognized as incubators of disease. Infants would be nursed by a rural worker who had recently had a child of her own. The wet nurse might be a slave belonging to one of the child's parents, but we know from Egypt—where the extremely dry climate has allowed many Roman legal contracts written on papyrus to survive buried in the sand—that families often hired wet nurses, whether a free woman or someone else's slave. When older, the child would return to the parental household to be cared for under the mother's supervision.

Dolls were among a girl's most precious possessions, and poignantly, they were often buried alongside their owners. Hundreds of dolls made of wood, terracotta, or ivory have been discovered in archaeological excavations from across the territory of the Roman Empire, often in the graves of girls who died in childhood. The dolls were made from a wide variety of materials. In poorer households, they might be made of cloth, like modern rag dolls, but the traces of these once ubiquitous cloth dolls are thin. (In all but the driest conditions, fabric disintegrates over time, so those that do survive tend to be from Egypt, the empire's most arid region.) Higher up the social ladder, however, dolls were made of more durable materials. They might be of fired clay or carved from wood or bone, or even from ivory or alabaster in the richest households, and it is mostly these upper-class dolls that have been found by archaeologists.

The majority of dolls that survive were styled as upper-class *matronae*, with carefully modeled faces, hair, and, in many cases, jewelry. The hairstyles of these dolls often closely imitated the coiffure of the reigning empress. The fact that the dolls were unclothed and thus needed to be dressed encouraged the girls playing with them to practice the rituals of self-adornment that so occupied the grown women of an aristocratic household. Indeed, giving a small daughter "something to do" while her mother was being dressed might have been a way to keep her from getting underfoot while at the same time allowing her to watch and learn.

Curiously, the Roman dolls that survive almost all represent mature women rather than children or babies. In other words, when upper-class girls played with dolls, they were not preparing themselves to take care of babies; this was a role that generally fell to female slaves. When girls of Tacita's class played with dolls, they were practicing for the high-stakes world of aristocratic womanhood. To the girls of the ruling classes, dolls represented not the world of childhood but a looming future in the world of adults.

Alongside the ivory combs, small mirrors, and cosmetic compacts often found among girls' grave goods, the dolls tell us that their owners were learning how to live in a world where appearance was currency. One scholar has even argued that the girls themselves were meant to learn something about the regal bearing of a female aristocrat from the rigid poses that the doll's moveable limbs could be guided into.[2] Another has made the intriguing suggestion that the reason so many of the surviving dolls are styled to imitate the empress of the day is that girls of prosperous families were encouraged to imagine themselves as part of the group of women at the top of the social pyramid.[3] Training girls to be at ease in scaling this pyramid was a serious business, and it was important to start early.

The most famous surviving Roman doll belonged to Crepereia Tryphaena, the daughter of a wealthy family who had originally been slaves of the emperor's household and grew rich thanks to their imperial connections after being freed. Tryphaena died on the eve of her marriage around age twenty, in the late second or early third century. Her marble sarcophagus bears a tableau of her family's sorrow at her death: a carved bas-relief of the bride herself lying on her deathbed, with a veiled woman, perhaps her mother, sitting at the side of the bed. Near the headboard, a man—possibly her father—leans toward her, bent over in grief. The sarcophagus was sealed with Tryphaena's body inside and placed next to the sarcophagus of another member of her family, Crepereius Euhodus, at the bottom of a well.

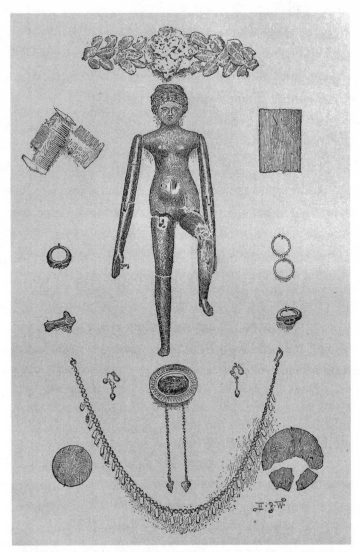

FIGURE 1. In addition to her ivory doll, Crepereia Tryphaena's tomb contained a bridal crown made from gold hammered into the shape of myrtle leaves. Among the other grave goods were a gold-and-turquoise necklace, a carved amethyst brooch, golden rings and earrings, a pair of ivory combs, and two small silver mirrors. Line drawing by Harold B. Warren, published in Rodolfo Lanciani, *Pagan and Christian Rome* (London: Macmillan and Co., 1895). *Photo courtesy of the author.*

The two sarcophagi were found in 1889 when workmen were digging foundations for the new Palace of Justice in Rome, on the north bank of the Tiber next to Castel Sant'Angelo. The excavator, Rodolfo Lanciani, who was among the most distinguished archaeologists of the day, gives a memorable description of the scene of the sarcophagus's opening when the grave was excavated.[4] A crowd had gathered around the workmen to mark the moment with "most solemn honors," and they were surprised and delighted to find her adorned with a bridal crown of gold hammered into the shape of myrtle leaves and accompanied by elegant grave goods, including a necklace, a carved amethyst brooch, rings, and earrings, all made of gold, along with an amber hairpin, an amber distaff and spindle, and an ivory-and-bone chest containing ivory combs and two small silver mirrors. One ring bore a cameo carved with the name "Filetus," which a poet writing at the time of the discovery suggested must have been the name of her promised husband.

But what people found most moving in Tryphaena's burial was the ivory doll buried with her. The doll had a beautiful carved face and an elaborate hairstyle of the epoch of Marcus Aurelius. Its clothes had disintegrated, leaving its long slim body exposed, with jointed limbs, tiny fingers and toes, small, high breasts, and a belly button.

The mind of a modern English speaker naturally turns to the first Barbie dolls of the early 1960s, with their exaggerated eyes, upswept hairstyles, and long-legged bodies, but the journalists of 1889 saw the doll in a more poetic light. Writers immediately began to rhapsodize about the "bambola di Tryphaena," musing that the young bride had not yet had the chance to leave her doll at the altar of Venus on the day before her wedding, a custom recorded by the Roman antiquarian Varro.[5]

The marriage ritual in the Roman period was not like ours, even for Christians—the concept of a church wedding would not emerge for several centuries. Instead, the marriage ritual revolved around the houses of the bride and groom.[6] It consisted of two connected ceremonies, scenes that relied on an audience for their stagecraft. In one, the bride left her own home and was led through the streets toward her husband's house, with her family accompanying her. The procession was a once-in-a-lifetime opportunity for the family to display its wealth in the bride's adornment as she traveled through the streets. It was also a moment when she was expected to perform her own reluctance to be married—paradoxically, her unwillingness was understood as a sign of her fitness as a bride: a mark of her love for her own family and her worthiness as a future mother.

The culmination of the procession was the moment when the bride arrived at the groom's door and received gifts from him. Traditionally, he would give the bride a gift of fire and water, the two elements that would help her to sustain the family and tend the hearth. By offering the gifts, a husband confirmed his acceptance of the bride, and by accepting them, she proclaimed her consent to become his wife, with all the roles and responsibilities this involved. This exchange of gifts was the central axis of the marriage ritual. It established what the Romans called marital *consensus*—the intention of the husband and wife to share a hearth and raise children together. Among propertied families, witnessed documents often confirmed the property arrangements, but no such documents were required. The sole requirements were the actions that established the bride's consent and the couple's shared marital intention.

One of the Roman terms for marriage is *domum ducere*, referring to the groom's act of leading his bride into his house. But curiously, the groom did not have to be physically present at a Roman wedding.[7] In fact, he could leave the gifts for her at his home with instructions for someone else to welcome the bride and present them to her. The wedding was really about the bride's entry into the husband's house to become the mistress of his hearth and her acceptance of this duty. It was the gifts, not the groom's presence, that confirmed her status as a legitimate bride and future mother of sons and daughters.

In his celebrated study of rites of passage, the anthropologist Arnold Van Gennep spoke of how these rituals make vivid a moment of uncertainty, when a person has left behind an old role or status and has not yet entered into the corresponding new one.[8] He spoke of this in-betweenness as a state of liminality, from *limen*, the Latin word for the beam spanning a doorway, whether above or below. The Roman bridal procession is the perfect illustration of this idea, capturing the anxieties and anticipation of a girl's transition from daughter to wife in the physical passage from one home to the next.

One Roman writer speaks of the bride as so heavily veiled that she was unable to see; her companions had to guide her forward. Roman brides walked blindly into an uncertain future, and no one could predict what life would be like in this particular family with this particular husband. Modern writers debate whether the flame-colored veil, the *flammeum*, was red or orange, while Roman antiquarian writers suggest that it was the color of blood, to signify the fertility of the bride. Other writers suggest that it is meant to evoke the veil worn by the *flaminica*, the priestess of Jupiter, a female public figure recognized as an icon of marital concord. Interestingly, we know that in Roman Africa up to the sixth century, even Christian families aspired to have their sons and daughters appointed to become *flamines*—the priests and priestesses of Jupiter, god of the harvest and father of the gods.[9] In other words, pagan fertility customs continued into the Christian period, and Tacita may well have participated in these customs. Many Christians felt a kind of cozy familiarity with the pagan gods not unlike the affection modern people sometimes have for the traditions of their grandparents or perhaps a family heirloom: something charming but slightly awkward that one finds a place for out of piety for the past.

Another ancient pagan idea carried into the Christian period was that of Venus, the goddess of love, as the sponsor of the bride. In pagan art, we see Venus adorning the bride on the day of her wedding, taking the role played by the bride's mother or female family members. The idea of Venus presiding over the bride's adornment was important both in the sense of awakening sexual fertility but also arming the bride with a radiance that would inspire her husband. Beauty had practical value as a tool to support marital concord and establish harmony in the household.

One of the most exuberant examples of a Christian invocation of Venus as the bringer of concord is a wedding gift that is now in the British Museum as part of the Esquiline Treasure.[10] In around 390, four or five years after Tacita's engagement, the casket was given to the bride Projecta, a daughter of the Roman senatorial aristocracy. The silver box weighs eighteen pounds, and it is decorated on the top and sides with biblical scenes hammered in silver. Around the lid a wedding blessing is engraved: "Secundus and Projecta, live happily in Christ!" But on the lid, given pride of place, is a portrait of the pagan goddess Venus sitting in a scallop shell and gazing into a mirror in her left hand to admire her own beauty. (The casket itself seems to be intended as a luxury storage chest for Projecta's cosmetics.) Clearly the wealthy friends or family who commissioned this gift saw no contradiction in decorating a gift for Christians with a sexually charged image of the pagan goddess Venus preparing herself for a night of love.

Also visible on the casket is a portrait of Projecta and Secundus, which captures how a Roman bride was bedecked with jewelry to signify the family's wealth and the value they placed on her, often with shining white pearls to signify her purity and radiance. We also see brides with their pearls on Roman marriage rings, which often bear a tiny portrait of an ideal couple, similar in spirit to the tiny statuettes of a bride and groom that adorn modern wedding cakes.

Visible too in these rings is the *dextrarum iunctio*, the joining of right hands that signifies the hope of concord between the marriage partners (and between the two families). It was the bride who was responsible for maintaining this concord. We will see this in the stories Augustine remembered from his mother, Monnica, about her friends who had difficult husbands; by her reasoning, it fell to the wife to use her sweetness and charm to bring the husband around to her point of view.

This job of engineering concord had repercussions not only for the bride's happiness, of course, but also for the wider community. In marriage, two families yoked themselves together to produce the new generation. For the great families, these alliances could have political consequences. But even in the smaller provincial families, marriage was a way of knitting together the different households into a wider social fabric.

One reason young women were encouraged to see marriage as a vital and positive turning point in their lives was that it was a moment of danger and uncertainty—and it could end in ruin. We know from Monnica's experience that moving into a husband's house involved challenges and difficulties that a young woman was not always prepared to navigate. A wedding was a mixed blessing: everything we read in Roman literature suggests that it was a matter of excitement, a great moment of coming of age, but also an occasion for grief. Again and again, marriage poems and images of weddings in Roman art portray the bride in tears.[11] Leaving her home and family, which had loved and cherished her, for an uncertain future required courage. This is the fear captured in a bride's gestures of reluctance in the marriage ceremony, as she closes the door on her childhood and steps forward into the unknown.

And in truth, a bride could expect to find herself at the bottom of the social ladder of the new household she was joining. Legally, she did not actually join her husband's family. It was as if she were on loan to them, joining her husband's household on probation and at its margin. The liminality of her position did not end with the ceremony. Having left her own family behind, she was expected to reinvent herself as the person who could provide what her husband's family needed most: the next generation.

This was a daunting role for a young woman, so a great deal of energy went into presenting it as an honor. To be the mother of Roman sons was a heroic destiny, and brides were encouraged to view their own reluctance as a sign of their readiness to do the job well. A girl who was attached to her childhood home and did not want to leave it could be expected to stay close to the hearth of her new home as a chaste and fertile wife and mother. Her love for her family did her credit, evidence of her qualities as a loyal and family-minded individual. Chastity and fertility went together, since an honorable matron had no sexual interest in men other than her husband. Her virtue and dignity signaled that she was single-minded about producing legitimate children for her husband's clan.

But the role came with a cost. A bride could expect to move some distance away from her own family. She would come under the sphere of her mother-in-law, who—if she was living—would in all likelihood be living with one of her sons. Since men generally married at around the age of twenty-five, by the time a son married, his father would be around fifty and less likely to still be alive than his mother, who had married at a younger age.[12] Mothers who survived childbirth had a good chance of remaining alive until their sons married. This meant that the bond with her new mother-in-law was one of the most important relationships for a bride. And in Tacita's case, of course, we know quite a bit about the woman who was meant to become her mother-in-law.

Augustine's mother, Monnica, was openhearted but not undemanding. She almost certainly saw austere and self-controlled conduct as essential for a young woman, but at the same time, she was aware of the difficulties brides faced because she had experienced them herself. Indeed, long after her death, Augustine remembered numerous stories about his mother's early years of marriage, which suggests that she made it a point to try to warn him that his little bride might be worried and homesick.

Monnica may have had a pastoral aim in telling her son about the hostility she had faced as a young bride from her husband's house slaves. It seems possible that she told the story to help Augustine make sense of a condition Tacita's parents set when they settled the betrothal: they had stipulated that he must send away the woman he had been living with. This last fact tells us something very important about Tacita's parents: they were looking out for her. Someone had thought ahead about the difficulties she might face in her new home.

If Monnica told Augustine the story of her own experience as a young bride at a moment when he was distressed at having to send away the woman he had come to love, she almost certainly believed that a clean transition between Augustine's successive partners was best for everyone. But she must also have known that things would be difficult for the woman who was being forced out.

Looking at the situation from the point of view of Augustine's spurned concubine, being displaced by someone who had youth and wealth and social standing was understandable, but it was a bitter pill to swallow. Had she remained nearby, she could easily have felt tempted to vent some of her frustration and anger at the younger woman who had displaced her. And if she had earned the affection of the other household slaves and dependents, these people could create difficulty for the bride long after the concubine had been sent away.

This makes Monnica's firm hand in dismissing her seem more understandable, though no less brutal. There was a choice to be made between the well-being of the young bride and that of the concubine. Monnica seems to have felt that duty lay with protecting the bride.

And Tacita's parents were not wrong to be worried for her well-being in her husband's house. We know less than we would like to about ancient domestic violence, because it was the kind of thing elite writers (who are disproportionately the ones whose work survives) preferred not to acknowledge. But the evidence suggests a correlation between domestic violence and a husband's extramarital affairs.

A famous murder trial from the second century illustrates this point. The victim was the senatorial heiress Appia Annia Regilla, the granddaughter of two Roman consuls. In 139, when she was fourteen, Regilla married the fabulously wealthy forty-year-old Herodes Atticus, a favorite of the emperor Marcus Aurelius.[13] Because of his wealth, Herodes was considered a great catch, even though he was known to be violent. He turned out to be an affectionate husband, but the rumors of his temper had not been exaggerated.

After their marriage, Regilla and Herodes left Rome and returned to his native Athens. The two had five children together, but Herodes was known to have other lovers. When Regilla was pregnant with their sixth child, he ordered one of his freedmen to beat her as a punishment for some unspecified transgression, and she died as a result. Normally a tragedy of this kind would have been kept quiet, and the bride's family left to cope with their loss in silence. But Regilla's brother was consul at the time, and he brought charges against her killer, despite the distance between Athens and Rome of almost eight hundred miles. It was on account of her brother's standing, and the sensational trial, that the story of Regilla's murder was preserved for posterity, but the murderer was acquitted, and the facts of the case were probably not as unusual as we might wish. Strangely, after Regilla's death, her husband mourned her extravagantly, perhaps to get out in front of speculation about his part in it. He built numerous shrines and memorials to her memory, as well as a monumental theater, which still stands in Athens—though it bears his name, not hers: the Odeon of Herodes Atticus.[14]

Regilla's case was by no means unique, and there is evidence that women were aware of the perils of dangerous husbands and shared stories about them. An example probably written in Tacita's lifetime or shortly afterward is found in a pious Christian romance, the *Passion of Anastasia and Chrysogonus*.[15] This anonymous narrative tells the story of a group of Christian martyrs during the Great Persecution at the beginning of the fourth century. It begins when the heroine, Anastasia, is turned in to the authorities because of her Christian faith and brought before the tribunal of the prefect of Illyricum, Probus. We have already encountered a real prefect of Illyricum called Probus: Sextus Petronius Probus, who held office some sixty years after the Great Persecution. The women of his family were literary patronesses and had a special devotion for St. Anastasia, so it seems likely that the tale of Anastasia is a work of historical fiction written under their patronage. The prefect Probus seems to be a cameo role for a fictional pagan ancestor modeled after the family's more recent Christian patriarch.

What fascinated and horrified Christian readers about the story of Anastasia was the distressing nature of her marriage. The daughter of a pagan senator and his Christian wife, Anastasia is married to a despicable pagan husband named Publius. To avoid sleeping with him, she claims that she is ill. At the same time, she begins dressing as a beggar and visiting Christians who have been thrown into prison on account of their faith. The reaction of Publius when he becomes aware of these visits is swift and fierce: he imprisons Anastasia in his house, appointing guards to make sure she cannot even look out a window. When news of this reaches the Christian community, an old woman is found who can carry a letter to Anastasia. Anastasia replies with a short, autobiographical narrative, explaining how her husband married her for her wealth and then did his best to spend it all. Now he has accused her of sorcery—the writer clearly believed, perhaps rightly, that this was the charge on which Christians had been persecuted in pagan times—and she is being mistreated so severely that she fears for her life. The Christian holy man Chrysogonus replies to Anastasia's letter, consoling her with the news that other Christians are praying for her and that the watchful eye of God is witness to her suffering. Then, as if in answer to their prayers, they learn that Publius is dead. Things get worse for Anastasia, however. She is interrogated by the pagan authorities, and the emperor Diocletian orders her to wed the pagan high priest Ulpian, who takes her to his house and shows her the treasures that await her if she accepts his hand in marriage. Next, he shows her the instruments of torture that she will face if she tries to resist and gives her three days in which to make her decision. On the third day, Ulpian comes to her, intending to force her to have sex with him, but when he tries to touch her, he is struck blind. Soon afterward he dies, the second abuser to face death as a result of her prayers.

While the story of Anastasia is told in a way that seems designed to hold readers spellbound with horrified fascination, the fear that men like Herodes Atticus, Probus, and Ulpian inspired was something Christian preachers felt the need to address. John Chrysostom, bishop of Antioch in the 380s, wrote a series of sermons and treatises on family life that show how openly his congregation talked about domestic violence.

Drawing on the stories he had heard in the community, his sermons warned the men in the congregation that God was watching them in their treatment of their families. Chrysostom was famous for his ability to hold an audience spellbound, and in his description of the regime of terror that a jealous husband could create for his wife, one can see his gift for vivid description. "There is surveillance and scrutiny," he warned. "Her entire life is filled with terror and trembling."[16] His analysis of the tactics of intimidation a husband could bring into play is almost novelistic. "Not only are her comings and goings the subject of interrogation," he says, "but even her words, glances, and sighs are meticulously cross-examined." Even as he conjures the concrete reality of her circumstances, he makes vivid the emotional effect on her. "She is compelled to be as still as a stone, enduring everything silently, confined to her rooms worse than a prisoner."[17] It is not certain whether Tacita would have known of such cases at such a tender age, but it is not impossible. If stories like the tale of Anastasia were read aloud around the fireside, the children would have been just as likely to listen as the adults. And while the narrative links Anastasia's ill-treatment by her husbands and the hostility of the pagan authorities, its great effect relies on a cultural awareness that the adverse conditions of her marriage were anything but fiction, even under Christian emperors.

How much scope was there for a girl to refuse a husband? We know that Roman law expected that the bride's consent be obtained, but whether she could really withhold it against parental pressure is another question entirely. A Christian historical romance written perhaps a century after Tacita's death, *The Passion of Eugenia*, gives us a glimpse into the different kind of future that was becoming possible for young women who did not want to marry.[18] It tells the story of a fourth-century governor's daughter, a pagan who grew up to become a Christian saint. In the story, Phillip, the prefect of Egypt, approaches his daughter Eugenia to tell her that he has received an offer of marriage for her from a young man from a good family. Eugenia replies that she needs to know more about the young man's character to make an informed decision. The honest Phillip commends her for her good sense, and Eugenia asks for a few days to think about it. She decides to go to the family villa in the countryside outside Alexandria, bringing some servants along as chaperones, and tells her father that she will give him her decision upon her return. Eugenia is reading a book as she is carried in a litter on the road out of the city, a Christian tale of a first-century maiden—Thecla of Iconium—who heard the apostle Paul preaching while sitting in the window of her pagan family's house. So compelled was Thecla by the apostle's words that she decided to refuse to marry the young man she was promised to and left her family to join the entourage of the apostle, following him wherever he went on his journey as a Christian missionary. When Eugenia reads the story, she decides that she wants to be like Thecla. By choosing the path of virginity, she can imagine herself as one of Paul's followers. (In fact, a fourth-century letter of spiritual instruction to the daughter of a Christian family encourages her to imagine herself as Thecla, following in the apostle's footsteps, whenever she reads the letters of Paul in the New Testament.[19])

We do not know whether the anonymous writer of the tale of Eugenia was a man or a woman, but we can see how the women of the upper classes had begun to question whether they should accept the traditional role of wife and mother. In earlier periods, women who had been unable to find husbands had dedicated their virginity or their widowhood to God as a way of claiming protection from the churches. This was initially a form of social welfare. But from the fourth century, a new group of women who had every opportunity to marry—the daughters of wealthy families—began dedicating themselves to virginity as a positive choice.[20] Some of what we read about these women suggests that they were looking to remain within a community of women, a choice that felt more familiar—and safer—than joining a strange man's family as a bride. Other women whose husbands had died found encouragement from the church to enjoy their independence as widows rather than marrying again, as both law and custom had traditionally encouraged them to do. (Such a choice was only realistic, of course, if the woman's financial situation made it possible; for most women, remarrying was a way of seeking financial security.)

A letter written by St. Jerome in 383 to one of Tacita's contemporaries in Rome, the thirteen-year-old Julia Eustochium, illustrates the kind of praise aristocratic virgins could expect to receive from the church if they chose not to marry. "Women of the world, you know, plume themselves because their husbands are on the bench [as judges] or in other high positions. And the wife of the emperor always has an eager throng of visitors at her door."[21] But Eustochium should see them as her inferiors: "Why do you, God's bride, hasten to visit the wife of a mere man? Learn in this respect a holy arrogance; know that you are better than they."[22] Many saw the minority of Christians who chose the path of virginity as representing the height of dedication to the spiritual life. For girls who did not want to marry, virginity offered a welcome alternative to a marriage arranged not for love but as a way of strengthening the family's position.

The question remains, what did Tacita's family see in Augustine? We know that his family was far less wealthy than hers—he is open in the *Confessions* about the fact that he was marrying her for her money. We also know that he did not come from a particularly distinguished family: his parents were small-scale provincial landowners, not people whose social credentials meant something at court. What he did have, at least in theory, was a promising future; it was well known in these circles that a provincial with literary talent might have remarkable prospects.[23] We know, for example, that the emperor was sometimes in the audience when Augustine gave speeches and that he was in favor at court; there was even the possibility on the horizon of a future appointment as a provincial governor.[24] Tacita's family may have joined Augustine's own in placing their hopes in his gifts.

Two cases for the marriage of girls in court circles at this period both illustrate the updraft of social mobility, though the girls in question were the daughters of generals rather than of literary men. Aelia Eudoxia was the daughter of Flavius Bauto, whose appointment as consul Augustine celebrated in a speech of January 385. A Frankish soldier, Bauto had risen through the ranks to become head of the Roman army, *magister militum*, in the 380s. In 385, when Eudoxia was three or four, Bauto shared the honor of appointment as consul with the boy who would become his son-in-law—Arcadius, the eight-year-old son of the Eastern emperor Theodosius. Ten years later, Eudoxia would marry Arcadius, now himself emperor.[25]

Eudoxia seems to have moved east when the court fled Milan on account of Maximus's invasion in 387. In 388, when she was six or seven, her father Bauto died, and she joined the household of Promotus, who was *magister militum* after her father. (No information survives about her mother.) When Promotus himself died, Eudoxia stayed on with his widow, Marsa, a dedicated networker who brought years of building relationships to bear on the task of supporting her young protégée. It may have been the widow Marsa who engineered Eudoxia's engagement to Arcadius shortly after his father died and he became emperor in 395; the other girl being considered as a possible bride was the daughter of the man who had been her husband's most bitter rival.[26]

Eudoxia grew up to become a powerful force politically, although she was constantly pregnant. After her marriage in April 395, she lived for only nine more years, but during those nine years she produced seven children, five of whom survived. During her short tenure as empress, she played an important role in imperial politics and as a patron of the church. Sadly, she developed an infection during the birth of her seventh child in October 404, when she was in her mid-twenties, and died of postnatal hemorrhage.

The story of another contemporary of Tacita and Eudoxia, the Berber princess Savina, takes an interesting turn in its second act.[27] Savina also married and had children, but she survived her husband and enjoyed her independence as a rich widow. Her marriage tells us something about the role these young women played as political pawns. Her father, Gildo, was a Berber prince who had served in the Roman army that put down the African rebellion of the 370s. Around the time Maximus invaded Italy in 387, Gildo was given the title count of Africa and sent to defend the region against the armies of the usurper. The count seems to have proven himself invaluable, drawing a significant portion of the usurper's armies away from Italy. Meanwhile Savina was given in marriage to Nebridius, nephew by marriage of the Eastern emperor Theodosius through his late wife Flaccilla. When Gildo left for Africa, Savina remained in Constantinople to guarantee that her father would not betray the emperor.

Years later, after Theodosius's death, Gildo did indeed turn traitor and tried to establish an independent state in Africa under his own rule.[28] But by this time Nebridius had died, and Savina had established herself as a Christian widow, claiming her refusal to remarry as an act of Christian piety. It is because of her pious widowhood that Savina's story has come down to us; after her husband's death, she took up a correspondence with St. Jerome, one of the great proponents of Christian asceticism. As the mother of a son and a daughter, Savina was by no means a virgin, but in her widowhood she became a minor heroine of the ascetic movement nonetheless.

Of course, Tacita didn't marry Augustine in the end. In the absence of facts, it is impossible to know how the broken engagement affected her. Was she "ruined"? Was she secretly relieved? Did she recover easily from the sudden change of tone in how the grown-ups around her were talking about her future? And what, in fact, were they saying and thinking?

Tacita was an heiress, and on that basis we can make an educated guess at how things played out from her parents' point of view, based on how money moved through the ancient world as a form of power, closing doors as readily as it opened them. In the world of great Roman landowners, the kind of family who could produce a daughter with a dowry sizeable enough to attract Augustine's ambition would not have taken the rejection of their daughter kindly. They may well have seen it as a declaration of war.

So it may have been no accident that in early autumn at the end of the harvest vacation, Augustine let it be known that he would not be returning to work once the new term began. He gave a chest infection as an explanation for why he could not lecture, but this was surely not the whole story. Perhaps he simply needed to get out of town. We know he left Milan for several months immediately after announcing the end of his engagement and only returned to the city in the new year. Might he have been afraid of retaliation from Tacita's father? One would give a great deal to know.

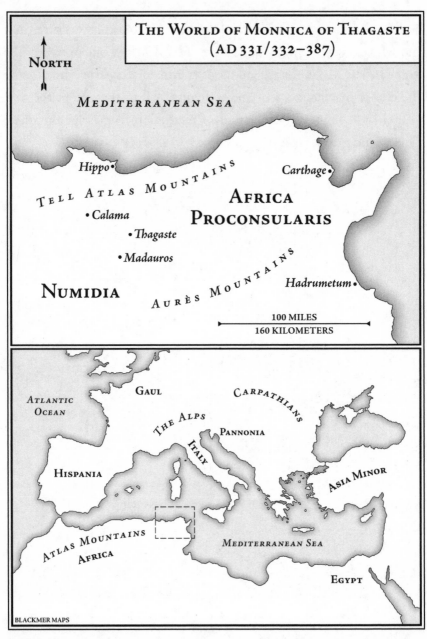

THE WORLD OF MONNICA OF THAGASTE
(AD 331/332–387)

NORTH

MEDITERRANEAN SEA

Hippo•

TELL ATLAS MOUNTAINS

•Calama

•Thagaste

•Madauros

NUMIDIA

Carthage•

AFRICA
PROCONSULARIS

AURÈS MOUNTAINS

Hadrumetum•

100 MILES
160 KILOMETERS

ATLANTIC
OCEAN

GAUL

CARPATHIANS

THE ALPS

PANNONIA

ITALY

HISPANIA

ATLAS MOUNTAINS
AFRICA

ASIA MINOR

MEDITERRANEAN SEA

EGYPT

BLACKMER MAPS

MAP 2. During her early life in the semirural world of eastern Numidia, Monnica of Thagaste could hardly have expected to spend her final years in Italy, in the imperial capital. Thagaste, her home during her married years, was known for its lion market. *Credit: Kate Blackmer.*

~ CHAPTER THREE ~

MONNICA

I F HER YOUNGER SON HAD NOT GROWN UP TO BECOME A
Christian bishop, Monnica of Thagaste would have left no trace,
barring the gravestone discovered in 1945 in the Italian port of
Ostia Antica—the city where she died, far from her home in North
Africa.[1] But Monnica remains unique among ancient women. She
was a storyteller whose tales run like a bright thread through her son's
writings, and in this way they came to influence the shape of Christianity during the critical moment when it was evolving from outsider
sect to world religion. Sometimes no more survives of Monnica's stories than an image or a thought-picture plucked from the flow of family life, but they are the last vestige of a deep tide of emotional insight
that she handed down to her children and, through her younger son,
to medieval Christendom.

Monnica's stories reach back beyond her own childhood to her
father's boyhood around the beginning of the fourth century, during
the reign of the last pagan emperors. Sifting through the fragments

and images that remain and looking for the earliest captured memory, we come to an arresting image: a young woman carrying a boy on her shoulders.[2]

The boy was Monnica's father, and the image comes from a story told in Monnica's family about his childhood. It captures something important about life in the towns and villages of Roman Africa: the sturdy strength of the older girl and the dependence of the small boy, the warmth of the companionship between them, and the paradox of slavery as a system of power so deeply accepted that it was considered unremarkable.

When we imagine a child riding above the world on an older child's shoulders, we instinctively think of the children as smiling. And yet, disturbingly, the very fact that the older girl was using her strong limbs to carry the boy on her shoulders tells us that she was not a person of consequence. If we stop to think, we might guess—correctly—that she was a slave.

Monnica told the story to her children because the older girl was her father's nursemaid, and she grew up to be Monnica's own nursemaid when the boy on her shoulders married and started a family of his own. By the time Monnica was a child during the last years of the first Christian emperor Constantine the Great, the smiling girl had grown up to become a figure of fear commanding respect and obedience. Curiously, we don't know whether Monnica heard the story from her father or the nursemaid. If her father told it, he may have been explaining that this enslaved woman, who was now in charge of Monnica and her sisters, was to be loved as well as feared. But if her now much older nursemaid told the story, she may have been aiming to soften the image of a stern father by emphasizing that he too, after all, had once been a boy. Or she may have wanted to remind the young mistress of the standing she had earned in the household as its long-serving guardian and as a person on whose kindness the master had once depended. Or she may have been attempting to do both. Stories told to children almost always have a moral, and sometimes they have more than one. Whatever its origin, the image invokes connection, across lines of class, family, and generations.

As Monnica remembered her childhood in conversations with her son, she singled out this seemingly marginal person, a slave handed down through the family from her grandparents to her father, as a figure of great influence in her early life. "She claimed that her strict training had come not from her mother's diligence," Augustine remembered, "but rather from an old slave who had carried my grandfather on her back when he was a small child, in the way small children are often carried by older girls."[3] The old woman wielded a double-edged weapon of affection and authority. "Because of her long service and because of her old age and high moral standards she was held in great esteem by her masters in that Christian house."[4]

Monnica seems to have taken it for granted that in practice, the hard hierarchical lines of slavery and freedom could be blurred without challenging the system altogether. Now entering old age, the nurse "was entrusted with the care of the master's daughters and discharged her duty diligently, and when it was necessary, she was fierce with a holy seriousness and a sober care in instructing them."[5] In slave societies, a slave who has built up a status as the representative of the master or mistress is often the one who does the unpleasant work of disciplining other slaves and the younger members of the master's family. Monnica's parents preferred to do things this way, so that their own time with the children was more pleasurable and less of a chore.

To our modern way of thinking, the old woman's techniques for training the children's sense of self-control are alarming. For example, despite the North African heat, the children were routinely denied drinking water. "Outside mealtimes, when they were fed modestly at their parents' table, they were not allowed to drink even water, even if they were burning with thirst."[6] The daughters of the house worked through the day on their spinning or weaving, and as they waited for sundown, not complaining about their thirst became a point of pride.

We may flinch at this Spartan ruthlessness in dealing with small children, but the intention was not unkind. Although they might suffer at the time, the girls would benefit in the future. Parents who hardened their daughters aimed to make them resilient and even fearless in their conduct. Young women who had grown up under a regime of austerity and self-control were a valued commodity in the web of provincial life in Roman Africa. And they would grow up to be confident in the knowledge that they could endure any challenge with dignity.

The mothers and nursemaids who imposed such hardships knew that a time would come when each daughter would be handed over to strangers. The likelihood of the daughter's marital home being close enough for frequent visits to her parents was not high. And even familiar families had their secrets. A seemingly generous bridegroom might turn out to be a cruel husband; a seemingly solicitous mother-in-law might choose to turn a blind eye. There was no way of knowing what a daughter might face in her married life. No one could guess from outside what took place behind the closed doors of another home. So the best strategy was to prepare a daughter to face hardship—and hold her ground when she needed to—quietly but firmly. Seen in this light, Monnica's upbringing was perhaps harsh and challenging, but it was designed to make her invincible.

The constant interaction between slaves and free members of the family emerges quite vividly in the stories of Monnica's childhood and early marriage. Retracing the key moments of Monnica's early life as she remembered it, we come next to an incident in her own child-hood around the time of the death of Constantine in 337. This was the quarrel between Monnica and her slave companion. Though they were of roughly the same age, the relation between the two girls was by no means equal: Monnica was the daughter of the master with his lawful wife, while the mother of the other girl was a slave. (The status of her father is unknown, but it would have made little difference.)

Monnica's family were Christian and Roman citizens, though her Berber name reaches back to both the family's pre-Roman past and its pre-Christian roots. The "Mon" in her name honors Ba'al Ham-mon, the god of the harvest known as Saturn to the Romans.[7] But like other Christian families of that era, Monnica's people not only owned slaves but may well have fathered children by them. Some children of household slaves were the half siblings of the master's children, while others were the product of relationships—a few of them stable and consensual, to the extent that consent was possible in such a situation—between male and female slaves. In both cases, the enslaved children would grow up alongside the master's free chil-dren, in a curious half-servant, half-playmate role that helped to keep the free children out from under their parents' feet. Evidence from nineteenth-century plantations suggests that the enslaved children of free men by enslaved women sometimes experienced a curious status of semirecognition and sometimes affection in the eyes of a father who was also a master.[8] This added complexity to the already blurred lines of hierarchy among slave and free children in the same house-hold, but it did not fundamentally change the balance of power.

We know a kind of rivalry emerged between Monnica and Illa, the handmaid who served as her companion—Monnica remembered the awkward balance of power that had governed their relationship and told her own children about it. We don't know what emboldened the child's sense of her own right to defy Monnica. A slave girl criticizing the master's free daughter was surprising but not unheard of. Despite the advantage of status, the lawful daughter had to show herself worthy of her privilege. Otherwise the handmaid, whose watchful eye witnessed every fault, could gain the upper hand in the ongoing game of psychological advantage. To her credit, Monnica seems not to have downplayed the stories in which she herself was at fault.

The story of Illa's challenge captures a particular humiliation. Monnica liked to sip wine from the cask when the girls were sent to fetch it for the table, a habit that one day gave Illa an opening to wound her pride. "The little handmaid with whom she used to go to fetch the wine had an argument with her young mistress when they were alone together, insulting her with the pointed accusation that she was a drunk. This stung."[9] Retelling the story years later, Monnica added that she had tried to learn from the humiliation. Rather than defending herself, "she reflected on her ugly habit and gave it up."[10]

The moral of the story, as Monnica told it to her son years later, was that even the most unpromising situations can yield an opportunity for spiritual growth. Illa may well have envied Monnica and wanted to catch her out, but even if her intentions were malicious, it did not mean no good could come of her action. This mysterious fact was a sign of the hand of God. "In her anger, the handmaid wanted to upset her little mistress, not cure her.... But You, Lord, ruler of heaven and earth, you turn the rushing depths to Your own ends.... [E]ven from the disease of one soul You drew forth healing for another."[11] Human beings muddle forward without any real understanding of what they are doing, but God is behind everything, guiding them into challenges that will bring forth new insight—if only they can open their minds to learn from the experience. If we accept her son's somewhat rosy memory of his mother and his quick judgment of Illa's effort to humiliate her, Monnica's ability to listen and learn when faced with her flaws was one of her great gifts.

Reading these stories, we notice many things about the household Monnica grew up in. Both of her parents were living, and she had at least one sibling, a sister—the story about father's old nursemaid makes clear that more than one daughter had been consigned to her stern rule. But curiously, it is Monnica's relationships with slaves— not with her parents or sister, whom she mentions only in passing— that receive the lion's share of attention in the stories she tells her son. Why do the relationships between enslaved and free members of the family loom so large?

Like other Roman girls of the prosperous classes, Monnica spent her childhood surrounded by slaves.[12] One often thinks of Roman slaves as laboring on agricultural estates, but in fact some lived in very close proximity to the families who owned them, as domestic servants or helpers in the family business. From the slave's perspective, this was not an easy life. Even if the standard of living was higher than for those working in the fields or in a chain gang, the conflicting demands made by different family members had no real limit. And there was nowhere to turn, no impartial judge to adjudicate if the master, mistress, or another member of the family behaved cruelly or unreasonably.

Further, living together at close quarters meant that class lines were readily blurred. Routine cruelty was taken for granted but individuals could sometimes test limits and boundaries, which might bring material benefits but also heightened tensions. Complex dynamics and even rivalries could develop between slaves and masters, as with Monnica and Illa. This was especially true if the slave children were related by blood to the master's family, in cases where the master or his male relatives had fathered children by slave women.

Sometimes the sense of family relationship made things easier—if relations were friendly, a slave might receive gifts or better portions of food or be treated with something like respect or affection. But if the relationship was strained or hostile, harassment could be constant. If slaves sometimes spoke up in their dealings with the more powerful members of the household, we should not be fooled into thinking that they took no risk in doing so.

Monnica grew up to become a Christian saint. Yet, sadly, this does not mean that she challenged the injustice of the social system of her day. Fourth-century Christians were encouraged to accept the injustices of their society, whether they were beneficiaries or victims (as a slave owner who was also female, Monnica was largely, but not exclusively, a beneficiary). Still, there is something welcome about the fact that Monnica noticed the hypocrisies of the system she was brought up in and called attention to them when she raised her own children. We may have Illa to thank for that.

One of Monnica's strongest convictions was that a person's status in the world has no bearing on the value of what the person says or does: this was the lesson of Illa's rebuke. What matters is the value of what a person says and what they make of what they have to work with. Long after Monnica's death, her son would advocate fiercely against the idea, widely accepted in the Christian society of the fourth century, that an individual's social status reflected his or her standing in the sight of God. In this way, Illa's words and actions shaped Monnica's experiences and her opinions, and they in turn shaped those of her son and thus fed into the stream of medieval thought. So Illa's voice had a long echo across history.

Up until the time of Monnica's marriage, we do not know her whereabouts, only that she almost certainly lived somewhere in

Roman Numidia. But with her arrival at her marital home in Thagaste, she appears on the stage of a wider history. Her husband, Patricius, was a town councilor in the prosperous market town—a personage of note, albeit a minor one, in a place that mattered. Augustine's roots there would remain important to him long after he left.

The town where Monnica lived out her married life stood at the crossroads of the Roman and Berber civilizations in the northeastern highlands of Numidia, nestled along a river in a landscape of fertile valleys. It was a hub linking the agriculturally rich interior to the trade routes bound for Rome. Two to three days' travel would carry the ancient traveler to Hippo Regius, the splendid port city of the Numidian kings—as the ancients reckoned distance, this was not far at all. The road in the other direction led to Carthage, the capital of Africa Proconsularis; in fact, the main east-west road connecting Hippo Regius to Carthage ran through the town. The road running southward led to Madauros, roughly a day's journey away on foot. This was the capital of learning in the region, where Augustine himself would study.

Though not far from the rich agricultural land of the coastal plain, the area around Thagaste has an alpine character and is both elevated and densely forested, though it lies close to the point where the Atlas Mountains fall down to the plain. The town was a natural citadel, shielded against would-be invaders by its rugged topography. But its medieval and modern name, Souk Ahras, meaning "the lion market," tells us something important about its character.

Up to the early twentieth century, leopards and barbary lions were hunted in large numbers in the mountains around Thagaste. These beasts were known in antiquity as "the terror of the forest," and yet they had great economic importance. They were the object of a constant traffic flowing toward the great cities with their gladiatorial games. Above all, they found their way to Rome. There, the morning sessions of what we think of as the gladiatorial games were organized around events focused on killing animals—the *venationes*, or beast hunts, similar to modern bullfighting—while the more expensive human-to-human combats were reserved for the afternoons. These morning sessions required thousands of animals yearly. Hosting such games gave the Roman aristocrat a peerless opportunity to display the quintessential "conspicuous consumption" of the day—to throw money away and be loved for it by the Roman crowd.

The first-century writer Petronius tells us that the African hunters had once prayed to Monnica's namesake, the god Hammon, for a successful hunt.[13] While a Christian emperor would eventually ban the games, they still engendered a robust traffic in hunting and exporting animals during Monnica's childhood. Set on a major trade route, with forest all around, Thagaste was the perfect place for a lion market.

Africa was among the more prosperous regions, with hundreds of small cities dotting the fertile countryside. The region's wheatfields generated the *Annona*, the grain that fed the people of Rome. And the ships bound for Rome carried not only grain to feed the Roman people and wild beasts to entertain them but also young men trained in the arts of the Latin language.

In the countryside around Thagaste, the *lingua punica* was still spoken, but the schools of Africa were famous for producing boys whose Latin speeches were so mellifluous that their curious provincial accent was all but forgotten. Many of these boys grew up to put their skill with precise language to work in the bureaucracy of the Roman government. The Carthage offices of the proconsul of Africa housed four hundred salaried clerks, secretaries, and minor officials, a mere fraction of the wider operation.[14] Administering an empire required an annual infusion of literacy on a massive scale.

If the lions and leopards were notionally bound for Rome, with its massive population and extravagant displays of wealth, the human traffic in ambitious young men flowed to wherever the imperial administration had its offices: to its provincial capitals and to its center, a moving target based wherever the emperor had settled his court at the time. During Monnica's lifetime, emperors rarely held court in the Eternal City. For strategic reasons, Constantine and his sons had resided and held court in the northern and eastern cities, within reach of the frontier lines most likely to need attention: Trier in the Rhineland and Milan just south of the Alps, or Byzantium, Nicomedia, and Antioch in the East. In these cities, a young man could rise beyond what his family could understand or even imagine. But in Monnica's case, it is likely that she saw the possibilities that lay open to her sons; whatever her faults, she was by no means lacking in imagination.

After an upbringing "in modesty and sobriety," Monnica married early. "When she was old enough to marry," her son remembered, "she was handed over to a man and served him as she would a master. She worked to win him for You, speaking of you through her virtues, by which you made her beautiful, lovable, and admirable to her husband."[15] The "You" of Augustine's address here is God, with whom ancient Christians tended to maintain an inner dialogue both formally, in prayer, and more informally, as though God were a confidant or even a family member.

Some Roman women married slightly later, in their mid-teens, but Monnica married soon after becoming eligible at the age of twelve. Her family was prosperous, and her African roots were deep, though her family were Roman citizens. Patricius came from an indigenous

African family that had received Roman citizenship in the early third century, and Monnica likely came from a similar background. Since the name Monnica suggests Berber ancestry, we can surmise that her North African roots reached back to a time not only before the Romans but before the Phoenician traders who had arrived to found Carthage in the time of Queen Dido. Like many provincials, Monnica would find that her loyalties were divided when Roman rule in Africa was called into question, as it was repeatedly in the civil wars of the late fourth century. But as a woman, she had reason to be grateful to Rome. Roman law allowed free women substantial property rights, and in a society where child brides married fully grown men, women could expect a long widowhood. After her husband died when she was around forty, Monnica would become an independent woman of means.

We have no firm information about the age of her husband, Patricius. As Roman men tended to marry at around twenty-five, he was probably her elder by a decade or more. The custom of the time dictated that he should try to marry the daughter of a local landowner slightly more powerful than his own father, and there is no reason to believe that he did not achieve this aim. If this was the case, Monnica would have had at least the advantage of social standing in their unequal partnership. But even where wealth was on the side of the bride, age as well as the privileges of gender swung the balance of power to the groom.

As a Roman citizen, Monnica also had the protection of the law. Roman law granted a woman rights that her counterpart in later societies did not always share: not only the ability to own property in her own right and to run a business but also to protect herself from a cruel or dishonest husband and bring a lawsuit against him.[16] As with men, women remained under their father's legal power while he was alive. Both men and women up to age twenty-five would have a legal guardian if the father was no longer living or they had successfully petitioned for dissolution of his paternal right, and for women who were not under the father's power, there would still be guardianship even after they reached their majority unless they had three children.[17] Crucially, a woman's husband could not himself act as her guardian. One of the functions of guardianship was to give a wife's family the means to protect her if something went wrong in the marriage.

A daughter's marriage offered her parents a chance to shore up their business and social networks and extend what they had achieved into the next generation. In theory, an arranged marriage required the consent of the bride, but taking a stand against her parents could not be easy for a girl in her teens. The Christian literature of the day celebrated numerous cases where a daughter rejected a groom proposed by her parents and chose a life of virginity instead, but none in which the girl's motive was the hope of marrying someone else.

For Monnica, marriage was fraught with challenges. At first, the problems were caused not by her new husband directly but by the other women in the house. Her son remembered that "at the beginning, her mother-in-law was stirred up against her by the whisperings of malicious handmaids."[18] A dispute of this type would normally be referred to the *paterfamilias* if it began to escalate, but the story makes no mention of Monnica's father-in-law. Her mother-in-law was a widow, it seems, with her adult son acting as head of household.

Monnica felt she could not go straight to Patricius to resolve the situation, however. She may have suspected—or known—that the female slaves felt bold because one of them was his mistress. Or perhaps, as a child bride, she was simply afraid to speak to the grown man who visited her bed at night. She later told her children that she felt her best chance was to win over her mother-in-law's affections.

This she did through "her attentions, and her persistent patience and gentleness, with the result that the mother-in-law spoke to her son about the chattering tongues of the handmaids."[19] Once trust had been established between the two free women, the mother-in-law turned against the slaves. "They were disturbing the domestic harmony between herself and her daughter-in-law, and she demanded that they be punished."[20] The war with the handmaids had escalated, but now Monnica had the upper hand.

Patricius "gave a whipping to the ones she accused, out of concern for household discipline and the harmony of his family," and order was restored. "Afterward, no one dared say a word, and they lived with a memorable goodwill and kindness between them."[21] In telling the story to her children, Monnica had clearly forgiven her mother-in-law and tried to see things from her point of view. But we hear nothing of the point of view of the slave women who were central to the conflict.

We know from fourth-century sermons that the relationship between free and enslaved women in Roman households was often colored by violence. "When women get angry with their female slaves," warned John Chrysostom, "they fill the whole house with their shouting. Many times, if the house happens to be situated on a narrow street, even passersby can hear the woman's shouts and the slave's outcry."[22] Chrysostom knew that this kind of commotion was a source of shame: "Immediately all the neighboring women pry into the situation and ask, 'What's going on in there?' 'That harridan,' one replies, 'is beating her slave.' What could be more disgraceful than this?"[23] Preachers expressed their disapproval of this state of affairs but recognized that it was endemic.

Other sermons make clear that the source of tension between slave and free women was often jealousy around sexual relationships involving the free males of the household. Obviously, such sexual attention was often unwanted, and compliance was easily imposed by force. But even in the cases where the slave partner was a victim and not an accomplice, sex between masters and slaves could provoke jealousy in a wife who found herself demoted by her husband. Meanwhile, husbands pushed back ferociously against the idea that adherence to the Christian faith required them to give up the customary privilege of taking sexual advantage of their slaves.

In cases where the slave was not unhappy to have been singled out for the master's attention—whether due to genuine sympathy or a sense that she might stand to gain from his favor—the vitriolic envy of the slighted mistress of the house could become electric. Indeed, one of the fourth-century church councils specifically offered advice on cases where a mistress became enraged by sexual jealousy and killed her slave rival.[24] Anyone could see that it made no sense for a mistress to vent her fury at her husband on a slave who had no control over the situation. But although shameful, it was not uncommon.

So when Monnica was sent to join the household of Patricius, her parents would have had an idea of the difficulties she might face. They may have reasoned that if he had a lover among his slaves, there were worse failings in a husband. On the whole, a young man who kept an established concubine was understood to be showing a certain interest in respectability, preferring a stable arrangement to the brothels that were fixtures of every Roman town.

Monnica's father would have known, from his close relationship with the woman who had raised him and supported him in raising his own children, that the most successful relationship between a householder and a slave had the tone of a partnership. However unequal the relationship, establishing a sense of shared purpose, which involved an element of trust, could make all the difference. This thinking was certainly idealistic, but from the slave owner's point of view, such ideals were not naive or even necessarily altruistic. Establishing a veneer of harmony could make a noticeable difference in a master's sense of his home as a place of comfort rather than conflict. Painful realities were best kept beneath the surface.

Even in a well-run household, displacement or demotion of a slave who had played an essential role always came at a cost. Slaves were seen as people without honor, so there was no dignity to be offended, as the master saw things. But the restlessness and resentment of a slave who had come unstuck from an accustomed role or routine had the potential to unsettle the whole household—and this was truer still if the disrupted role had involved a sexual component. A wise master found a way to tread carefully in these cases.

If the animus against Monnica was indeed caused by sexual jealousy or by a handmaid's fear of losing privileges earned through sexual service, this tells us that neither Patricius nor his mother bothered— or was able—to give the situation the expert attention that it required. A more becoming way of handling the displacement of Patricius's slave mistress might have involved assigning her new and interesting duties that made her feel she had been promoted. But there is little evidence that either Patricius or his mother used strategies other than brutality in controlling the slave members of their household.

So we can deduce that Monnica had left a household where a veneer of benevolent authority reinforced the master's power and joined one where tensions were left to spin out of control. We can detect a hint of pride in her stories of how she rose to the occasion. Still, it is tempting to imagine that Monnica had support from an invisible source. It would not have been unusual for her parents to send her closest childhood companion with her when she married, to act as her personal servant in her new life. If this was the case, Illa would have been a formidable ally.

The stories parents tell their children are usually ones they think will be useful, either to explain their own actions or to warn the children of an obstacle they hope can be avoided or deftly managed. As we know, Augustine risked stumbling into a worrying sexual triangle at the time of his own engagement, and this may explain why Monnica told him such detailed stories of her troubled early marriage—and perhaps why Augustine listened as closely as he clearly did. It was a warning not to fall into the same trap as his father had done.

As landowners, Monnica and Patricius played a pivotal role in the web that bound their little world into the wider frame of the Roman Empire. Theirs was an intensely hierarchical society: 10 percent of the population was enslaved; at the other end of the spectrum were the five or six hundred illustrious families of the Roman Senate, which had their base in Rome but owned land across the empire. Many of these families had vast estates in Africa. The scions of such families only rarely visited their holdings, and the local population dealt largely with their representatives—estate managers and secretaries. But one of these great landowners arrived in Carthage every year to serve his term as proconsul of Africa.

It was the smaller landowners, however, who held the system together. They were the indispensable people who ran the municipal councils, who paid the taxes—even if they did so on the backs of their slaves and tenants—and who kept the people below them in the pyramid in check. For Patricius, it was a world of giving and calling in favors. There were sometimes money troubles: in a world where the rich had their wealth tied up in land and slaves, even the more prosperous families could face cash-flow problems after a bad harvest or a drop in grain prices. Monnica must have counted herself lucky that

Patricius was expansive and well-liked. Power in this kind of world is about having friends, a network of people who will do what they can for you when you are in trouble.

Monnica bore Patricius three surviving children. The first, probably the older son, Navigius, seems to have been born when Monnica was in her mid-teens. Then there was a girl, who was not with them for long because she married—though later in life, as a widow, she was close to at least one of her brothers. Monnica's younger son, Augustine, was born when his mother was twenty-three.

But the marriage was not an easy one, even after Monnica had won the trust of her mother-in-law. Patricius was repeatedly unfaithful to his wife. She may have been grateful for his infidelities if they allowed her to escape the cycle of almost continuous pregnancy and childbirth experienced by many Roman women. On the other hand, there may have been numerous pregnancies but only three that produced a surviving child. Only about a quarter of Roman children survived their first year, and roughly half reached adulthood, so Augustine may have had siblings who died in childhood.

Augustine tells us that Patricius was warmhearted but volatile. "He was exceptional both for his kindness and for his irascible anger"[25]—in other words, someone who could not be trusted to manage himself. So Monnica intervened, becoming one of those wives who try, as quietly as they can, to contain their husbands' tendency to get into trouble. In this, her patience and willingness to look for opportunities where others saw only difficulty would stand her in good stead.

When her son Augustine looked back at this period of Monnica's life, he showed an unusual interest in the dilemma faced by the wife of an unpredictable and sometimes violent man in that highly patriarchal culture. "She knew not to oppose an angry husband, neither in action nor even in speaking."[26] Even if the law would protect

76

her against serious abuse, there was a sense that a wife was more respected if she did not ask for help. This was a society that saw the social hierarchy as ordained by God, and every wife understood her place as second to that of her husband. Monnica did not see her effort to "manage" Patricius as invisibly as possible as a failure to advocate for herself. Rather, it was a way of maintaining their joint standing in a community that valued women's strategic deference.

If met with unjust criticism, Monnica would make her case, but she was cautious about the timing; as she saw it, it was a question of having the wit and self-control to choose her battles. "When she saw he had wound down and become calm, and the moment was right, she would explain her thinking, in case perhaps he had acted without sufficient reflection."[27] As a beloved younger son, Augustine was naturally inclined to take his mother's side. But he has been criticized for praising her handling of a potentially threatening imbalance of power, steering perhaps too close to faulting women who were not so fortunate.

Monnica herself seems to have taken for granted that wives who did not manage their husbands' tempers could expect physical abuse. When other women complained about the behavior of their husbands, she was more practical than sympathetic. "Speaking as if she were joking but meaning it in earnest, she would blame their tongues, saying that the marriage agreement they had heard read out was in effect a sale making them the husband's slave. In light of their status it made no sense to try to lord it over their masters."[28]

To a modern ear, this is alarming, and of course it sounds dangerously close to blaming the victim. Yet, in that harsh world, Monnica's first concern would have been to help her friends de-escalate situations that had spun out of control. If Monnica had found a fleeting sense of agency in her efforts to manage her husband, she would have wanted to share what she had learned.

As Monnica told the story, when she shared her advice with her friends, "they were amazed, knowing what a ferocious husband she had to put up with."[29] Everyone knew that Patricius's volatile temperament could be threatening, especially when he had been drinking. "But there was never a sound or a mark to suggest that Patricius had beaten his wife, or that the domestic peace was broken, even for a day."[30] Monnica was left feeling that her advice and example had been useful to others and that they admired her for handling a difficult situation with skill and diplomacy. But Augustine is perhaps rather jejune in the conclusion he draws: "Those who followed her advice found by experience that it was something to be grateful for; the ones who did not, were humbled and mistreated."[31]

In his later life as a Christian bishop, Augustine would write letters and sermons offering advice on marital harmony. In these letters he tended to suggest that most husbands could be steered toward acceptable behavior if only the wife would approach him with charm and patience. A bishop also had a duty to admonish any man who treated his wife unkindly, and there is no evidence that he failed in this regard. Yet the task of encouraging wives to make light of their husbands' behavior seems to have come to him more easily.

If Augustine reveals any weakness of judgment in this arena, however, he came by it honestly. His was a world in which there was little scope for a direct challenge to male dominance. And there was also, perhaps, a psychological aspect to his insistence. Children who grow up in abusive households often internalize the distress caused by a parent's behavior. They tend to believe, however wrongly, that if only they could find the right formula to placate the abuser, the abusive behavior would cease. So there may be an emotional charge behind Augustine's fierce belief in his mother's methods.

One imagines that as he tells the story, Monnica's now grown son is seeking closure and looking for a way to put uncomfortable memories to rest. Even if the young Monnica's attempts to steer her husband away from frightening behavior or violence were largely successful, witnessing them must have distressed Augustine and his siblings. For Monnica, the presence of a sympathetic son—especially one who paid as close attention to her struggles as Augustine's memoir reveals that he did—could only be a source of strength. One can understand why the boy was the object of such intense affection.

For a mother in the Roman provinces, a beloved son was both a consolation and a route to a better future. Monnica and her husband spotted Augustine's gifts early on. They made sacrifices for his education, putting off other expenses to pay his school fees, knowing as they did that the ability to write brilliant speeches could be the ticket to anything from a stable living as a schoolmaster to upward mobility in the imperial administration or even a career in politics.

As Augustine looked back years later, he credited Monnica's ambition as the force that drove him first to the provincial capital in Carthage and then, after Patricius's death, to Italy—first to the old capital at Rome and then to the real center of power, the imperial court at Milan. Augustine's considerable successes would offer a satisfying answer to the years of enduring the temper of a swaggering provincial *paterfamilias*.

The plan that Monnica laid for her son rested on the idea that what a person had to offer did not depend on birth or circumstance. What mattered was patience and strength of character. It was a stroke of considerable fortune that such a clear path out of Thagaste lay open. But as things turned out, the opportunity did not come without cost. It brought consequences that were not at all what Monnica had hoped for.

FIGURE 2. Queen and founding ruler of the African city that bore her name, Cyrene was a figure of legend and an icon of feminine daring; she was remembered by the fifth-century poet Nonnus as "a deer-chasing second Artemis, a lion-killing Nymph" (*Dionysiaca* 13, 300–301). This mosaic from the second or third century shows her in a calmer moment. (Museum of Lambaesis, Algeria.) *Photo courtesy of the author.*

~ CHAPTER FOUR ~

UNA

THE MOTHER OF AUGUSTINE'S SON WAS AMONG THE HUM-
bler of the women he immortalizes in his *Confessions*—and
the one whose position was most precarious. Just as with Tacita, we do not know her name, although the name by which scholars
have come to refer to her, "Una," has roots in a historical source. *Una*
is simply the Latin word meaning "one" or "someone." She was the
woman with whom Augustine lived for over a decade when he was
a schoolteacher: "In those years I had someone, though not in lawful marriage.... [B]ut there was only one woman, and I stayed faithful to her bed."[1] This is the closest he comes to introducing her in the
Confessions, withholding her name in a twisted gesture of respect. But
since we want to bring her into focus, it is almost impossible to avoid
imagining her as a person who had a name. So "Una" will have to do.

It is natural to want to hear Una's story from her own point of
view, but the *Confessions* is the only historical source that records her
existence. Augustine calls the relationship "this thing without which

my life would have seemed to me to be not a life but a punishment."[2] His sense of her vacillates between quiet reverence and the hyperbole of a besotted poet, convinced that no one had ever loved a woman so deeply: "My heart had fused with hers."[3]

Of course, we have no way of knowing how Una felt about the liaison. We have no insight into how it started: whether he formally engaged a free concubine or simply made sexual use of a slave. We can only speculate as to whether they bantered and flirted when they first met or the tenor of their first encounter was openly coercive. We do know that Augustine came to depend on her and to love her. But, like most men who take up with women whose involvement is rooted in coercion or economic need, he almost certainly had no great understanding of what his beloved thought about or felt for him.

Still, we can piece together a blurry picture to supplement the daunting thinness of the trace she left in the world. There are a few clues, and there are some things about which we can make educated guesses. For example, although no story survives of when and how the relationship began, it is almost certain that it had started by the time of Patricius's death in 372, the year Augustine turned eighteen. We know this because Una bore him a son, called Adeodatus, the following year. The roots of the arrangement may reach back a year or two earlier, because we know that Monnica had expressed concern about her son's sexual restlessness the year before he went on to Carthage for his advanced studies.

This means that Augustine was no more than seventeen or at most eighteen when Una fell pregnant, and this in turn suggests that the liaison probably began when she was in her teenage years. Una may have been a trusted slave or freedwoman of the family who was slightly older than Augustine and had been assigned to the role of caring for the master's son. Whatever the case, he found her intoxicating. After at least a dozen years together, he remembered that with her he was "trying to satiate an insatiable lust, and the habit held me violently captive and tortured me."[4]

We have only a very limited understanding of Una's legal and economic circumstances. It goes without saying that she was not an important person in the eyes of the ancient world: whatever her reason for accepting the meagre sliver of stability that service as a concubine afforded her during her teens and twenties, the very fact of her occupation assures us that she had no better prospects. She may have been a slave or a freedwoman, or even a freeborn person of low status. Augustine mentions explicitly that the relationship was not a marriage, and the fact that he felt it necessary to do so suggests that she was a free citizen who could be mistaken for a wife. The question of her legal status would have influenced her reasons for accepting the liaison, but in either case it was a move in the direction of respectability.

Respectability was a curious thing in the Roman world, a line drawn between those who could expect to be protected from sexual exploitation and those who could not. Being born into the right circumstances made a decisive difference in one's prospects and outcome, of course. But respectability could also be a performance. A nobody who was able to act the part exceptionally well held a sort of wild card in the social order. For women, this involved broadcasting an aura of sexual unavailability if at all possible, though a fair bit of luck was required to pull it off.

The idea was to get a man of higher standing to choose you as his favorite. Even a slave had a fighting chance in this arena: if she could find a man on the rise and be selected as his concubine, she could gradually reinvent herself as his socially acceptable consort, trusting that by the time he had achieved a higher standing in society, the traces of her origins would have begun to fade. In some cases, the relationship could lead to manumission and marriage to the man himself. We know this happened regularly from surviving gravestones in which a husband tells the story of his dead wife's journey from slavery into freedom and respectable marriage in her epitaph.[5] Legal literature also recognizes the phenomenon; the Roman jurists return repeatedly to the case of the man who grants freedom to a slave concubine in order to marry her. The practice is treated as perfectly legitimate, except in the case of senators, whose wives were expected to have been born into respectable families to begin with.

This possibility of freedom and social mobility is of course the great difference between Roman slavery and the slavery of the eighteenth and nineteenth centuries. Slaves were people who had been taken captive in war or piracy or born in the wrong place and time. There was no racial divide between slaves and citizens, and the Romans did not share the view of the Greeks that free citizens were inherently superior to slaves; slaves were simply unlucky. Masters were encouraged to think of slaves as people who might one day earn their freedom. The Romans were notoriously philosophical about the fickleness of fortune: being captured by pirates and sold into slavery, they reckoned, could happen to anyone.

In any case, while the question whether Una was enslaved or free is important, her status did not influence her reasons for wanting the relationship to be a success. Even if there was no marriage, affection paid dividends. Nostalgic memories of the time spent together could foster a sense of her value in later years. When he had reached his prime and hers was behind her, he might still help her every now and then.

We must be content to remain without answers of any kind for other important questions, including the all-important one of Una's

character. Was she a long-suffering paragon of humble loyalty? This
is the picture Augustine paints of her. Or was she a spirited and clear-
eyed operator? If she was a free citizen, her intent all along may have
been to hold Augustine's interest as long as she could while she put
aside money and then to set herself up with a small business, perhaps
with Augustine's help, when he moved on. If she was a slave, the prize
at stake could well have been her freedom.

It had always been common for young men of good family and character to maintain a stable, unmarried relationship during the years
between puberty and mature adulthood. Once he had attained the
age of majority, the man would enter into an arranged marriage, ide-
ally with a girl from a local family slightly richer and more powerful
than his own. Marriage could offer a potent form of social cement,
and when a man married, he also formed a partnership with his
wife's father—if the father was living—and her male kin. The right
father-in-law could be both mentor and financial backer.

Up until the mid-fourth century, committing a son to a local heiress as early as possible was seen as the best way to secure his future,
even if the marriage itself were delayed until he reached maturity.
These alliances were often forged when the prospective bride and
groom were still in infancy. A powerful local father-in-law could
be a source of patronage and wealth for the young man and for his
children.

But in the second half of the fourth century, new routes of
upward mobility were opening up. Provincial families began to plot
new strategies for maneuvering their sons into positions where they
could attract the notice of powerful men connected to the imperial
administration, in hope that one of them might have a daughter with

a sizeable dowry. This involved thinking carefully about the timing of a son's betrothal.

In the 370s, when Augustine came of age, families who could afford the luxury were keeping promising sons off the marriage market until they reached maturity. An accomplished man in his thirties could attract a better dowry and a more powerful father-in-law than he might have done earlier on the strength of his prospects. The "right" father-in-law might want confirmation of a protégé's value before committing his daughter. So it made sense for the young man's parents to delay his marriage until he had reached his peak. Any match for which a young man was eligible was one he ought to try, socially speaking, to outgrow.

As a result, liaisons with low-status women became even more important. Directing the passions of socially climbing sons toward a single, stable partner made them look more promising and responsible than did random coupling with whomever was available. In the best scenario, the concubine would be one of the slaves or former slaves of the young man's family, trusted women who could turn to other duties when it came time for the young man to marry.

If the concubine was not one of his family's slaves or freedwomen, she would take sole responsibility for any offspring. The Roman rules of marriage made clear that the father bore no responsibility for children born out of wedlock. In any case, once the young man had raised himself to a position suited to the ambitions of his family, he was expected to marry. With luck, he would find a bride whose standing was higher than he might have hoped for as a young man; if not, the parents had at least done their best.

But this strategy of leaving young men in unmarried "starter" relationships as their careers matured had an unexpected emotional cost, and Una's case gives witness to the brutality of the practice. By the time Augustine was ready to seek a wife, they had been together for over a decade, and their illegitimate son—who had become his father's protégé though not his heir—was on the verge of manhood.

Yet, when he describes their sexual relationship, Augustine makes clear that by then their relationship was, for him, both a first reckoning with love and a matter of sexual obsession. "In those years I had someone (*unam*)—not that I knew her as a lawful wife, but rather, my restless lust had sought her out without plan or reason."[6] His somewhat mournful description emphasizes the distinction between lawful marriage and the yoke of lust. He is unhappy with his own role in the relationship but adamant about how he felt about her.

Despite his love for her, he recognizes that their relationship was not what it ought to have been. "But she was the only one, and I was faithful to her. I learned by experience how wide a difference there is between the discipline of a marriage partnership for the sake of having children, and...an arrangement based on lust, in which children are born without being wanted."[7] He is frank about the fact that his son, Adeodatus, was an accident, though it was not long before both parents fell under his spell: "Once born, they force their parents to love them."[8]

But what would happen to Una and their child when he married? Augustine may have intended to settle some sort of retirement sum on the boy's mother, but he would have faced difficulties if he tried to adopt Adeodatus as his legal heir. Roman law frowned on attempts to blur the distinction between legitimate and illegitimate offspring. In this sense, with respect to his son, Augustine may have been, like his own mother, besotted with a boy whose intelligence dazzled him—he is very clear on this point—and whose company he cherished. Yet he was aware that he could not in all honesty claim him as an heir, either before a Roman magistrate or in the sight of God. Although the tone is one of self-criticism, there is also an elegiac quality to Augustine's account; it is a story that will end badly. The relationship with Una came to an abrupt end. And sadly, the beloved son who was its legacy would not survive long into adulthood.

Turning to Una's point of view, we have to start from the problem of her status; there was no corner of Roman life where status did not influence how people were treated, how others thought about them, and even how they thought about themselves. But Una's story is also the story of the fluidity of Roman life. Every Roman began from a starting point, a birth position, that would seem disturbingly restrictive to most modern people. But there were ways to edge out of one position and into another, and this was notoriously true for women. For example, if a female slave could persuade her master that she would make a better wife than any woman he might find among the free citizenry, it was in his power to free her and marry her.

If you look very closely, it is sometimes possible to find traces of a person who either succeeded in moving from one social status to another or who was caught—whether by death or by the course of events—in mid-flight. Una may well have been such a case, a woman whom chance had connected to a man who had it in his gift to help her to reinvent herself, if she could encourage him to forget, week by week and month by month, that his intentions toward her had not been honorable. Augustine's remarkable comment about their child— as someone who was not supposed to be born but who, once he had burst forward into life, was impossible not to love the way a parent loves a child—is telling. It almost certainly had its echo in the unexpected and unwanted feelings that Augustine found himself feeling for Una.

But Una herself had to be more clearheaded about their relationship. It is not impossible that she returned his love, but even if she did not, she had every reason to edge the relationship away from one of thoughtless exploitation toward one in which Augustine felt a sense of loyalty. If she could manage this, she had everything to gain. Sadly, there is clear evidence that the venture—if, indeed, there *was* such a venture—was not a success. Augustine too was trying to reposition himself, and for him to succeed it was necessary for Una to fail.

Augustine's hints about his mother's role in his search for a concubine suggest that Una was a slave or freedwoman belonging to Patricius or Monnica, perhaps even the child of one of the slaves they had grown up with. One clue to this family connection is that Augustine kept Una's son with him in Milan when the liaison ended. It was not common for a natural father to retain custody if the boy was not otherwise a dependent of the household. Concubinage conveyed no rights to the female partner or her children, and the children bore no legal relationship to their father. Concubinage had something in common with marriage, but it was many steps down the ladder. Only a woman with very few options would see concubinage as an opportunity—but Una was a woman with very few options.

Augustine emphasized that he and Una were not married, which suggests that at least by the time she reached Milan, she was a free woman. (Otherwise there would have been no danger of anyone thinking that their relationship had the status of a marriage.) But this doesn't mean that Una was freeborn. As mentioned above, Roman legal writers repeatedly mention cases where owners granted freedom to slave concubines, and disturbingly, it was within the owner's right to demand that a former slave whom he had freed should serve as his concubine. An owner who freed a slave automatically became the slave's patron, and this placed a number of obligations on the former slave; in the case of a female slave, sex was explicitly one of the services she was expected to provide if required.

Before trying to make sense of the situation faced by a woman whose owner or patron offered her this status—or imposed it—we must understand a few things about Roman sex and reproduction. The most important is that, from the Roman standpoint, male sexual interest in women was fundamentally predatory. A far-reaching dual standard defined women's social status partly through their success at resisting male sexual attention, whereas the successful exercise of sexual prowess was an equal and opposite way for men to claim status. Within this system, slaves and other low-status people were notoriously vulnerable to sexual exploitation, coercion, and violence. Male and female slaves—many of them children—were expected to serve the sexual needs of their masters, though because of the dual standard, mistresses were discouraged from exploiting their slaves in the same way.

Marriage was a very specific kind of relationship, and one that was rarer than it is in the modern world. The right to marry was restricted to Roman citizens, and the principal value of doing so was the resulting contract that ordered questions of inheritance. In other words, marriage cemented a reproductive collaboration between two separate families, establishing a secure answer to questions about property—that is, which among a man's biological offspring could claim rights as his heirs. The jurists referred to the agreement between a man and a woman that he would recognize her offspring as his heirs as "marital intent." Recall that a wife did not join her husband's family; she remained part of the family of her father, even if she lived, as most wives did, with her husband.

Although Roman law did not aim to control male sexuality, it adhered to the principle that a man should be legally entangled with the newborn children of only one sexual partner at a time. Divorce was freely available in Roman law, so sequential monogamy was an option even in the fourth century, when Roman law was administered by Christian emperors. But polygamy was disallowed. The Greeks and Romans believed that a man should have only one wife, though many minority groups within the Roman Empire followed non-Roman norms and legal traditions that allowed for polygamy. For example, in Judaism, the multiple wives of the Old Testament patriarchs were accepted as a precedent, and the practice was carried forward by rabbis across the Roman period and into the Middle Ages.

Christianity, of course, had imposed the idea that its bishops should only have one wife, and one might reasonably guess that the early Christians found a "one man, one woman" principle in the story of Adam and Eve. But this wasn't the case. By the fourth century, some preachers railed against the double standard for women and men, but the church fathers recognized that the book of Genesis moves seamlessly from describing Adam's partnership with Eve to the multiple wives and concubines of Abraham and the later patriarchs. So they did not read the story as a sign that the creator intended for Adam and Eve to be an exclusive pair. Instead, they pointed to Eve's encounter with the serpent of Paradise and the eating of the fruit of the Tree of Knowledge, with its disastrous consequences, as the reason for women's subordination to men.

Christian preachers also recognized that in a slave society, the sexual exploitation of slaves was central to the life of every household; just as slaves were ubiquitous, so was the use of their bodies by people who owned them, and indeed by others. (By law, free men were permitted to force sex on another man's slave, though causing physical harm to the slave was condemned as damaging the owner's property.) Slaves were understood to have no honor, so protecting them from sexual exploitation was seen as unnecessary, and no laws or widely held norms restricted how many slaves a man could sexually exploit. Procreation was not the aim of these unions, but any resulting children brought economic benefit to the slave's owner, since they inherited their mother's enslaved status and became her owner's property.

Sexually molesting a woman who had been adopted as her owner's concubine, however, was not advisable. It was seen as an affront to the owner's right to enjoy his property undisturbed. Similarly, if the owner had freed a slave concubine or taken a concubine from among his family's freedwomen, molesting her without his permission was seen as a violation of her patron's right to expect her sexual fidelity. Roman law was clear on the fact that, like wives, established concubines were expected to be faithful to their male partners, especially if the partner was also her patron.

Since the focus of marriage was to provide clear guidance regarding a man's legitimate heirs, male citizens would often progress through different types of union at different points in the life cycle. In youth or old age, a man might reasonably want to avoid begetting heirs. A young man's first sexual experiences tended to be with slaves or prostitutes if he could afford them, while a widower whose legal heirs were grown would often take a concubine rather than a second wife in order to avoid creating confusion in his estate.

A free male citizen could also expect to sleep with other low-status people in addition to slaves, male or female (though Christian writers frowned on sexual exploitation of other men). Payment was sometimes involved with prostitutes (who might be slave or free), but the sex was not necessarily consensual: neither law nor custom ordered punishment of a man who forced sex upon people of low status.

Established concubinage and marriage were viewed as mutually incompatible. By definition, a woman was not an established concubine if her partner also had a wife at the same time. But both marriage and concubinage were understood to be compatible with the male partner's use of incidental low-status sexual partners. The religious or philosophical writers who frowned on simultaneous access to multiple partners were generally viewed as eccentric. Whether slave or free, low-status people were exposed to the threat of forced sex with whatever man noticed them and decided to molest them.

A female sexual partner of high status outside marriage was out of the question, however. The important thing was not to step on a highborn man's toes by bothering his daughter or—God forbid—his wife. Assaulting or seducing a highborn woman (or man, for that matter) invited the serious criminal charge of *stuprum*, the violation of a respectable person's sexual honor. The marriage laws of the emperor Augustus had established penalties for *stuprum* as well as adultery; assaulting or seducing a married woman was a capital crime. (Indeed, adultery was only recognized if a married *woman* was involved, since it was understood to be a crime against her husband.) In principle, only slaves, noncitizens, procuresses, and prostitutes were identified as "safe" objects of extramarital sex. But a circular definition seems to have come into play; the jurists recognized *stuprum* only where the victim was understood to be a person of status or respectability, and respectability was a luxury that the poor could not afford.

Roman law provided a smooth and draconian clarity for the child-custody issues that might emerge from nonmarital unions. Or rather, it negated them by providing a firm and irrevocable ruling in advance. Indeed, under Roman law, it was the intent of the couple with respect to a child's custody that distinguished concubinage from legitimate marriage. A man who sought legal heirs could marry and divorce freely, but at the time of conception, he must establish "marital intent" with the prospective mother of the child. Equally importantly, he must establish it with her father or guardian, if she had one. Roman marriage did not require a written contract or formal ritual: the only material point was an agreement of intent between the two spouses— although ancient tradition also imposed a symbolic requirement that the couple spend three nights together in succession.

Oddly, while Roman law required no paperwork for a man to take a wife, he was required to sign an affidavit (*testatio*) declaring that the union was not a marriage if he took a concubine whose social status was high enough that he might reasonably have married her. This would become important if he died, as legitimate children had a right to a share of his estate, while illegitimate children did not. Some jurists opined that any stable sexual union with a freeborn woman should be recognized as a marriage.

Roman lawyers most hated ambiguous cases—for example, the elderly widower who takes a concubine instead of a second wife so as not to force his grown-up children to share their inheritance, then later becomes fond of his children by the concubine and wants to adopt them as legitimate heirs. Surviving paperwork from a number of lawsuits in the third and fourth centuries gives evidence that this did happen. But it was a messy business, and Roman law frowned upon it.

Although it seems strange to us, it was seen as entirely honorable for a man to have children whom he did not intend to support, but delaying decisions about whether he would do so was discouraged. Children—especially male children—became more valuable as they became older. This was in part because of the mortality rate in infancy and youth. The longer a child survived, the better the odds for the future. Child mortality meant that a man who had thought he had plenty of heirs might suddenly find that he had fewer than expected and might thus find himself regretting that his living children were by the wrong mother.

If the lack of any material sexual protection for female slaves and women of low status was intimidating and even dangerous, this does not mean they had absolutely no chance of fighting back. What male owners and patrons most feared was the concubine who did everything to please a man up to the point of marriage—and then turned against him.

A fascinating case survives from a lavish funerary altar dedicated to the memory of an eight-year-old girl, Junia Procula, that is now held in the Uffizi Galleries in Florence. The front of the tombstone shows a portrait of the child. Her hair is styled in the distinctive corkscrew ringlets of the Flavian empresses, a clue that allows us to estimate the date of the portrait. An inscription records that her death left her parents "wretched with grief" and marks their intention to add their own bones to hers in the grave upon their deaths. But on closer look, a troubling story emerges: while the name of her father, Marcus Junius Euphrosynus, is clearly legible in the inscription, that of her mother has been hacked away. This suggests that sometime after the child's death, the father placed a curse on the mother's memory, a *damnatio memoriae*, and made a vow never again to speak her name.

One might be tempted to imagine that the couple's marriage fell apart after the death of their child, but a second inscription on the back of the altar tells a far more disturbing story. It begins by invoking the speaker's hatred of a woman called Acte: "Here is written an everlasting curse on the freedwoman Acte, sorceress, faithless, deceitful, hardhearted. A nail and a hemp rope to hang her neck and boiling pitch to burn up her evil heart." Next the inscription summarizes her misdeeds from the perspective of her abandoned husband: Acte was a slave whose master freed and married her, but sometime afterward, she ran away with another man, taking along with her two slave children—a girl and a boy—who were her husband's property. "She abducted attendants—a handmaid and a boy—from her patron while he lay in bed, leaving him, an old man abandoned and robbed, to despair."[9] The children may have been Acte's own offspring from the time when she herself was a slave, in which case one can see why she wanted to take them with her, though it was clearly against the law.

Given the *damnatio memoriae* against the mother of the child to whom the altar is dedicated, it is reasonable to suggest that Acte was first the slave and then the wife of Marcus Junius Euphrosynus. On this reading, Acte stayed peaceably with her husband while their daughter Junia Procula was living, but at some point after the child's death, she left him—although unlike other married women, those who had first been slaves and then freed for the sake of marriage did not legally have the right to initiate a divorce.

There is no way of knowing whether Acte's departure was the product of a well-laid and long-nurtured plan to escape from the household where she had lived as a slave or an act of impulse, the result of a fleeting opportunity that she snatched when it came. But the episode tells us two things worth taking into account in trying to understand Una. The first is that Acte's husband, the one who represented her as wanting nothing more than to be buried with him and their daughter, had no idea what his wife was thinking or feeling about their life together.

The second, equally important, is that even women whom the law had classed as nonpersons could sometimes find ways to act on what they thought and felt.

To a child, the difference between enslavement and free but grinding poverty was probably not especially noticeable. Household slaves in high-born families knew that they were far better fed and clothed than other slaves or the free poor. Many children were orphans. Some had mothers, but so many women died in childbirth that by no means all of them did; if not, an older sibling or relative might take an interest, but other children simply had no one looking out for them.

And given the predatory sexual landscape of ancient Rome, every Roman child of low or slave status had a series of far-reaching decisions to make as soon as he or she was able. Children were already familiar with sexual exploitation and probably sexual assault, particularly since the sleeping arrangements of the poor did not allow for individual bedrooms. Slaves slept in doorways and corridors and some at the foot of their owners' beds. (Others were expected to sleep in the bed itself as their masters' sexual playthings, even as children.)

Some children would learn early on to leverage their sexual attractiveness as a source of power, aiming to withhold not sexual availability—it could not be withheld, really—but at least some element of charm or recognition that the predators might crave but could not control. These children might grasp at a certain kind of fragile agency. Others would simply try to endure whatever befell them.

As a child, Una was probably aware, dimly at first, that as she grew, she was ever more a target of sexual attention. So a game of evasion had to begin. She would have to find and mobilize a network of allies and potential protectors: people who would steer the attention of predators away from her or claim not to know where she was. Relatives or older friends who felt protective toward her—if there were any—might offer to stand in for her, perhaps even successfully. If this happened, she knew she was loved.

In either case, it was clearly a stroke of good fortune if a free male from the master or patron's family began to show an interest in taking her on as a regular partner, especially if he was not physically repulsive or disturbingly old. Belonging to a man of standing meant most other men would leave her alone. So when Augustine made his interest known, Una probably breathed a sigh of relief. By his own evidence he was self-important and not particularly considerate, but he was reasonably well off and certainly not too old. When their baby came, he fell in love with it. When he began to travel, he wanted to bring her and the boy along, first to Rome and then to Milan. Things could have been a great deal worse. And the future? It was a problem to be faced when it came.

PART 2

∞

THINGS FALL APART

FIGURE 3. This fifth-century mosaic from the floor of the great dining hall in the House of Bacchus at Cuicul in Numidia celebrates a staged *venatio* rather than a hunt in the wild; the mosaic is probably a souvenir of gladiatorial games sponsored by the *dominus* in whose house it was displayed. (Museum of Djemila, Algeria.) *Photo: Angela C. Davies.*

CHAPTER FIVE

A SON OF AFRICA

THE LIVES OF OUR FOUR HEROINES WOULD COLLIDE IN Milan in the years between 385 and 387. To make sense of how and why this happened, we need to reckon with Augustine, whose account of the events in the *Confessions* is the closest we have to a reliable source. This does not mean we should trust him: his is only one version of the story, and saints do not always make reliable narrators.

The *Confessions* opens with Augustine's childhood in Numidia, an increasingly volatile world where the old rules no longer seemed to apply. For much of Augustine's childhood, Africa was embroiled in civil war. From the early 360s, when Augustine was six or seven, a particularly despicable count of Africa had governed the African provinces so corruptly that he was spoken of openly as an enemy of the people. In the way of things, Romanus would almost certainly have succeeded in fleecing his subjects and retired from office a wealthy man, but events came to a crisis shortly after 370, when Augustine was in his early teens.

In the early 370s, the Berber prince Nubel died and his sons fought over the right to succeed him, and Romanus made the mistake of meddling in the dynastic politics of the Numidian royal family. He backed the wrong brother, and Firmus, the brother who became king, did something unexpected: he turned against Romanus and the Roman power.

The victorious Firmus now raised a rebellion that swept eastward across Numidia from his stronghold in Mauretania, toward Carthage, where Augustine then was, around the time of his father's death. By 375, when Augustine was twenty-one and Monnica was a widow in her early forties, the rebellion had reached Calama, two days' journey west of Thagaste.

Along with the other landowners east of Calama, Monnica would have been listening closely to try to glean when and how the rebels would reach Thagaste. Quite possibly she was rooting for them—Rome was by no means universally loved—but this can't be established with certainty. But before the rebels reached Thagaste, the imperial army finally put them down. The leader of the imperial forces was the Spaniard Count Theodosius, master of the cavalry to the emperor. Two of his generals, his son Theodosius the Younger and their fellow Spaniard Magnus Maximus, would play an important role in the empire's future.

Trouble was also brewing in the African towns and villages for a different reason: a dispute over the powers of heaven. Africa had been a seedbed of Christianity for nearly three centuries. In the time of Augustine's great-grandparents, Christianity in the Roman world had been an "outsider" religion, practiced by a group that was sometimes persecuted but at other moments benefited from a widespread fascination with Eastern religions.[1] The third century had seen a flowering of religious and philosophical exploration of the inner human being and the transcendent nature of the soul, a heady atmosphere that has been likened to the spread of Eastern religions in the West in the late twentieth century.

Up to this point, the Christians had not been organized into a single international church. A helter-skelter web of local communities had grown up across the empire organically, often with two or more rival organizations in the same locality. Christians shared a sense of themselves as spiritual pilgrims whose first allegiance was to a heavenly kingdom, but sometimes little else. In the face of intermittent persecution, loyalty to the faith was sacrosanct.

Then, in the second decade of the fourth century, the emperor Constantine declared himself a friend of the Christian faith, and this changed everything. Treating its adherents preferentially in his legislation and building monumental churches on imperial property, the emperor transformed the faith from the creed of fringe communities into a cult worthy of heads of state. With precipitous speed, Christianity became a conduit of power and political favor, and this quickly led to conflict. Schisms and theological controversies erupted among churchmen as they sought to establish new rules for access to patronage and privilege, a struggle that was ultimately over the soul of Christianity itself.

Some Christians were unwilling to accept the standardization of Christianity under the emperor's patronage. One faction saw themselves as the church of the martyrs: these were the Old Believers who rallied under the leadership of Donatus, a bishop of Carthage elected shortly after Constantine's conversion.[2] Neglected by the emperor's representatives at the time when he was choosing who would receive his patronage, they retaliated by arguing that their outsider status kept them closer to the faith of the church as it had unfolded in the age of persecution. These Christians were known for their courage and their loyalty to the faith but also for a certain austere and uncompromising character.

These political and religious tensions largely remain below the surface of Augustine's narrative in the *Confessions*, but they are crucial to understanding his account of his childhood. For example, he offers a lively description of his earliest years, which, despite its good humor, is also a serious contribution to the debate among African Christians of his day about whether children were born innocent or whether they should be baptized early in life to save them from hellfire should they die in childhood.

He begins, somewhat disarmingly, with his earliest awareness of the world around him. He tells us, "Back then I only knew how to suckle, to be soothed by pleasures, to cry when my body vexed me, nothing more."[3] There is a wry self-irony in his description of childhood experiences that he, of course, does not remember. "Later I began to smile, at first when asleep, and then while awake. This is what people told me about myself, and I believed them, since we see other babies doing it, though I don't remember doing it myself."[4]

There is an important theme here that he keeps coming back to: how the will of a child is often at odds with the world. Babies and toddlers cry not only because they are uncomfortable but also because they want things that are dangerous, or impossible, or simply wrong.

In Augustine's thinking about his early childhood, one hears the wisdom drawn from his own experience with parenting, but his way of looking at himself from the outside seems to reflect the affectionate stories told by Monnica. He muses on his first efforts to try to control the adults around him: "And when I didn't get my way, either because I wasn't understood or because I asked for something harmful, I was angry that my elders would not obey me, and that these people wouldn't be my slaves."[5] The ironic tone of what comes next again seems to reflect the point of view of other family members. "So I got my revenge on them by howling."[6] Then, seeming to relish the absurdity of his own line of reasoning, he returns to his own experience as a parent: "I've learned, from those babies in a position to teach me, that this is how they are."[7]

Baptism involved washing with blessed water, anointing with holy oil, or both, and all Christians believed that the ritual could cleanse a person's soul of any guilt for past misdeeds. But the Old Believers, the faction Monnica had grown up in, believed that since children were born innocent of sin, it was better to wait to baptize them until adulthood. The cleansing of baptism was a once-in-a-lifetime opportunity to wash away one's past sins, so baptizing a child was seen as depriving him or her of a chance, later in life, to make a clean start.

But in adulthood Augustine would join the opposing party, which felt that, given children's vulnerability to disease and the possibility that they might not reach adulthood, depriving them of the spiritual safety conferred by baptism was wrong. He also believed that children were not quite so innocent as his opponents claimed. "With my own eyes," he says, "I have witnessed a little one who was possessive; he couldn't yet talk but he glared with a pale face and a bitter expression at his fellow nursling."[8] He is speaking of a simple fact of daily life: "Is there anyone who doesn't know that this happens?"[9]

Augustine also has a very different reason for being interested in his childhood frustrations. The experience of children illustrates something important, as he sees it: that people often don't understand the real significance of their own actions or how their actions fit in to the wider human picture. Children are the obvious example of this, he reasons, but the point holds true for adults as well: fear rather than wisdom often brings someone into line. What is needed, he thinks, is a benevolent authority to guide them and when necessary to impose a limit on their ability to act on their badly judged impulses.

In his account of his school years, Augustine remembers the authority of adults around him as benevolent but also terrifying. "As a little one," he tells God, "I prayed to you with no little feeling, to keep me from being beaten in school."[10] The adults only smiled at him because they understood what he didn't: that the fear and the beatings had a purpose.[11] In retrospect, it really wasn't important that his teacher was not a saint. "He was the type who writhed more with anger and envy if his colleague bested him on some trivial point than I did if my playmate beat me in a ball game."[12] But what mattered was that there was a point to it all—even if the point wasn't apparent to the child.

Schooling also aimed at bringing the boys into line with the expectations of an empire as cruel as it was glorious. Augustine's discussion about how the boys were trained reflects a colonial sharpness in the obsession with rhetoric that held sway in the African schools. The acquisition of splendid language was a demanding discipline, and the pain involved was not only that of the beatings the boys received if they were found to fail. There was a harsh emotional logic in what the boys learned: they were preparing themselves for a life of disappointing people. Putting people off or finding the words to justify an uncomfortable decision handed down from on high would be their daily lot if they were lucky enough to join the imperial bureaucracy.

Augustine tells us a story that conveys something of how the African schoolroom entangled the pursuit of beautiful speech with the demands of empire. A competition was set in which the pupils would perform famous speeches from Virgil, which they themselves had recast into prose. "The prize was glory, and for the loser shame and the fear of a flogging."[13]

The poem in question was of course Virgil's *Aeneid*. The task was "to speak the words of Juno in her rage and anguish when she could not turn the Trojan king away from the path to Italy."[14] It was a task to which boys in many ancient schoolrooms had applied themselves, according to a pedagogy that saw "a woman scorned" as the operatic height of human expression. "That boy won most applause who best captured the dignity of the queen's character in expressing her grief and rage, and clothed her sentiments in the most appropriate words."[15] The idea was to extend the boys' range and to hone their sense of the fit between language and emotion.

The exercise also carried an implicit message about the cost of empire. The *Aeneid* is, among other things, a story about departure and the pain that comes with it. Aeneas successively abandons Creusa, his Trojan wife, and afterward Dido, his Phoenician lover, because his fate is to reach Italy, win Lavinia, and establish a new people. If we view Juno's rage with North African eyes, we see in it a new significance. Juno would bring Aeneas to Africa and to Dido—the African queen whom he would have to betray to pursue his destiny. Dido was the avatar of the painful longing that the boys learned to express and explore. Augustine would remember how involving he found her story with some bemusement: "For what is more pitiful than a pitiless wretch weeping for Dido's death for love of Aeneas, but not weeping for his own death caused by failing to love You, my god, light of my heart?"[16] He would return to Dido's grief in remembering his own departure for Italy years later. But the connection between the wanderings of Aeneas and the wanderings in store for the boys in the schoolroom he would only make in retrospect. As a schoolboy, he learned that Africa had been a detour on a hero's path to glory.

Augustine acknowledges the crucial influence of his mother's great Christian faith, but he is quieter about the fact that Monnica counted herself among the Old Believers. We know this because she held back from baptizing her son as a child, one of the practices of which the sect disapproved. While Augustine was still a boy, he became seriously ill, so much so that he thought he would die. Even then his mother refused to take the step of baptizing him, which, given her beliefs, would be an admission that she expected him not to survive. "I demanded baptism in your Christid.... I demanded it in the name of my mother's piety and of our mother church." He tells us she was "deeply shaken," but she held firm.[17]

It is hard to know whether Augustine's talk of his sexual awakening in his teens, while he was a student in Madauros, is a form of backhanded boasting. "I burned with the flame of desire, gorging myself on hellish pleasures, and I dared to cast forth the tendrils of various shady love affairs."[18] He makes clear that by love affairs, he means "slimy bodily lust and the gushing of puberty."[19] His sense of how he was spinning out of control is almost exuberant: "I was thrown about, gushing out, and boiling away with my promiscuity."[20]

In 370, when he was sixteen, his parents decided to retrench financially and brought him home from Madauros. The plan was to send him on to the greater center of learning at Carthage, but financial issues had to be settled first. He writes, "Money was being arranged to pay for a stay further away in Carthage, more through my father's enthusiasm than his actual means.... [M]y father went beyond the limit of the family's means to spend whatever was necessary for his son to study, even in a faraway place."[21]

His enforced period at home, though, only made his sexual agitation more acute. "The brambles of desire towered over my head, and there was no hand to uproot them." To the contrary, Patricius was goading him, he felt. "When my father saw in the baths that I was hitting puberty and putting on the signs of restless young manhood, he was thrilled, just as if this meant he was already begetting grandchildren."

Visiting the municipal baths was a sociable activity in the Roman world, and groups of men would enjoy the steamy rooms together in a state of complete undress. Patricius's excitement at his son's puberty seems to have been partly delight at the prospect of grandchildren—"He gleefully told my mother"[22]—and partly a kind of swaggering pride at his son's sexual coming of age.

Understandably, Augustine cringed at the attention to his genitalia in a public setting. Looking back, he channels the anxious feeling into a religious frame, proof that his society had the wrong priorities. "He was feeling the heady glee in which this world forgets You, its creator, and instead loves what You've created."[23] Here, as often, the choice to write in the second person as an address to God creates the effect of a theatrical aside.

Augustine remembers Monnica's reaction to his sexual maturity as even more cringe-worthy. "I remember how she took me aside and with urgent insistence warned that I shouldn't engage in promiscuity, and especially that I shouldn't have an affair with someone else's wife." A rakish teenager at the time, Augustine dismissed all this as "womanish warnings, the kind of thing I would have been mortified to take seriously."[24] One wonders whether, with this attitude, he would have cooperated had she taken the matter in hand and begun to look for a wife.

In Augustine's retelling, the matter of his sexual awakening becomes a reason to suspect his parents of failing to set him on the right path. Just as they had failed to baptize him, now they failed to find him a wife to control his lust. Looking back, he connects his parents' failure to steer him into marriage with their worldly ambition at a time when he was all too easily toppled by the moral dangers of the unmarried state. "My family did not bother to save me from my downward spiral with marriage. Instead, the bother was about having me learn the best possible way of speaking."[25] In short, his parents were willing to risk his soul for the sake of ambition.

Even his pious mother was unwilling to commit him to marriage at this stage, and Augustine criticized her for letting her ambitions for his career stand in the way of good sense. "The reason she took no action was that she feared her ambition for me could be thwarted by a wife."[26] Looking back, he wants to underscore that even his pious mother's hopes for him were worldly: "This was not the hope she had for me in You for the world to come, but the hope of eloquence that both my parents shared for my career."[27] To a modern eye, Augustine seems to be trying to dodge responsibility for his own actions, but we should remember that while his father was living, the question whether he should marry fell not to him but to his *paterfamilias*.

Reading between the lines in this account, we arrive at an important and long-neglected question. Was it Monnica who brokered the relationship Augustine began in his late teens with Una, the woman with whom he lived for more than a decade, the mother of his son? If marrying off a son in his teens was no longer the habit of ambitious provincial parents, other ways had to be found to steer him away from reckless sexual wanderings. We can't know for certain, but it would have been characteristic for Monnica to settle on one of the female dependents of the family to serve as his concubine until he was in a position to marry. If this was the case, it would explain his somewhat reproachful way of talking about the decision to keep him from marrying just yet.

What Augustine wants his reader to notice here is the doggedly determined interest in his career that his parents seem to have shared. He was being groomed to become a master of rhetoric. "Their only concern was that I learn the best way of speaking, to persuade through the craft of words."[28]

Monnica and Patricius were encouraging him to hone his rhetorical skills, but without particularly caring, at that stage, that honing those skills involved encouraging him to stretch the truth. "I was more praiseworthy, the more of a fraud I became."[29] He felt restless about it all, he remembers, but he complied. Only later did he begin to suspect that empty ambition might have been the cause of the restlessness.

During the year in Thagaste, he found that social pressure only added to his craving for debauchery. "I was stumbling along in such thorough blindness that with the boys my age I was ashamed to be less shameless than them. I listened to them tossing around stories of their exploits, glorying in them more the more awful they were."[30] He was, he tells us, a shy boy who loved company, and this was a powerful motivation for getting into trouble. The way to earn standing in the group was to outdo each other in misbehavior. "And I wanted to do things not only for their own sake, but really because I wanted their praise."[31] Transgression held no real attraction for him, he avers, but if it brought him closer to the other boys, he was more than willing to join in.

In Book Two, he tells a memorable story of stealing fruit from a neighbor's tree. "There was a fruit tree near our vineyard heavy with fruit," he begins, "but the fruit was unappealing in either shape or flavor."[32] The incident, which takes place at night, is passed over very quickly. "After playing out in the streets until the middle of the night, we made our way to the tree to make away with its fruit. We took away a huge load, not to eat but to throw to the pigs.... [W]e simply wanted to do something that was not allowed."[33] The point of the story is the bliss of sociability, and it is difficult not to sympathize with the young Augustine's craving to join in the bonding of pointless crime. He was willing to pay a high price for the pleasure of belonging.

What makes the tale so memorable is Augustine's introspective, rambling analysis of why he joined in the theft. It wasn't because of need or even craving: "I had plenty of better fruit; I stole this only in order to steal, since once I had picked it, I threw it away. I dined on the crime itself, which was what I wanted to taste."[34] He considers how most crimes are committed for the sake of one of the "lovely material things" that people crave or for emotional stakes like honor and revenge. "When people look into a crime and try to establish its motive, they usually aren't believed unless the explanation is based on a desire to have things or avoid losing them."[35]

From his petty theft of pears, he has now built up his logical pyramid to reach the crime of passion. "Someone committed a murder. Why did he do it? He coveted the man's wife or land, or wanted to steal in order to live, or he was afraid of the victim taking something from him, or he had been wronged and was burning for revenge."[36] So the question of the crime without motive reaches its absurd extreme: "A person doesn't commit murder for no reason, just the desire to kill, does he? Who would believe that?"[37]

But then he concludes that people really do commit crimes just for the fun of it. There is no other way to explain why he would steal pears from a neighbor's tree when he could easily have pears that were much nicer by legitimate means. "The thing I loved in that theft was the theft itself, nothing else, though the theft was nothing, and I more miserable because of it."[38]

And yet, beyond the charm of committing such a pure and pointless crime, there was the sense of camaraderie with his friends. "And yet I wouldn't have done it on my own. . . . [W]hat I loved was the company of the others with whom I committed the crime."[39] Looking back, he wonders whether what he felt with these other boys was really friendship, since it mostly took the form of goading one another into misbehavior. Transgression was a social currency. "But when someone says, 'Let's do this!' it feels shameful not to be shameless."[40]

Not long afterward, Augustine left for Carthage as his parents had planned, though he mentions that his mother was now financing his education.[41] While Madauros had been roughly equal to Thagaste in size, he now found himself in a massive and cosmopolitan city. And while the wealth of the old Numidian kingdom had always been based in agriculture, Carthage had been the city of Phoenician sea traders back to the time of the Trojan War, dazzling the rest of the Mediterranean with precious metals, dyes, and spices. But eventually, the wealth and the swarm of ambitious people made him draw back: "Suddenly all my empty hopes became contemptible, and I longed for deathless wisdom with a fire in my heart I could hardly understand."[42]

He owed the change to Cicero. "At my impressionable age," he tells us, "I was studying works of rhetoric, an art in which I longed to shine, with the unworthy and pointless goal of puffing up my pride."[43] But one of the set texts had an unexpected effect on him: "In the normal course of studies I came to a book by a certain Cicero, whose tongue everyone praises."[44] The book was the *Hortensius*, which explains the importance of studying philosophy. For Augustine, the message hit home: "It wasn't . . . to sharpening my tongue that I applied the book, and what I valued in it wasn't the style of the writing, but what it was saying."[45]

Now he began the search for wisdom in earnest. Since he had been raised a Christian, this led quite naturally to an attempt to make sense of the Bible, but he didn't get very far. "Then I undertook a close study of the sacred scriptures, to get a sense of them. And I found that the subject matter was neither obvious to the arrogant nor straightforward to the simple, but lowly at the beginning and more lofty and mysterious the deeper one progressed."[46] At that stage, he couldn't make sense of them.

Looking back, Augustine sees his dismissal of the scriptures as a sign not of their inadequacy but of his own arrogance. To a self-important student of oratory, they "seemed trivial next to the majesty of Cicero. My high-headedness was unsuited to its manner, and my critical eye could not reach its meaning."[47] It would be years before Augustine came into contact with a Christian thinker who could talk about the Bible in a way that was not off-putting to someone who thought of himself as an intellectual.

And so, instead, he joined the sect of the Manichaeans. This offshoot of Christianity had a complex mythology based on the idea of a cosmic battle between the forces of light and darkness. Originating as it did in Persia, the sect had a whiff of exoticism that attracted Augustine and his friends. Equally appealing was the fact that it had always been illegal in the Roman Empire, both because it was classed as a dangerous superstition and because its followers were suspected of being spies for the Persian emperor.

After Augustine left for Carthage, his father died. It is difficult to know whether Patricius's death was expected; ancient people lived with the reality that a sudden fever could kill anyone within a matter of days or even hours. In any case, Augustine gives only a brief, sterile notice of his father's passing, in a later chapter of the *Confessions*, as if he is trying to avoid calling attention to it. Whereas he returns again and again to muse about his relationship with his mother, with his father there is a feeling that much is best left unsaid. Despite his standing as Augustine's *paterfamilias*, Patricius's presence in the *Confessions* is limited, reduced to a sketch of godless machismo.

Augustine does report that Monnica was successful in persuading Patricius to become a Christian before he died, and he saw this as one of her great achievements. But the fact of Patricius's death while Augustine was still a student casts a sad light on his crowing in the baths about the prospect of grandchildren. It wasn't Augustine's last conversation with his father, but it is the last one he tells us about.

After Patricius's death, Monnica aimed the full force of her energies at steering Augustine away from his potentially dangerous affiliation with the Manichees. "My mother, Your follower, was crying out to You for me more than most mothers weep for the bodily death of their children."[48] Augustine asked her to move in with him now that she was a widow, and at first she hesitated. He tells us, "She was beginning to dislike the idea in her disapproval and loathing for the curse of my folly."[49] In the end, she consented to the plan thanks to a dream.

Monnica's dream seems curiously suited to the fact that her son was training to be a schoolteacher. "In this dream, she saw herself standing on a kind of wooden measuring rod, and a luminous young man came toward her, smiling at her joyfully although she was broken by sadness."[50] When the young man asked her why she was so mournful, she responded with the story not of her lost husband but of her son. "She answered that she was lamenting because I was damned.

Then he ordered her to look and see, that where she was, so would I be. And when she looked, she saw me next to her, standing on the same measuring rod."[51] The dream, she decided, meant that moving in with Augustine would not be taken to mean that she approved of his lifestyle—it was a chance to convert him.

What happened next captures something of the easy back-and-forth between the two of them. "When she recounted her dream to me, and I was trying to get her to see it as meaning that she should not give up the possibility of being with me, right away and without hesitating she said, 'No—he didn't say, "Where he is, you are"; he said, "Where you are, he is."'"[52]

Now they both settled in for a long impasse. Augustine was incorrigible: "Yet close to nine years followed in which I stirred around in the deep shadows of error, sometimes trying to climb out, but then falling further back again."[53] And yet Monnica was even more dogged: "But she, a chaste, pious, and sober widow of the type You love, even more lighthearted with hope she didn't lighten her weeping and groaning; she didn't cease her prayers to You at all hours."[54]

Finally, she sought the advice of a Christian bishop who had grown up in the Manichaean sect. "She asked him to give me an interview and refute my mistaken ideas, leading me away from evil and toward the good." The bishop refused, explaining, Augustine writes, that "I was still unteachable, because I was full of hot air due to the heresy's novelty." From his own experience, he said, Augustine would discover that the Manichaean teaching did not offer sufficient intellectual rigor to interest. "Leave him alone, but keep praying to the Lord on his behalf. On his own, in his reading, he will begin to understand where he has gone wrong and how badly he has strayed."[55]

But Monnica still persisted: "She kept up with her begging and her copious tears, to try to make him see me and talk to me." At this point, the bishop did his best to shut her down. "'Go away,' he said, 'just keep doing what are doing. It's impossible that the son of these tears will be lost.' In talking with me later on, she often remembered that this had been like thunder from heaven."[56]

Later, Augustine returns to his mother's assiduous prayers on his behalf. "Could you, the God of mercies, have scorned the broken and humbled heart of a chaste and sober widow?"[57] He recounts her many acts of piety: she was "busy with almsgiving, and serving and attending to Your holy ones, not missing a day for making an offering at Your altar, coming to Your church twice a day, morning and evening, not for pointless gossip and old women's talk, but to hear You in Your own words, and for You to hear her in her prayers."[58] Surely, he suggests, Monnica was someone whose prayers deserved to be heard.

She most feared, Augustine remembers, the possibility that he would die while still in the grip of the Manichaean superstition. To her Christian understanding, this meant that when he died, instead of being together with her in Heaven, he would be trapped by the powers of Hell.

In 375, the twenty-one-year-old Augustine returned to Thagaste to take up his first teaching job. The saddest story from Augustine's twenties concerns an old school friend with whom he became close during this year in Thagaste. "He was incredibly dear to me," Augustine says, and the friendship was "all too sweet."[59] Part of the sweetness lay in the fact that Augustine had converted his friend to Manichaeism, though he later came to regret this. "I led him into those superstitious, dangerous Manichaean fairy tales that made my mother despair over me. In his mind, he was lost along with me, and my soul couldn't do without him."[60]

But then, a year into this intensely close friendship, the unnamed friend fell dangerously ill and became delirious for a number of days. "When he was suffering with a fever, he lay a long time in a deathly sweat, unaware of what was happening around him, and when it was believed that there was no hope for him, he was baptized without knowing it." Augustine was present at his side during the whole ordeal and did not object. "I thought nothing of it and I imagined that his soul had kept what it had gotten from me, not what happened to his body without his knowledge."[61]

When his friend became conscious again, the worst seemed to have passed, and Augustine tried to laugh with him about the fact that the Christians had gotten to him while he was asleep. But "he shrank back from me as if I were a deadly enemy and warned me with immediate and singular candor that if I wanted to be his friend, I should stop saying such things."[62] Augustine was "stunned and distressed" by how seriously his friend seemed to be taking the episode, but he decided to stay quiet and talk with him about it all later, when he was feeling better. But this never happened: "After a few days, the fever came again while I wasn't there, and he died."[63]

Now Augustine fell into a miserable depression. "The sorrow of this overshadowed my heart, and whatever I looked at was death. My hometown was a torture to me, and my father's house a place of singular misery."[64] He had finally found a soulmate, and his being taken away so quickly was unbearable. "My eyes were searching everywhere for him, but he wasn't there. And I hated everything, because nothing had him in it, and nothing could now say to me, 'Here, he's coming,' as they did when he was alive but not with me."[65] This loss was the beginning of a long readjustment in Augustine's understanding of human attachments; he had only begun to see how fragile and fleeting our connection is to everything and everyone we find to love in the world around us. "Only tears held any pleasure for me, and they had taken his place as my heart's delight."[66]

At twenty-eight, after he had returned to Carthage for several years to serve as a teacher, Augustine suffered another blow that darkened his outlook. He had long waited for the chance to consult with the Manichaean bishop Faustus, whose arrival in Carthage promised to give him a chance to clear up some inconsistencies he had noticed in the Manichaean teaching. But the long-awaited encounter with Faustus brought only disappointment. Augustine could see why others loved him: he was a generous and humane teacher. But he was by no means a great light intellectually, and he could do little to reconcile the contradictions that his brilliant pupil had discovered. Obviously neither Faustus nor Augustine could have known that they were unfairly matched. Augustine was on his way to becoming by far the most influential intellect of the Latin Middle Ages. But if Faustus was as good a teacher as Augustine believed, he was delighted by the questions Augustine laid out for him, even if he was unable to answer them.

W e know very little about the shakedown that must have taken place in the late 370s, after the Revolt of Firmus. With such conflicts, a family could not be sure whether its network of friends and patrons would be left standing once the new dispensation was in place, so extending the network as widely as possible was essential. In the event, things turned out well for Augustine and his family because the Roman senator Quintus Aurelius Symmachus, a major African landowner who had been stationed at Carthage as proconsul of Africa in 373 and 374, became prefect of Rome in 383 and 384. He maintained a healthy network of contacts in Carthage, one of whom "discovered" Augustine there in 383 and offered him the chance of a lifetime.

Augustine records that in the summer of 383, a Manichaean friend with contacts in Rome told him that a teaching job had become available there for the coming September, offering not only better compensation and greater glory but also, word had it, students who were more serious about their studies than the rabble-rousers of Carthage. He applied for the post, and his application was successful.

The move to Italy was abrupt—so abrupt that his critics accused Augustine of having fled. In truth, the accusation was not unreasonable, since 383 was a difficult year for Carthage's Manichaeans. Early in the year the Eastern emperor, Theodosius—son of the Theodosius who had quelled the rebellion of Firmus—had passed a law condemning the sect as enemies of the state, and there was a danger that the law would be applied stringently even in the Western provinces, with those convicted sent into exile or even executed as traitors.[67] In all likelihood, Augustine's sudden departure was sparked by his friends' fears that he was too visible an advocate for their cause.

If so, the attempt to sidestep a looming crackdown was not an overreaction. While there is no evidence that the law of 383 resulted in convictions in Africa, three years later, in 386, a second round of legislation resulted in formal proceedings against the Manichees in Carthage, and more than one of Augustine's friends and associates were condemned. Augustine himself was named in the proceedings, but by then he was in Milan.

The different outcomes of 383 and 386 seem to have their roots in the wide discretion of the proconsul of Africa to choose whether and how laws arriving from the emperor would be implemented. In 383, the incumbent was Eusignius, a Christian moderate who would later take a stand against the imposition of doctrinal uniformity. He was recalled to Italy around the time Augustine arrived there in the autumn of 384, and evidence suggests that he tried to dampen the escalation of religious tensions in Milan as he seems to have done in Africa. But the tide was turning against this kind of open-mindedness. Part of the difference between 383 and 386 was in the sensibility of a different proconsul, but it may also have been that the world was changing.

In any case, from Augustine's point of view, Rome was certainly safer than Carthage. Surely he could more easily lose himself in the crowd in Rome, no longer the imperial capital but still the empire's largest city, with its population of nearly half a million. When his Manichaean friends arranged the sudden opportunity to take up a teaching post there, he accepted with alacrity. This gave him a ready-made excuse to leave Africa just as the situation in Carthage became threatening.

Augustine's friends encouraged him warmly, but against his going he had to count the formidable will of Monnica, who by now was also in Carthage. "My mother... lamented desperately at my going and followed me down to the sea. But I deceived her even as she vehemently clung to me, demanding that I either stay or take her with me."[68] Taking advantage of her Christian piety, he waited until she went to pray at the shrine of St. Cyprian, the great third-century bishop of Carthage, near the harbor, and then slipped away to board his ship without telling her. "The wind blew, and filled our sails, and the shore was lost to sight."[69]

Of course, he was not present on the shore to witness her disappointment, but he describes it vividly nonetheless. Turning to God, he considers how she must have felt. "She loved to have me with her in the way mothers do, but with her it was far more so than most, and she had no idea what joy You were going to create for her from my absence."[70] In the end, as he later came to see things, the suffering would be repaid, but neither she nor Augustine knew this at the time. "She didn't know, and so she wept and wailed."[71]

"And what was she begging of You, my God, by so many tears but that You would not allow me to sail? Yet in Your wisdom You understood the root of her longing, and took care to make me what she continually prayed for, You did not grant what she prayed for just then."[72] Now God has become the parent and Monnica the child crying bitterly for something that she can't have because, as the parent knows, it will only harm her. Monnica's love and her wishes were provisional and uncertain; it was her prayers that would ultimately do the most good. And Augustine's own desires were being put to the service of God's purpose, however obliquely. "You goaded me to make me tear myself away from Carthage, and You placed the attractions of Rome before me to draw me there, using people who love a life of death and do senseless things in this world, and promise empty rewards in the next."[73] Still, for the moment, he was going to abandon her.

It has long been remarked that Monnica's weeping on the shore intentionally echoes that of Dido weeping for Aeneas, about which Augustine has so much to say in the *Confessions*. It is worth noticing Augustine's self-irony in telling the story in the way he does, for he makes it clear that he was a poor substitute for the hero of epic: while Aeneas had fled a great love in order to found an empire, Augustine evaded his mother in order to find more biddable students.

The episode also evokes Augustine's discussion of his own tears for Dido, in Book One. Now, as he looks back, Augustine recognizes that his pleasure in Dido's suffering was misguided. Only his mother, he tells us, could see the more authentic reason to weep: that her son had let himself be trapped, by his earthly passions, in the world of death. Augustine recognizes that the very voice of God is speaking in Monnica's cries and warnings.[74] Just as Augustine the schoolboy had wept for Dido, who committed suicide for the sake of love, now Monnica weeps for Augustine out of fear for his own death—not only of the body but of the spirit. In speaking of his mother's tears, he stages a surprise for the reader: in the *Confessions* it is not Monnica but Augustine himself who most resembles Dido.

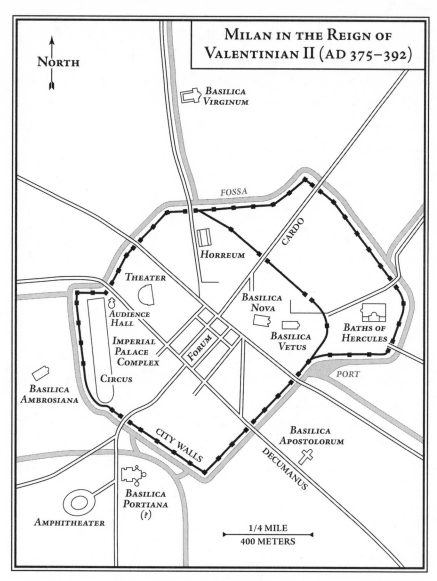

MAP 3. From the reign of the emperor Maximian Herculius (286–305), Milan had benefited from imperial investment in its public buildings. Under the Christian emperors of the fourth century, this included two cathedrals, the Basilica Vetus and Basilica Nova, and the splendid Basilica Portiana close to the palace. Between 374 and 397, Bishop Ambrose added a group of churches in the cemeteries outside the city walls, one of which, the Basilica Martyrum, would serve as his own burial place. *Credit: Kate Blackmer.*

CHAPTER SIX

THE EMPRESS AND
THE BISHOP

To UNDERSTAND HOW THE TRAGEDY OF AUGUSTINE, Una, and Tacita unfolded, we need to understand the heightened atmosphere of the Christian churches in the 380s. In Milan, the threat of civil war and of barbarian invasion encouraged both the clergy and the laity to feel that God had turned against the Roman people. All parties agreed that the anger of the powers of heaven had to be mollified at any cost. The empire was in danger, and the failings of the Roman army were a symptom, not the cause.

Bringing Christianity out of the shadows had been Constantine's greatest gamble, and now, nearly a half century after his death, whether the gamble had paid off was still not clear. Before Constantine, the Christians had been outsiders, a minority group that was at best tolerated and sometimes persecuted, and their bishops had been informal leaders without real power. But Constantine had secured the legal status of the Christians, granted them property, and even gone so far as to give Christian bishops the right to act as representatives of the government. Suddenly, the bishops commanded both power and wealth.

The effect of this had not been entirely what the emperor expected. Soon the churches in the empire's great cities had split into factions.[1] Constantine had made clear that he expected the bishops to give up their quarreling. But in the end, this accomplished nothing more than to allow some to enjoy the patronage and protection of the emperor, while the others—finding themselves returned to their old status as outsiders—anointed themselves as heirs of the early Christian martyrs.

Confusingly, in different cities the conflict turned on different questions. Carthage was torn apart by one dispute, Alexandria by another. The only constant was that the arrival of imperial patronage had unsettled the churches. Nobody had reckoned with how the rival bishops would begin to stir up support from among the restless unmarried men of the cities and their surrounding villages. Soon the disputes began to escalate into violence. Of course, the violence itself was not new—the cities of the Roman provinces had always been prone to rioting. The novelty lay in how theological ideas became the rallying point for urban conflict.

Many of these theological quarrels remained local or regional, but occasionally the spark would travel from city to city. The most far-reaching of these fourth-century disputes was one that rose in Alexandria over the relationship linking Jesus of Nazareth, the Son of God, to God the Father and the Holy Spirit. Originally, the presbyter Arius taught that the Son of God was a human being born like any other creature, while his rival Athanasius, later bishop of Alexandria, taught that the Son of God was much more than a historical person: he was also the Word of God—the Logos—which had been spoken at the creation of the world. The creed proclaimed at the Council of Nicaea in 325 captured the idea by speaking of the Son of God as "eternally begotten of the Father." After Nicaea there was no enduring "Arian" movement—Arius himself quickly modified his views to try to keep the peace. Still, the Nicene party discovered that constant accusations of heresy against their rivals was a powerful tool for populist crowd-building, and the fact that "Arianism" was an empty accusation made it particularly useful as a slur to aim at whomever the Nicene bishops disagreed with.[2]

The Nicene Creed was still a cause to contend with when Augustine reached Milan. Rome had been a center for the Nicene faction, but Milan, a city closely associated with the emperors Constantine and Constantius, had largely followed their lead in dismissing its bishops as troublemakers. With the arrival of Bishop Ambrose, however, the fortunes of the Nicene party in Milan would change decisively. After his father's death, Ambrose had spent his early adulthood in Rome, living with his widowed mother and his sister Marcellina, a professed virgin, not long after the time when the hero of the Nicene cause, Athanasius of Alexandria, had spent eight years in exile there (338–346). Although Ambrose was by no means a theologian in his early years, his mother and sister were part of the circle of the pope Liberius (352–366), a champion of the Nicene faith. Marcellina was her brother's closest confidante, as well as the source of some of the most compelling stories Ambrose's biographer collected after his death. Ambrose would be remembered as the empress Justina's fiercest opponent, known for a passion against her that can only be described as misogynistic, but we should not imagine that Ambrose had no sympathy for women.

Ambrose had made his name in the frontier region of Pannonia in the 370s, while Valentinian the Elder was campaigning there against the invading armies of the Quadi. The future bishop was a lawyer in the court of Sextus Petronius Probus, a former proconsul (governor) of Africa who served as praetorian prefect of Italy, Illyricum, and Africa from 368 to 375.[3] Probus was one of the most rapacious power brokers of the Roman Senate. During his time on Probus's staff in Sirmium, Ambrose came to his notice as a brilliant lawyer and became his protégé.

It was probably during his term as praetorian prefect that Probus developed an allegiance with one or both of Justina's brothers, who played an important role in her husband's administration. When Valentinian the Elder died in 375, Probus played a key role in elevating Justina's son, his namesake, as emperor alongside his older half brother. So the later conflict between the empress and Probus's protégé Ambrose was not inevitable. If anything, they had reason to be friends.

The elder Valentinian was still alive in 372 when Ambrose became governor of Aemilia-Liguria in northern Italy, a role based in the provincial capital at Milan. The city was one of Valentinian's principal residences, but it was also known as a stronghold of the Constantinian dynasty. Justina's kinsman, the emperor Constantius, had held court there for many years, and the bishop, Auxentius, had made his name as a principal supporter of the creed published at Rimini in 359, the faith of the imperial family who rejected Nicaea.

Neither Probus nor Ambrose could have known how long Ambrose would remain in the city; a governor normally only remained in post for a year or two. But in 374, nearing the end of his appointment, Ambrose made a shockingly unexpected career move, one that would keep him in Milan indefinitely. When Auxentius died, Ambrose was invited to become the city's bishop, and he accepted.

The circumstances of Ambrose's election were unusual, to say the least. When Auxentius died, Governor Ambrose was called upon to quell an emerging riot.[4] The gathered Christians of Milan were arguing over who would succeed Auxentius, with the Rimini and Nicene factions each refusing to accept a bishop from the other party. As governor, Ambrose had responsibility for public order. He arrived at the scene and put his gift for bringing a crowd under control to work. Suddenly, his biographer records, the voice of a child was heard crying out, "Bishop Ambrose!" Then the fractious crowd, moved by "miraculous and unbelievable harmony," invited Ambrose to take up the post himself.[5]

To a modern eye, Ambrose was a surprising candidate for ordination. To begin with, he was not yet a baptized Christian. He came from a senatorial family, and his father had been a praetorian prefect, probably under Constantine II (d. 340). His father died while Ambrose was a child, and Ambrose grew up with his siblings and widowed mother. Ambrose himself was initially viewed as a neutral party mediating between the religious factions that divided Milan, despite his mother and sister's support for the Nicene cause.

One of Marcellina's stories captures the atmosphere of the household in Rome after their father's death. Christian bishops were regular visitors to the pious ladies of the household, and when his mother or sister would kiss the hand of one of them, Ambrose would make fun of her afterward, offering his own right hand with a smile and announcing that he too was sure to be a bishop someday. This was taken as an absurdity—in the middle years of the fourth century, few bishops were men of standing, and it was not a plausible career path for the son of a praetorian prefect. So Marcellina would refuse to kiss the offered hand, as she remembered afterward, and tell her brother to stop being foolish.[6] Only years later did the story acquire a new significance.

This family background may explain why a Roman senator at the height of an already distinguished career was willing to receive ordination. In some ways, the idea made sense: the role of bishop was evolving swiftly in the third quarter of the fourth century, and the fact that it was not yet very clearly defined created opportunities for men who were not afraid to take risks. And the cities themselves were alive to the possibility that recruiting bishops and other clergy from the higher echelons could strengthen a city's ties to the imperial government. As it happens, Ambrose saw potential where others saw nothing worth noticing. The people of Milan were right to believe they had found a man who would be a gifted advocate for their city in years to come.

During his first years as a bishop, Ambrose made a concerted effort to educate himself in the fine points of the Nicene faith and quickly put his outstanding education to the service of the church. Drawing on his philosophical training and his knowledge of Greek, he began a program of translating Greek Christian writers (who were known for their theological sophistication) into Latin. When the emperor Valentinian I died in 375, Ambrose dedicated a treatise on the Trinitarian controversy to Gratian, exploring the mysterious doctrine that the Son of God had already been present, one with God, at the beginning of time.[7] With this, Ambrose sealed his position at the center of the Nicene coalition, although where Gratian's own loyalties would settle was not yet certain. But Gratian did not move his court to Milan until 381, so Ambrose had ample time to build his power base there without interference from the imperial family.

We know very little about Justina's life in the years between her husband's death in 375 and Gratian's move to Milan in 381.[8] There is some evidence that she stayed near Sirmium for at least a few years after her husband's death, but the timing of her movements is impossible to pin down. One surviving story suggests a clash with Ambrose while she was still in the region. The story paints her as a patroness of the church, a role for which women of the imperial family were often celebrated. But in Justina's case, we hear the story from a hostile source, Ambrose's biographer Paulinus of Milan, and he gives it an unpleasant spin.

In 375 or 376, Bishop Germinius of Sirmium died, and Ambrose traveled to the city to consecrate a new bishop—a serious undertaking that involved a journey of roughly thirty days in each direction. Why Ambrose became involved is uncertain. He may have had friends there from his time on the praetorian prefect's staff in the early 370s, and the Nicene faction there may have sought to involve him as a trusted supporter.

When Ambrose arrived at the city's main basilica, he found a crowd of hostile women who attempted to drive him from the building—they seem to have felt that whoever controlled the building would control the election. Ambrose's biographer Paulinus suggests that Justina was the architect of the commotion: she had packed the crowd with supporters from her own faction.

Even as described by his fawning biographer, Ambrose's conduct on this occasion strikes the modern reader as vindictive. Braving the throng of hostile women, he seated himself on the bishop's throne. When one of the *puellae* (the word could refer to either a girl or a woman of low status) took hold of his vestment and tried to drag him down into the crowd, Ambrose threatened that God would punish her for laying hands on a bishop. She died not long afterward. Ambrose himself drew the moral afterward that her death was a fitting punishment for her gesture of disrespect. There may also have been a suggestion that when women show loyalty to a female leader, God may turn against them.

Yet if Ambrose was a master of misogynistic rhetoric, his view of women was not one-dimensional. No one was more fulsome in praising the heroines of the faith when it served his purposes. And, like many other firebrand preachers, Ambrose had female followers of his own. His movement accorded a special place to virgins and widows—women like his sister. Ambrose's treatises on widowhood and virginity are electric with praise for female moral courage. Here, for example, is his view of the prophetess Deborah from the book of Judges: "A widow, she governs the people; a widow, she leads armies; a widow, she chooses generals; a widow, she determines wars and orders triumphs." Widows, in other words, are people of spiritual power: "It is not sex, but a valorous spirit which makes a person's strength."[9]

So for Ambrose the fact that Justina was a widow was by no means a reason to dismiss her—quite the contrary. (We will see below that Ambrose counted a number of widows among his devoted followers, including Monnica of Thagaste, mother of Augustine.) But if women could be invaluable allies, they could also be useful as enemies, because many people loved nothing more than hearing a good man wax lyrical about the vices of a bad woman.[10]

The first of the great barbarian victories on Roman territory took place in August of 378, when Gothic armies won an astonishing victory at Hadrianople, close to the Eastern capital at Constantinople.[11] The Eastern emperor Valens was killed, and the Spanish general Flavius Theodosius was soon appointed to replace him. Theodosius chose for his main capital the ancient city of Byzantium, which Constantine the Great had renamed as Constantinople, "Constantine's city."[12] Constantine was remembered as the founder of imperial Christianity, and a city bearing his name was the perfect home for a

Christian emperor who wanted to display his piety and cultivate the goodwill of the people. From late 380, when he arrived in Constantinople, Theodosius began to use the city's churches as a showcase for religious processions designed to broadcast the closeness the imperial family felt with their God.

His wife, Aelia Flaccilla, played a pivotal role in this new imperial Christianity, and she found an ally in the new bishop of Constantinople, Gregory Nazianzen, who had arrived in the city only shortly before her husband. In the new urban ritual built around the imperial family, the empress's prayers could anchor the empire's safety when her husband was away at war.

Sadly, Flaccilla died in late 386. But Bishop Gregory's funerary oration remembering her virtues survives, and it captures the mood of trustful partnership between the bishop and the palace.[13] In his oration, Gregory paints a picture of Flaccilla as a "model of wifely love" who embodied the emperor's benevolence toward his people. Her kindness and piety had earned the love of her husband's subjects, Gregory declares, and this had made them love their emperor in turn. On her death, the city was bereft: "This ornament of the empire has gone from us, this rudder of justice, the image of philanthropy or, rather, its archetype...this model of wifely love has been taken away."[14] We can't be sure how much of what Gregory says is specific to Flaccilla herself—many such epithets were part of an emerging repertory of praise for imperial women. But we do know that Theodosius and his court made distinctive use of the virtue of female family members as a rallying point.

Gregory also talks about how the people of Byzantium had cherished glimpses of Flaccilla. Although normally hidden within the curtained chambers of the palace, she sometimes traveled through the city in the chariot customary for a triumphal procession or in the imperial wagon adorned with gold and draped in purple, the chants of the people rising through the streets as she passed.

Central to Gregory's picture of Flaccilla are two virtues that were comparatively new to the repertoire of womanly praise: Christian piety and humility. Another writer spoke movingly of the humility with which Flaccilla had served the needy and those suffering from illness: she "ministered to the wants of the sick, herself handling pots and pans, and tasting broth, now bringing in a dish and breaking bread and offering morsels, and washing out a cup and going through all the other duties which are supposed to be proper to slaves and handmaids."[15] Gregory laments, "This zeal for the faith has departed from us, this pillar of the church...the common haven of those who are heavy laden."[16]

When Gratian brought his court from Trier in the Rhineland to Milan in 381, the city could easily have become the stage for new Christian civic rituals centered on the imperial family similar to those that Theodosius and Flaccilla were instituting at Constantinople. Milan was certainly well suited to the role. Like Constantinople, it had inherited monumental buildings from the age of Constantine, and its strategic position meant that successive emperors had often held court there between campaigns. The Western court would remain in Milan for another twenty years; not until after the Goths besieged Milan in 402 did the Western capital move again, to the more easily defended coastal city of Ravenna.

But the difficulty of defending Milan was not the only reason things played out differently there than they did in Constantinople. A psychological factor was also in play: on the face of things Gratian and his young wife, Constantia, were natural candidates for religious ritual centered on the imperial family, but they had failed to produce a cluster of adoring children to reassure the people of their good fortune. As things turned out, the signs of misfortune were accurate. Both of them died in the summer of 383, only two years after the court's arrival in Milan.[17]

During his short time in Milan Gratian made a number of bold moves designed to broadcast his reverence for the Christian God, but perhaps unwisely, he did not choose to build consensus around his wife as a symbol of harmony and unity. Instead, he encouraged an increasingly strident bishop to set the factions of city and empire against one another.

The most controversial of Gratian's moves was aimed at the pagans: he stripped the goddess Victory's altar from the Senate House in Rome.[18] Originally erected by Augustus in 29 BC to commemorate his defeat of Antony and Cleopatra at Actium, the altar was revered as an icon of the peace and prosperity Rome's first emperor had brought to his empire. Gratian also withdrew the state subsidies that supported many of the acts of worship to the traditional gods and refused to accept the Senate's offer of the robes of the *pontifex maximus*, the chief administrator of Roman religious law, a role filled by the emperor since the days of Augustus himself.[19]

It was no accident that Gratian did these things with the backing of Ambrose's Nicene coalition. While his father, Valentinian, had been known for a policy of religious toleration, Gratian seems to have fallen under Ambrose's spell. One cannot fault him for being impressed by Ambrose's work on behalf of the Nicene cause: with the Eastern emperor Theodosius to rely on for military strength, Bishop Ambrose for persuasive Christian rhetoric, and a representative of the older generation, the inimitable Petronius Probus, as a fixer, the Nicene coalition was beginning to seem unstoppable.

Each of Gratian's actions was a provocation to the remaining pagans in the Senate, who must have suspected that a half century's uneasy balance between pagans and Christians was coming to an end. Some years earlier, Constantius II had tried to eradicate paganism, but he had failed: indeed, his reign produced what might be called a pagan backlash. His nephew and successor, Julian—remembered as Julian the Apostate—had grown up Christian but returned to the old gods when he gained control of the empire soon after his uncle's death. After Julian's death in 363, no Christian faction immediately gained a decisive upper hand.

But now the Nicene party's ambitions were coming into focus, and they were terrifying to the party's enemies, both pagan and Christian. In the East, Theodosius seemed to believe that he owed it to his God to eliminate not only paganism but any Christian group that did not follow his own creed.[20] And in the West, Gratian was taking cues from Ambrose, who was equally committed to the Nicene cause.

But Gratian's good fortune did not last. In 383, a Spanish general, Magnus Maximus, allowed his troops to proclaim him emperor. A Nicene, Maximus had successfully fought against the Picts in Britain, and he now crossed the channel to challenge Gratian in battle outside Paris. Most of Gratian's armies defected, and in August 383, the emperor himself was killed. Maximus took control of Gaul, Britain, and Spain. This left Gratian's younger brother Valentinian, now twelve, perilously exposed. Maximus set up his court in Trier in the Rhineland and prepared to invade Italy; Ambrose was able to broker a delay, but it was obvious that it would not last long.

In the years between the death of Gratian in 383 and Maximus's invasion of Italy in 387, Ambrose was waging a religious war on several fronts. Gratian's death had put him in a curious position. On the one hand, he had a channel open to the usurper Maximus due to their shared Nicene faith, while Justina and her close associates, including her son, were adherents of the Creed of Rimini.[21] On the other hand, he wanted to take advantage of any chance to erode the position of the pagans at court and in the Senate.

In May 384, the Senate appointed a new urban prefect for the city of Rome, a role viewed as one of the highest honors of a senatorial career. The appointee was Quintus Aurelius Symmachus: like Probus, a titan of the Senate, but one whose profile was genteel, old-fashioned, and literate rather than forward-thinking and rapacious. It should come as no surprise that Symmachus was a pagan. Symmachus and Ambrose seem to have had a pleasant relationship despite finding themselves attached to opposing factions in the matter of religion; indeed, some scholars have suggested they were cousins.[22]

A duty of the urban prefect was to represent the views of the Senate in formal correspondence with the emperor, and one of Symmachus's first tasks was to discover whether Valentinian intended to continue his brother's hard-line religious policy. Symmachus's third formal missive (*relatio*) to the emperor, known as the *Third Relation*, captures something of what the Senate—still largely composed of pagans and moderate Christians—felt about Gratian's religious overreach.[23] They hoped that Valentinian would reverse his brother's policy and break free of Ambrose's influence. The main thrust of the *Third Relation* is to plead with Valentinian to restore the Altar of Victory to the Senate House, but it opens out to become a wider plea for the value of religious tolerance.

Symmachus begins his case with concerns that he believes will build consensus with his Christian listeners. He begins with the importance of Victory herself to Rome, all the more so at a time when the threat at the frontier was so acute. "We are not on such good terms with the barbarians that we can do without an Altar of Victory!"[24]

And yet the importance of the goddess's altar lay as much in its way of regulating relationships among the Romans themselves: "Where else are we to take our oath of allegiance to Your laws and ordinances? What religious sanction is going to deter the treacherous from giving false evidence?"[25] As he builds his case, Symmachus turns to consider the value of tradition and of piety for previous generations.

Finally, he addresses the deeper principle behind the view—held by pagans and Christians alike—that it should not be the business of the Roman state to repress discussion of the search for truth in a spirit of concord. "And so we ask for peace for the gods of our fathers, for the gods of our native land. It is reasonable that whatever each of us worships is really to be considered one and the same."[26] At a time when ambitious men were making energetic efforts to divide the population into warring factions, the invitation to open inquiry that Symmachus puts forward in this speech is remarkable: "We gaze on the same stars, we share the same sky; the same world is all around us. What does it matter what practical system we adopt in our search for the truth? It is not by exploring only one avenue that we can arrive at so tremendous a secret."[27] Over a thousand years later, it is difficult not to be moved by how Symmachus defends the right of people to hold different views and the idea that we have a greater capacity to learn from one another because of it.

But if Ambrose was moved by Symmachus's call for unity, he found a way to resist the impulse. When he heard what Symmachus had written—even before he had had a chance to read it himself—he penned an open letter to Valentinian to warn him that any attempt to back down from his brother's antipagan measures would be seen as a betrayal of the Christian cause.[28] This was not exactly true: many Christians were not at all unhappy to see the forces of intolerance openly challenged. But as Ambrose saw things, that was an inconvenient truth.

Ambrose reminds Valentinian of what he had done for him by meeting with Maximus and of the debt of gratitude he ought to feel toward Theodosius, suggesting that in questions of faith, as in other things, he should be guided by a filial feeling toward his imperial colleague. With this, he lets it be understood that the young emperor's safety depends on the willingness of Ambrose and Theodosius to protect him.

In the end, Ambrose prevailed in the Altar of Victory controversy, and Symmachus, despite his eloquence, was disappointed. The idea that the emperor had the right and even the duty to eradicate religious dissidence was beginning to take hold.

Coincidentally, during the same summer, Symmachus was asked to recommend a teacher of rhetoric to a municipal chair in Milan, a prize appointment that offered the opportunity to give formal speeches at court.[29] He recommended a Manichaean from Africa who had only recently come to Rome but was already acquiring a reputation as a truly remarkable public speaker. Symmachus had been proconsul of Africa in 373–374 and had wide connections in the African provinces, but we cannot be sure that his recommendation of Augustine was based on personal acquaintance. Still, it is somehow fitting that as a member of an "outsider" religious group, Augustine received his big break thanks to an outstanding defender of religious tolerance.

In 385 and 386 Ambrose decided to provoke an outright face-off with the imperial family over who controlled the city's churches. We have seen that between 381 and 385 the Eastern emperor Theodosius and his empress, Flaccilla, had discovered in Constantinople that well-judged appearances of the imperial family could do a great deal to generate support for the emperor and his armies—indeed, when the emperor was away campaigning, his wife and children could spark popular support back in the capital simply by letting themselves be seen among the people.[30] The clergy, who could be remarkably valuable allies, were grateful for the attention this brought to their liturgies.

On the face of things, Milan was in principle the perfect place for this kind of collaboration between the bishop and the palace. The city had seen a wave of church building in recent years, sponsored by both the bishops and the imperial family. A new cathedral, the Basilica Nova, had been built in the city center before Bishop Ambrose's time, and he himself was overseeing—and financing—the construction of churches in the cemeteries outside the city walls.[31] But the relationship between cathedral and palace was developing very differently in Milan than in the Eastern capital. In 385 and 386 control over the churches became the point of contention in a clash between Ambrose and the palace known as the "Conflict of the Basilicas."[32]

The jewel in the ring of churches around Milan was one now known as San Lorenzo, which stood on the road running south to Ticinum (modern Pavia), directly south of the Imperial Palace and close to the amphitheater. The only suburban church of the period not linked to Ambrose, San Lorenzo may have been built at the same time as the Basilica Nova, before his time.[33] Because of its magnificent architecture and decoration—a dome sitting above four majestic colonnaded apses, built of brick and concrete with an interior crafted of porphyry, marble, and mosaic—one medieval bishop called it "the most beautiful church in Italy."[34] Both its splendor and its location close to the palace suggest that the church was an imperial foundation. It is unlikely that San Lorenzo was originally dedicated to the martyr St. Laurence—the earliest evidence for the dedication is from the sixth century[35]—and it has been suggested that the church can be identified as the Basilica Portiana, the church that stood at the center of the dispute between Justina and Ambrose.

Gratian's death in the summer of 383 had brought an end to Ambrose's undisputed supremacy in Milan. Valentinian and his mother, Justina, were proving far less pliable than Gratian and Constantia. Justina had ideas of her own: she was aware of the value of what Theodosius had achieved in Constantinople and of the opportunities Gratian had missed. The now indispensable dowager empress knew that her son needed to have his people see him in church, and she wanted these appearances to be carefully orchestrated by the palace. This was the root of the falling-out between the empress and the bishop.

In the fourth century, when Christmas had not yet emerged as a major feast of the church, the Christian year was anchored by Jesus's resurrection at Easter. For a bishop, Easter was the point in the calendar when baptisms of new Christians took place, while for the imperial family it was a moment when the earthly ruler could most meaningfully lead his people in prayer and celebration.

Unlike the bishop of Constantinople, who had cooperated with the palace to showcase the imperial family's involvement with the church, Ambrose saw the prospect that the palace might play a central role in important Christian festivals as a threat. He could not easily deny the right of assembly to an orthodox Christian faction, especially one associated with the palace, since final authority in the matter lay with the emperor. But his instinct was to resist letting the palace take center stage.

And Ambrose was an expert in the art of the possible. Faced with overtures from the palace seeking the use of ecclesiastical spaces, he made every effort to suggest that the palace was wrongly challenging his authority. He sustained his position by repeatedly surrounding himself with an unruly crowd of his followers, who vociferously accused the emperor's men of persecuting him. He built up the impression that he was in danger by enthusiastically offering to die for the faith if called on to do so by God. In this way, Ambrose defended a claim entirely unsupported by Roman law: that the church should be accountable only to God and not to the authority of the emperor. It may have been an idea with a long future, but it was utterly radical at the time.

By defying the emperor in such a bold and public way, Ambrose took a risk, but his ability to steer the mood of the crowd was astonishingly effective. By provoking the court, he was able to wrap himself in the mantle of the Christians who had stood fast in the faith during the age of persecution. Ambrose the bishop was becoming synonymous with Ambrose the martyr.

Things came to a head in the spring of 385, as the imperial family was making plans to celebrate Easter, and culminated during Holy Week. The most detailed account of this first crisis survives in a letter Ambrose wrote to his well-connected sister and confidante, Marcellina.[36] He could not have chosen a better recipient of his narrative. Marcellina was well connected, and his pose as an admiring younger brother sharing news of his troubles to a pious older sister was well calculated to earning the reader's sympathy. When Ambrose wrote to his sister about his conflict with the imperial family, he clearly meant for his account to be copied and circulated—in modern terms, he wanted to "control the narrative." In this, he was successful: his version of events has endured up to the present as the original source behind all surviving versions of the story. Ambrose's skill at piloting the Roman propaganda machine was remarkable.

So it is wise to pause for a moment to ask what Ambrose was trying to accomplish in telling the story of his refusal to allow Valentinian to worship at Easter in a church outside the palace walls. Later writers would remember the conflict as a matter of orthodoxy and heresy, but both parties subscribed to orthodox views as they were then defined. It is the balance of power between the palace and the church that most interests Ambrose in the letter to Marcellina. Who has the right to decide how the city's churches will be used on a given Sunday?

Ambrose begins his letter by signaling his close relationship with his sister, suggesting that she had had a premonition of his difficulties: "The day after I received your letter in which you revealed that your dreams were disturbing you, a mass of grave troubles was set in motion."[37] The problem, he tells her, was that the emperor and his family had made known their intention to celebrate Easter Sunday in the city's cathedral, the Basilica Nova, with a liturgy and had chosen a celebrant who adhered to their own creed. Legally, the palace's plan was not surprising or unreasonable. Ambrose's resistance, however, was unusual.

Ambrose says that a message from the palace arrived on the Friday before Holy Week. He presents it as an order: "Counts of the imperial consistory met me with the demand that I should both surrender the basilica and see to it that the people did not cause any disturbance."[38] He lets it be taken for granted that he had no intent of complying: "I replied as a matter of course, that a Bishop could not give up a temple belonging to God."[39]

The following day, he tells Marcellina, he organized his congregation to perform an acclamation—a rhythmical shouting of slogans, which normally took place in a political assembly or a sports arena—in the church. "No less a man than the Praetorian Prefect arrived"[40]—this was the religious moderate Flavius Eusignius, who as proconsul of Africa had declined to bring the Manichaeans to trial in 383. Eusignius was prepared to negotiate and suggested that Ambrose make at least one of the major basilicas available to the imperial family, not necessarily the cathedral. Instead of thanking Eusignius for being flexible, Ambrose called upon his congregation to express their indignation. "The people protested. We parted, with the Prefect saying that he would report to the Emperor."[41] Eusignius seems to have departed with civility, but his distaste for Ambrose's populist posturing can be imagined.

The next day, Palm Sunday, imperial officials presented themselves at the Basilica Portiana just outside the city walls and began to install the rich hangings that normally accompanied the emperor's appearances in public. This clearly indicated that they intended the emperor to attend a Christian liturgy. If the Basilica Portiana has been correctly identified as the surviving Church of San Lorenzo by the Ticino Gate, the emperor's embroidered hangings would have created quite a striking scene. The church has a four-apse shape similar to an imperial audience hall, and the drapes would in all likelihood have adorned the arches leading from the central hall to the apses. This was an enormous expanse. While the original interior is no longer visible due to rebuilding and remodeling, the basic shape has survived. The drop from the four great arches to the pavement in the (rebuilt) Renaissance church was forty *braccia* (23.8 meters or 73 feet).[42]

While the imperial hangings were being installed, Ambrose's people began to flock to the Basilica Portiana, although the bishop himself was in the baptistery next to the old cathedral, the Basilica Vetus, preparing his candidates for baptism a few days later, at Easter. Then, as he celebrated Mass, a messenger came to say that his people had taken one of the palace priests captive, a man named Castulus.

Ambrose's dramatization of his distress at the news is perfectly judged to divert attention from the fact that his followers were at fault. "Right in the middle of the offertory I started to weep bitter tears, and to beg God to come to our aid, and to prevent anyone's blood being shed . . . or at least that it was my blood which would be shed." Almost as an afterthought, he seems to notice that the thugs were from his own party and adds, "In short: I sent priests and deacons, and had the fellow snatched out of harm's way."[43]

Next Ambrose somewhat misleadingly implies that a police crackdown had targeted his group without provocation. "And so during the holy days of the last week of Lent, a time when by custom debtors are freed from their shackles, there was a loud rattle of chains, chains being hung around the neck of people who have done nothing."[44] Ambrose clearly expected his sister to discount the fact that some of his followers—those who kidnapped the priest Castulus—had in fact committed a crime. Instead, he skillfully keeps the focus on the idea that Milan's citizens are behind him and ready to suffer with him. "Persecution was raging, and it seemed as if they got the gate opened, they would break into every kind of atrocity."[45]

Finally, Ambrose says, "counts and tribunes" came to try to get him to vacate the Basilica (scholars are divided on whether the cathedral or Portiana is intended). "I myself was being pressed by the counts and tribunes to agree to an immediate handover of the basilica. They said that the emperor was exercising his legal rights, since all things were subject to his authority. I replied that if he was after what belongs to me, that is my land, my money . . . no matter what, that was mine, I would not resist."[46] But, he argued, this conflict was about something more important than personal property: "The things that are God's, I insisted, were not subject to the power of the emperor."[47] Now he invokes a story line from the acts of the early Christian martyrs, the martyr-bishop who refuses to allow Christian books to be confiscated by a pagan emperor. "If my family property is what is wanted, come and take it; if my person, I will offer it. Do you want to drag me off to prison? Or to execution? I am ready. I will not surround myself with a defensive wall of my people, nor will I cling to the altar, begging for my life. Instead, I will more gladly be sacrificed before the altars."[48]

With this rhetoric, Ambrose all but buries the fact that his position has no basis in law. Naturally, he also neglects to mention what Marcellina surely knew: that many of the emperor's senior advisors were themselves subscribers to Ambrose's own creed. Ambrose's behavior was outrageous, and yet the palace was treading very carefully.

With magnificent skill, Ambrose builds up the impression that his resistance to the palace's request is his only option. The imperial family's wish to join in prayer with their people in one of the city's churches at Easter may seem innocent, he suggests, but it hides a darker motive: a threat of martyrdom toward himself and his congregation. "I feared that their appropriation of the basilica would be accompanied by carnage, which would result in the ruin of the city as a whole. I kept praying that I might not survive the cremation of so great a city, perhaps of all Italy.... I offered my own throat."[49]

On Wednesday of Holy Week, the emperor's soldiers occupied the Basilica Portiana, which was filling with Ambrose's people, and surrounded the Basilica Vetus, where he was waiting with another congregation. Among the soldiers there were members of Ambrose's Nicene faction, however, and he reports with delight that some slipped away from their duties to come to the Basilica Vetus, where he was saying Mass. When they joined the congregation, his people received them with cheers.[50]

Ambrose then launches into a detailed analysis of his own preaching to his supporters, and here we begin to see how he focused the anger of his congregation on Justina. Surprisingly, he presents this choice to his sister not as a regrettable error of judgment but as a tour de force, inviting her admiration.

Ambrose reports that he began his sermon with the story of how the biblical hero Job was tested, paying special attention to how Job's wife goaded him even as he tried to endure the challenges God put in his way. Warming to the theme of the evil influence of women, Ambrose turns next to Adam and Eve: "After all, Eve tripped up even Adam, and that is how he came to disobey the instruction of heaven."[51] Then he reaches for the Bible's most famous stories of how women could seduce weak-minded rulers into persecuting prophets sent by God. "Do I need to add that Jezebel persecuted even Elijah most cruelly, that Herodias had John the Baptist killed?"[52]

Ambrose clearly feels confident that Marcellina will accept the idea that his difficulties with the court are only one case in a long stream of female attempts to undermine male righteousness. "One generation of women follows another. The objects of their hatred shift. Their intrigues change."[53] Ambrose himself, of course, is only the latest in a long line of heroes blessed with the courage to stand up to such provocation: "Men in high positions are summoned to appear in court, and a charge of 'an insult to the emperor' is trumped up.... [F]inally the order comes, 'Surrender the Basilica!'"[54]

By now it is clear that the "woman" Ambrose has in mind is not Job's wife, or Eve, or Jezebel. Though Justina is not named, there is no doubt about whom he means; as Ambrose sees things, the emperor would not be pushing so hard against him if it were not for the influence of the empress. This was a deft move rhetorically, both humiliating the emperor and allowing Ambrose to hold back from directly accusing the man himself.

It is a measure of the bishop's artistry that he holds back his insinuation against the empress until the climax of his narrative. In this

147

way he focuses the minds of his readers on his chosen antagonist just at the turning point where the rigors of his "persecution" give way suddenly to cheers of jubilation. When he had reached this point in his sermon, he tells his sister, good news arrived: the emperor had withdrawn his plan of celebrating Easter in the Basilica Portiana and the imperial hangings had been taken down.[55] Ambrose had won.

Recent research has shown that the palace had good reason to tread cautiously around Ambrose. Through his spies, the usurper Maximus was watching events in Milan very closely, and he was clearly delighted by Ambrose's challenge to Valentinian. A letter from Maximus to Valentinian in the spring of 386 makes clear that if Valentinian allows himself to be seen as a "persecutor" of Nicene Christians, Maximus will use this as an excuse to invade Italy, arguing that it will be necessary to step in to protect the orthodox faith.[56] The letter appears to be framed as fatherly advice, but Maximus sent copies to potential allies in the Nicene faction; indeed, the surviving copy comes from the archive of the bishop of Rome.

In other words, Justina may reasonably have wondered whether Ambrose's religious vituperation was a veil for something more sinister. Possibly he meant to encourage the people of Milan to be ready to welcome the usurper Maximus when the invasion came. Ambrose's pagan kinsman Symmachus was a supporter of Maximus, and it is not impossible that Ambrose too was leaning in this direction.[57] But if Justina had her suspicions, she had no way of confirming them.

Was Ambrose working in concert with Maximus? It is certainly not impossible. He had spent months at Maximus's court in the winter of 383–384 and had made a second embassy to Maximus on behalf of Valentinian's court, probably in the autumn of 385 or the spring of 386, to reclaim the body of the late emperor Gratian so he could be buried.[58] He may have felt that since Maximus was likely to invade, it was better not to tie the church too closely to a vulnerable regime. Whatever his motive, Ambrose had clearly begun to see that a theological charge of heresy was the firmest ground on which to rally the people to defy their God-appointed emperor.

Ambrose's shift away from the problem of church property toward reframing the conflict as a matter of persecuted religious conscience is visible in sources from the spring of 386.[59] In these more theologically oriented writings, a letter to Valentinian (Letter 75) and an appendix to it containing the text of a sermon preached against the palace favorite Auxentius, a bishop from Durostorum on the Danube, Justina receives no mention.[60] Ambrose seems to have seen Auxentius as a personal enemy.[61] He also seems to have recognized that Justina was not an ideologically motivated player. In orthodoxy and heresy he had found a theme with lasting potential to rally the crowd. Misogyny had played its part, but other tools were now at hand.

There was a second clash over where and even whether the imperial family would celebrate Easter of 386, which again escalated to violence. But something curious happened in the process of memory. When vivid stories are told and retold in successively modified versions, the ideological "message" that the stories are understood to carry sometimes evolves over time.[62] In the case of Ambrose and Justina, writers remembering the conflict began to graft the vivid scenes narrated in Ambrose's letter to Marcellina describing the conflict of 385—a conflict over church property in which Justina was Ambrose's chosen antagonist—into the theological frame set out by sources from the conflict of 386. It may be that this hybrid version of the conflict has its roots in Ambrose's own tendency to remember Justina's lack of support. In any case, it was this version that would endure in memory.

An early and influential case in point is Augustine's *Confessions*, which includes a thumbnail description of the Conflict of the Basilicas.

Augustine introduces his version of the story as he is musing about how strongly the liturgy affected him at the time of his baptism. It was Ambrose, he recalls, who had begun to organize Christian hymn singing—a custom borrowed from the Greek churches—for the first time in the Latin West. Although Augustine's topic is the emotional power of music, he takes a detour to mention the conflict during which Ambrose introduced this, and his version is centered on Justina. "Justina, the mother of Valentinian the boy emperor, persecuted Your man Ambrose for the sake of her heresy"—here he introduces an accusation of heresy borrowed from Ambrose's preaching—"which she had been drawn into by the Arians."[63] The mention of the empress is completely irrelevant to what he is trying to say about music and emotion, but the chance to invoke her as a latter-day Jezebel is too magnetic to pass up.

Augustine is fulsome in his praise of how the populist bishop managed to escalate the conflict into one that the people of Milan found terrifying but also exciting: "The God-fearing people kept vigil overnight in the churches, ready to die along with Ambrose, their bishop and Your slave."[64] The language of the bishop as a slave to God is revealing here. One of the key techniques of successful populists is establishing an emotional logic in which they claim to speak on behalf of God, or the people, or both.[65]

Looking back, Augustine emphasizes that although he himself was not present, his mother, Monnica, was one of the ringleaders in Ambrose's congregation. "My mother, Your slave, took a leading role in the troubles and kept watch all night; she lived on prayers."[66] We will see in the next chapter that Monnica's involvement may have had consequences both for Augustine's position at court and, indirectly, for the outcome of the conflict itself.

In his *Confessions*, Augustine also introduces a reference to Justina in his description of a later event, when a vision came to Ambrose revealing the burial place of two of Milan's early Christian martyrs. This was both a confirmation of divine favor and a practical opportunity to involve his followers in an exciting project, a new church that would house the bones of the martyrs. "Then through a vision You revealed to the celebrated bishop where the bodies of Your martyrs Protasius and Gervasius were, which had lain for so many years in Your hidden treasure house so that at the right moment You could bring them forth to check the ravings of a woman who was also a queen."[67] The new church would become a focal point for Ambrose's following, and Ambrose was keen to nurture their sense of themselves as a faithful people persecuted by an evil empress.

We see here how fully Augustine had bought in to Ambrose's rhetoric. That the imperial council Ambrose defied included several members of his own congregation and that he had fabricated an impression that the palace was out for blood when in fact it was trying to deescalate the situation seem to have been altogether lost on Augustine. He also seems to have taken for granted that Justina's motive for "persecuting" Ambrose stemmed from theological motives rather than a reasonable concern, shared with other representatives of a legitimate government, to assist the head of state in finding a space where he could lead his people in worship. To a modern eye, this tactic—a firebrand religious leader baiting moderate government officials—fits the profile of a disturbingly self-serving form of populism.

The empress would understandably have felt distaste for Ambrose's posturing, and she must also have been perturbed by his singling her out as a target of provocatively misogynistic invective. But Justina had not survived decades of violent regime change without learning to stay focused on what she meant to achieve.

One would give a great deal to know whether the empress also meant to take a stand for religious pluralism against the Nicene takeover, as the pagan senator Symmachus had done. The Nicene party had now attracted a powerful political coalition including the usurper Maximus, Bishop Ambrose, and the Eastern emperor Theodosius. But pushing back against these men's religious single-mindedness was almost certainly not Justina's main aim. First and foremost, her responsibility, as she saw it, lay in defending the dynasty of which her son was now the only living emperor. Her priority was her son's safety. His rightful place was at the head of his people in prayer: in this way he could win their loyalty and the favor of God, who could grant safety to them all.

And in the end, the trouble with Ambrose was less important than the danger that the emperor of the East, Theodosius, would come in on Maximus's side. This had to be avoided at all costs. Early on, Theodosius had shown signs of intending to avenge Gratian. In 384 he had planned an expedition to the Rhineland to confront Maximus, but it was either canceled or failed to prove successful, and his enthusiasm had waned.[68] A way had to be found to rekindle his interest. In the meantime, the thing to do was to buy time. The longer Maximus could be kept from invading Italy, the better the chance Valentinian and Justina would be ready for him when he came.

Given how little she had to work with, it is nothing short of remarkable that Justina achieved her aim. When Maximus invaded Italy in the summer of 387, she was prepared. At first, the prospect seemed less than hopeful: Valentinian retreated eastward to the port city of Aquileia, and Maximus occupied Milan. It was at this point, the pagan historian Zosimus tells us, that Justina took the initiative.[69] Taking her son and daughters with her, she set sail for the Eastern emperor's palace at Thessalonica. The party anchored in the harbor there while an embassy went to Constantinople, alerting the emperor to the situation of Valentinian and his family and begging him to avenge the outrage they had suffered. The approach was well judged. As Justina must have hoped, Theodosius made haste to Thessalonica to manage the situation in person. He welcomed the refugees but expressed his reluctance to involve himself further in what was on its way to becoming a full-scale civil war.

Now Justina played her trump card. Accompanied by her eldest daughter, Galla, who was then fourteen or fifteen, the empress threw herself at Theodosius's feet. She grasped his knees and began to plead with him. Surely he could not leave unavenged the death of her stepson Gratian, to whom, after all, he owed his own standing as emperor. Next she pointed out how essential he, Theodosius, was to her safety and that of her children and how hopeless they would find themselves without his support. If Theodosius felt that the empress's self-debasement was exaggerated, it only shows how profoundly he underestimated her intelligence. Justina knew instinctively what modern neuroscience has only recently established: that a state of preexisting agitation in a male subject greatly enhances his perception of a woman's attractiveness.[70] Her own display had merely been the warmup act; now—the historian Zosimus stops to emphasize the timing—she turned and called the emperor's attention to the extraordinarily beautiful Galla, who tearfully confirmed her mother's account of the family's despair.

As Justina had foreseen, the widowed emperor was spellbound by Galla's beauty. He begged the women to stop weeping and offered to step in as their protector, asking for Galla's hand in marriage. Now Justina had her opening, and her long experience stood her in good stead. She immediately made it clear that a marriage could only take place if the emperor would commit to a full-scale invasion of Italy. In short, he must restore Galla's brother Valentinian to his rightful place as emperor of the West and destroy the usurper.

Theodosius accepted Justina's condition, and shortly afterward he began to prepare for war. After the marriage, he arranged for a ship to carry his new wife and her family to Rome, a city whose walls were considered unbreachable and whose citizens had openly defied Maximus. There, Justina and her children would be both safe and symbolically restored to their rightful place while he undertook to capture the usurper.[71] After a year of campaigning, Theodosius fulfilled his promise: Maximus surrendered and was executed in August 388.[72]

Like her mother before her, Galla took a role of crucial political significance as a bride. It might be argued that her marriage restored the unity of the Western Empire, if only for a few more decades. Her future would be in Constantinople, the Eastern capital, her destiny to produce heirs for the Theodosian dynasty.

We have only an inadequate account of what befell her mother and her unmarried sisters after Valentinian's restoration. Some ancient sources suggest that Justina died in the same year as the usurper Maximus and did not live to see her son return to Milan.[73] Theodosius remained in Italy for a number of years after the invasion, and other sources suggest that Galla and Justina were present when he made his triumphant entry into Rome in the summer of 389.[74]

For Justina's part, the conflict with Ambrose had never been about theology or doctrine; it had always been about loyalty to her son and to the empire. It is also possible that she simply did not want to compromise the faith she had grown up with to please an impertinent bishop.

One would give a great deal to know whether things could have gone differently between Justina and Ambrose. Had Justina approached Ambrose with the type of calculated display of feminine helplessness that served her so well with Theodosius, she might well have found the bishop eating out of her hand. Instead, her unwillingness to defer to an inferior fanned the flame of his misogynistic populism, and while she saved her son, she failed to persuade the bishop to support the form of Christianity centered on the imperial family that would strengthen the Eastern Empire in the centuries to come.

The Christian churches of the Latin-speaking West, by contrast, would remember admiringly how Ambrose had stood up to Justina and later to Theodosius himself. Ambrose's stance of fiery independence became an icon of the idea that religious leaders should maintain their independence from earthly authority and be prepared to speak truth to power. In many ways, this is admirable. Yet by weakening the people's bond with the imperial family, Ambrose's displays of independence may have hastened the fall of the Western Empire.

Still, this was all in the future. Justina had achieved the goal she had set herself. She had protected her family and, for the time being, the Western Empire that God had entrusted to their care. Yet sadly, Valentinian's situation unraveled swiftly after his mother's death. He died in 392, possibly by suicide.[75] His sister Galla, the Eastern empress, also died in the early 390s, but Justina's spirit would live on. Galla left behind an infant daughter, Galla Placidia, who would grow up to follow in the footsteps of her grandmother. Justina's granddaughter became empress regent for her own infant son, Valentinian III, when the boy's father Constantine III died in 411.[76] It would prove to be a remarkably successful partnership. When Valentinian grew to adulthood, Galla Placidia remained one of his closest advisors. The two ruled the Western Empire together peacefully for nearly four decades until Galla Placidia's death in 450, a legacy Justina would almost certainly have found pleasing.

FIGURE 4. For men whose ambitions exceeded their resources, an advantageous marriage provided both financial backing and political patronage. Few had the opportunity to marry for love, but it was realistic to hope that with time the bride and groom would create a trusting partnership. This late Roman funerary portrait from the Archaeological Museum of Milan captures an aristocratic couple as they wished to be remembered, joining their hands in the *dextrarum iunctio*, a gesture symbolic of their marital concord. *Photo courtesy of the author.*

Chapter Seven

THE HEIRESS

ONNICA OF THAGASTE WAS A PROVINCIAL WIDOW of good family but modest means, so the idea that she played a significant role in the conflict between Justina and Ambrose may seem surprising. But Augustine remembers her as a ringleader in 386, keeping vigil in the basilica that Ambrose claimed to defend.[1] Even if there is some exaggeration in Augustine's account, it illustrates an important point: the bishop's genius lay precisely in his ability to mobilize sober-minded people of the middling sort and to involve them in his political grandstanding. The throng of middle-aged widows may have been his secret weapon.

There is also a more individual question to be asked about Monnica's relationship with Ambrose. Was it his influence that led her to relinquish the dream of seeing her son join the charmed circle that revolved around the palace? And if this was so, what in the bishop's preaching changed her mind? Was it a newly hatched disinterest in wealth and material connections or a newly heightened distaste for the imperial family's Rimini variant of Christianity?

There is also a third and more disturbing possibility. Monnica may have begun to pick up hints from friends in Ambrose's entourage that Valentinian was not likely to survive the expected invasion. In other words, the thought may have occurred to her that by encouraging her son to insinuate himself in the circle around Valentinian, she was pushing him to place his money on a losing horse. If this was the case, her feeling that it would be safer not to be too visibly counted among Valentinian's supporters may have been part of a wider ebbing away of popular support.

The date of Monnica's arrival in Milan is uncertain. We know Augustine abandoned her when he left Africa for Italy but not how they reconciled or when she came after him. It is tempting to imagine that she was in Milan in time for the first of Augustine's triumphs, his ceremonial speech in January 385 celebrating the installation of the new consul. Surely he would have alerted his mother to the fact that he was slated to deliver the speech, and equally surely she would have done her best to be there. But it is possible that she arrived later in the year or even very early the following spring. All we are sure of is that she was there in time for Easter of 386.

Whatever the precise moment of Monnica's arrival in Milan, she could look back with something like astonishment at the fruit her efforts had begun to bear. Across decades of invisibility in a remote provincial market town, she had poured all her energies into a single, shining hope: Augustine, her younger son. She had placed her trust not in her own ability to guide his path and shape his character but in the mercy of God and the intercession of the saints.

Other Roman women had placed their hopes in a son and been disappointed, but Augustine, it seemed, was going to make good on

Monnica's aspirations. He was a man of remarkable qualities, and she was now a matriarch—already a grandmother, if you counted the boy Augustine's concubine had given him. He had always been the listener of her two sons—the one with whom she had shared her stories and memories. At every step on the path forward, he had brandished his gifts with perfect accuracy, moving onward and upward, from his position as a schoolmaster in a dusty provincial city, to Carthage, and then across the sea to Italy. Now he had found a place in the rarified world that revolved around the emperor's court. Widowhood was not at all unpleasant if you had a son like Augustine.

It helped, of course, if your husband's absence, on the whole, was less a cause for sorrow than a source of relief. But Monnica knew that it was not yet time to rest on her laurels. Now, in Milan, her family's future depended on her. The men at court were lords of the universe; they could make or break fortunes as easily as a cat might trap a dormouse. If she could steer her boy into the arms of one of these men, one who had set aside a sizeable dowry for a marriageable daughter, Augustine's gifts would take care of the rest. If he could find the financial backing and connections to pursue a political career, there would be no stopping him. His brother and all of his cousins would surely thrive on the scraps he could throw their way if he found his place in the firmament of those men. But for now, the onus was on Monnica. Finding the right kind of wife for Augustine would be the final stone in the foundation she had laid for his rise. There was no reason—was there?—to see this last challenge as more daunting than the ones that already lay behind them.

Augustine had left Carthage for Rome in the summer of 383, and he had been in Rome for almost a year when the chance to move to Milan came. We know very little about the year Augustine spent in Rome, after first arriving in Italy, except that much of it was lost to a near-fatal illness and his longer recovery. His mother was still far away in Africa, but fortunately, the friends of friends who were his only contacts in Rome stood by him when he was ill, and he regained his health. And then, seemingly also thanks to these friends, another opportunity arose, this time through the senator Symmachus.[2] There was an opening in Milan: a municipally sponsored chair of rhetoric. Augustine couldn't have designed a better position for himself if he'd tried.

Augustine and his makeshift family were in Milan from the autumn of 384 to the summer of 387. Una and Adeodatus seem to have been with him from the beginning, with Monnica arriving not long afterward. Augustine does not recount when or on what terms his mother forgave him for abandoning her when he left Carthage for Rome, but he captures her sense of purpose in making the journey in an anecdote from the voyage. During the crossing from Africa to Italy, the ship encountered a storm, and Monnica reassured the sailors: "She promised them that they would arrive safely, because You had promised her in a dream."[3]

Divine protection would be even more welcome in Italy itself. It was in the summer of 383, just as Augustine was leaving Carthage for Rome, that the emperor Gratian was killed, and now Italy was on the brink of civil war. Augustine and Monnica now found themselves in the company of people who had everything to gain—or lose— depending on how things played out. The *Confessions* reveal little of the maneuverings and motivations of Justina, Ambrose, and Maximus, but Augustine recognized that Milan was a place where, for men with careers on the rise, there was opportunity and possibility. Everything was unsettled, and everything was there for the taking. As a wordsmith who had only begun to discover the full extent of his gifts, Augustine knew that in Milan a single speech, even one drafted by an unknown newcomer from the provinces, could make or break the speaker's fortune.

Like everyone around him, Augustine would have to find allies in this strange new world. With war on the horizon, knowing whom to trust might become a matter of life and death. He swiftly found himself forced to declare his loyalty to the current regime in very public terms indeed. The object of his ceremonial speech of praise in January 385 was the year's new consul for the Western Empire, the Frankish general Flavius Bauto, the man in charge of Valentinian's defense against the forces of Maximus. The speech itself has not survived, but the fact that Augustine gave it is evidence both of his own status as a celebrated orator and of the expectation that he showcase his loyalty to Valentinian's government.[4]

To Monnica, these larger political questions may initially have seemed an unwelcome distraction: one problem weighed on her mind above all others. Like Justina, she needed to protect the interests of her son. Augustine had a great deal to gain if he could find his footing in this dangerous new world. This meant finding a wife, someone whose wealth and connections would open the door to the opportunities that lay before him.

Like many pious mothers of sons, Monnica placed both practical and spiritual hopes in the influence of the right wife. Augustine was clearly floundering. It was tempting if not entirely fair to lay this at Una's door; after all, a woman of high social standing would have a better chance of being listened to by an ambitious man than someone whom society encouraged him to see as dispensable. And of course, a well-connected father-in-law and an enviable dowry might focus the mind.

For his part, Augustine was now an outstandingly eligible bachelor, even if he was not equipped with an excess of social or financial capital. In the *Confessions* he refers to his father, Patricius, as "a townsman of Thagaste of modest means,"[5] though his biographer Possidius records that the family were *honestiores*, from the upper classes.[6] So the hunt was on for an heiress whose wealth and family connections could propel him into the Senate and allow him to reinvent himself yet again.

The matter of the dowry was crucial. The tradition among senatorial families was to settle roughly a year's income from the parental holdings on each daughter as a dowry. This could amount to a colossal sum: the contemporary historian Olympiodorus reckoned that a "middling" senator drew an income of one thousand to fifteen hundred Roman pounds of gold per annum—roughly $15 million to $25 million in twenty-first-century dollars.[7] For an established family to offer a hand up in this way to a young man of great promise was seen as entirely respectable. Cicero himself had married for money, after all.

The hopes and expectations of his relatives would have weighed heavily on Augustine. A chain of interdependence linked his personal prospects in Milan to the well-being of a wider family in Africa, whose future depended on his ability to court fortune and curry favor on their behalf. In a world where brutality, bullying, and quid pro quo arrangements were the norm, the patronage, backing, and networks Augustine could secure for himself and his family would make a measurable difference to their prosperity. And in a time when civil war was becoming endemic, there was also the question of their safety.

Monnica herself had overcome a harsh upbringing and a difficult marriage, and she had done everything to foster her youngest son's career as her family's most viable hope for the future. Now, as a widow, what she could offer him in financial terms was modest, but her expertise in choosing a bride could be relied on. "My mother took the most trouble in this, thinking that once I was married, the saving baptism would wash me clean; she rejoiced that day by day

I was becoming more ready for it, and she was seeing her prayers and Your promises fulfilled by my faith."[8] The idea seems to have been that a young man would sow his wild oats, and afterward the right wife would keep him on the straight and narrow. In Augustine's case, this meant drawing him closer to the church and away from the Manichees.

But Monnica must have known that Augustine had fallen in love. By the time he arrived in Italy, he had spent over a decade in a faithful and loving relationship with Una. She and Adeodatus had followed him from Africa to Italy, and in Milan the three had made a home together. After Monnica's arrival, an explosive emotional triangle may have begun to brew thanks to her zealous effort to steer her son into marriage.

And yet, so much of what happened between Augustine and Una resulted from the unquestioned cruelty of the Roman approach to family life. A modern reader can only be disturbed by a mother's willingness to sell her son to the highest bidder, or by the son's willingness to be sold. But in Augustine's case, there was never any question about whether he would step away from the mother of his son when the time came—it was simply a question of when the time would come. Neither Monnica nor Augustine seems to have grasped what it would cost him to put the plan into action.

Up until now, Augustine had played his part in the game of family ambition flawlessly. He had achieved a kind of success for which most parents of gifted sons could only hope. Betting on their son's abilities, Monnica and Patricius had held back from arranging a marriage, intending to wait until their investment in his education began to pay off. Augustine knew that his family expected him to pursue a political career and that this was beyond his means without "a wife with some money."

Looking back in the *Confessions*, Augustine seems to recognize that the traditional strategy of marrying him early might have been wiser. His parents' hopes for him differed slightly, but "both of them were very ambitious for my career."[9] Patricius was ambitious in the conventional sense: "He hardly thought about You at all, and about me he thought only about unimportant things."[10] But Monnica was not insensitive to his moral education. Still, "she thought it would do me no harm, and would be a help to set me on the way towards You, if I undertook a traditional literary education."[11] Armed with a sizeable dowry, his natural talents, and a powerful father-in-law's connections, he would have the world at his feet. But following the path of ambition would not be without cost.

A curious thing about the time Monnica, Augustine, and Una spent in Milan was the devotion both Monnica and Augustine came to feel for Bishop Ambrose. As he told the story afterward, the three years in Milan were the turning point of Augustine's life. He remembered it as a moral revolution in response to a single decisive factor: his encounter with Ambrose.

Augustine writes, "And so I came to Milan, to Ambrose the bishop, known throughout the world to be among the best of men, your faithful servant."[12] This is how Augustine introduces his time in Milan: as always in the *Confessions*, he imagines he is explaining his thoughts to God, and in this case he sounds like a starry-eyed child caught in the orbit of a personality with powerful gravity. Nowhere does Augustine capture the contradictions of himself as a young man more fully than in discussing the great object of his admiration, Bishop Ambrose.

Scholars have debated for centuries whether the relationship between Augustine and Ambrose was as close as the younger man

seems to remember. There is something enthralling about encounter-
ing a veteran of one's profession whose talent commands an immediate
and reverent respect—and as a shrewd political player with the ability
to compel crowds of the faithful with his words, Ambrose and his silver
tongue were the epitome of Augustine's aspirations. He was a powerful
figure from a powerful family whose sheer force of will and clever-
ness could only impress Augustine, groomed as he had been to tirelessly chase career ambition as his North Star. Augustine seems to have
admired Ambrose not just for his piety but also for his agile maneuvers
and brilliance in bending the game of Roman power to his will.

Certainly, Ambrose came to occupy a vital place in Augustine's
imagination. In part, he was a substitute father, but even more importantly, he changed Augustine's understanding of the nature of human
affection, uncovering a sense that all human connection forms part of
a larger web of connection with God. He described this theological
premise in his preaching on baptism as a fellowship connecting the
living and the dead through the loving presence of God. This sense
of connectedness would be a source of consolation to Augustine. In
the next few years, the people he loved most were taken from him,
one by one: first Una, then Monnica, and finally, his beloved son,
Adeodatus.

Augustine was fascinated by Monnica's devotion to Ambrose,
and in his description of their relationship, we can see how public
preaching gave a man with Ambrose's rhetorical gifts a platform to
build up a following. Of course, the relationship was asymmetrical: it
was fundamentally about the inspiration she found in his words. "She
would run to the church and hang on Ambrose's words, which were
a fountain leaping up into eternal life."[13] But the feeling seemed to be
mutual: "He in turn was fond of her because of her extremely devout
way of life, which led her to be constantly in Church with a spirit

burning for good works."[14] The bishop clearly had a gift for making his followers feel valued.

Swiftly, Monnica committed herself to the bishop's ways and his Nicene cause. The dispute over the Trinity was not widespread in Africa, where both the Old Believers and the Loyalist party accepted the Nicene idea that the Son of God was of one being with his Father without much difficulty. But Monnica encountered many surprises in how her faith was practiced in Milan. For example, she was disappointed to learn that her Numidian custom of bringing bread and wine to share at the shrines of the martyrs was forbidden—the view in Milan being that the practice was too close for comfort to pagan "superstition." But her loyalty to Ambrose had already taken root: when she heard that the prohibition came from Ambrose, "she was most happy to hold back." Augustine, for his part, was surprised to find his strong-willed mother so compliant: "I doubt my mother could have yielded so easily in giving up a settled habit if the prohibition had come from someone she loved less than Ambrose."[15]

Ambrose's obvious charisma with women, especially with one such as Monnica, who was not a person of worldly importance, reveals a very different side than we have seen previously. But the passionate preacher who stirred up crowds and the courteous pastor who was attentive to a newcomer from the provinces were facets of the same man. If Ambrose commanded a dangerously loyal following in Milan, it was at least partly because the people genuinely loved him.

Monnica also saw Ambrose as a potential weapon in the battle for her son's religious loyalties. At the beginning of their stay in Milan, Augustine was still involved with the Manichees, and she thought Ambrose had the power to bring him closer to the faith of his childhood. Once she saw that Augustine was falling under his spell, she became all the more devoted to him. "She loved that man as if he were an angel of God, because she'd found out that it was through him that I had been brought to this back-and-forth state of balance, by which she took it for granted that I would pass from sickness to health."[16]

But if Monnica's affection for Ambrose was uncomplicated, Augustine felt there was a shadow over his own relationship with the man. "When he saw me, he would often erupt into praise for her, congratulating me for having such a mother. Yet he didn't know that she had a son like me . . . who was hugely skeptical whether I could ever find the path to life."[17]

Why Augustine the Manichaean attended the bishop's preaching on Sundays isn't entirely clear; it may have been an attempt to curry favor with the Nicene faction or a matter of professional curiosity—after all, this was a man renowned for his gifts as a public speaker. Or it may have been simply that the old habits of his Christian upbringing died hard, and there was a certain comfort in sharing the experience with his mother.

In listening to Ambrose's preaching, Augustine felt he had finally found the teacher whom he had sought so tirelessly, with such disappointing results, in Madauros and Carthage. Something about the older man's manner made the newcomer Augustine feel at home: "That 'man of God' received me as a father would and showed concern for my journey with a kindness most fitting in a bishop. I began to love him, but at first not as a teacher of the truth, for I had absolutely given up on Your Church, but as someone who was kind to me."[18]

Augustine seems to have been watching everyone around him, trying to find a way to shed his sense of alienation, but at the same time, he wasn't entirely ready to shake off his craving to prove himself to the world. His attraction to Ambrose was intellectual, but he was also drawn to Ambrose's visible success. "My mind was bent on intellectual challenge and impatient for argument. I saw Ambrose as happy by worldly standards, because so many important people showed him respect."[19] Part of Ambrose's appeal, to Augustine, was his seeming to be living proof that it was possible to win the game Augustine had been playing all his life.

Watching Ambrose, Augustine began to see how to square his own mental restlessness with his yearning to make a mark in the world. Augustine's relationship with his father had been a troubled one, and he clearly had mixed feelings about the expectations his family had for him. He was looking for a role model, and in Ambrose he had found someone he could genuinely admire.

But there was one curious fact about the bishop: instead of being the head of a family and showcasing a well-turned-out wife and children, he was unmarried. We have no record that Ambrose was a widower, so he may never have had a wife, which would have been an unusual choice for a Roman senator and provincial governor. His clerical status did not pose an obstacle, since Christian priests and bishops were often married in the fourth century—and in any case, when Ambrose was baptized and became a bishop, he was already in his thirties, so the decision whether or not to marry was well past him. It is possible that Ambrose had divorced—Christians seem to have divorced quite freely in the fourth century—but if so, his biographer thought it better not to mention the fact.

By the time Augustine knew him, Ambrose's unmarried status had taken on a religious coloring, even if this was not its origin. His sister and confidante, Marcellina, was a professed Christian virgin, and this offers another dimension to his easy relationship with women. Marcellina was an early adopter of the ascetic movement, which advocated sexual renunciation as a path to spiritual illumination. A hallmark of the movement as practiced in Italy was that women and men who set aside the messy business of sex, marriage, and child-rearing could share an "angelic life" in which platonic friendship between the sexes was possible. (All parties agreed that it was otherwise virtually out of the question in that highly sexed society.)

For Augustine, grappling with Ambrose's ascetic lifestyle was part of his attempt to make sense of the man himself. He was not an ordinary personage: his unmarried status was still a relatively new choice for fourth-century bishops. Traditionally, Christian communities had been led by married couples, with the wife quietly, but often very effectively, dispensing pastoral care under the aegis of her husband. But Ambrose was part of the ascetic movement: "His celibacy was the only thing about him that seemed a hardship."[20]

Like many charismatic people, Ambrose had a quality that invited people to imagine what it was like to be him. "I couldn't guess what hopes he had, what tests his high standing might present, or what solace he found when troubled."[21] There is something almost tender about Augustine's musings on the older man's possible inner life, especially since he seems to be using them as an outlet for disappointment that he wasn't closer to Ambrose. "Nor did he know anything of my turmoil, or the trap that threatened to swallow me."[22]

The problem, put simply, was that Augustine wasn't part of Ambrose's inner circle: "I couldn't ask him the questions I wanted to, in the way I wanted to, because I was blocked off from getting his ear, or getting a word from him, by the crowd of people bringing him their business."[23] It was all very frustrating.

Ambrose seems to have kept a kind of open house, as many Roman senators did, allowing a crowd of clients and followers to spend time in his residence whether he was paying attention to them or not. Often, he was reading, and this was a cause for surprise: "When he read, his eyes ran across the pages and his mind made out the sense, but his voice and his tongue remained silent."[24] Like other people of his day, Augustine was used to reading everything out loud—not only because the rhetorical schools focused on training the voices of their pupils but also for the more basic reason that in ancient Rome, writing was thought of as a way of recording the spoken word, and reading was a way of bringing the word back to life by converting it into sound again.

Augustine paints a curious picture of young men milling around in Ambrose's atrium and watching him with curious interest as he read to himself in order to work on his theological writings: "We were often with him—he didn't prohibit anyone from coming in or have arrivals be announced—and we saw him reading silently then, and never any other way." They were fascinated by him and also a little in awe: "We sat in long silence—for who would dare bother someone concentrating so intently?—and then went away."[25]

In Augustine's case, however, hanging around the atrium was also a matter of watching for a chance to talk to the man. "But that meant I had no chance to consult Your holy oracle that resided within him, unless I had something that I could spit out very quickly." He was sure that Ambrose could help him, if only he found a chance to lay out all the things that were bothering him: "The commotion of my mind demanded a listener who was free to listen when it was laid out before him, but the moment never came."[26] So although Augustine was part of the group who gathered around Ambrose, he never had the chance to establish the kind of intimacy that he craved.

Instead, he had to make the most of what he could get from Ambrose's preaching, and this turned out to be well worth the effort. Unlike in his disastrous encounter with Faustus, this time he had found someone who could answer his questions: "Of course, every Sunday, I heard him unfolding the scriptures' words of truth in just the right terms, and more and more I began to understand that all the twisty, wily knots of slander which the people who had deceived me had wrapped around the holy books could be loosened."[27] Finally, he had found someone who could speak to "my deep anxiety about what I could hang onto as certain."[28]

There is something awkwardly moving about the younger man's investment in the asymmetrical relationship that Ambrose's public preaching afforded. One might almost call it parasocial by modern standards: Augustine was bringing his questions to Ambrose and receiving answers, but Ambrose wasn't actually listening—Augustine was largely engaging with an Ambrose of the imagination, supplemented by Ambrose's public pronouncements. In this way, the younger man was practicing the skill of reading the signs and silences of the more established figure, co-opting him as a partner in an imagined internal dialogue.

Augustine's distant-but-intimate relationship with Ambrose can be seen as the beginning of a remarkably fruitful habit of finding and building a live imaginative connection with others that could overcome distance or physical absence. This allowed him to engage deeply with a wide variety of conversational partners, whether exchanging letters and essays with living individuals or musing on the writings and stories of the long-dead heroes of the faith. Of course, this habit would serve him well in the study of scripture and in what would become a lifelong habit of engaging with God in prayer. Ambrose was teaching him many things, and one of the most important may have been how to imagine his response if he were listening.

Now everything was beginning to seem clearer. Augustine had been attracted to Christian teaching for years, having been raised in a Christian family, but he had dismissed the Bible as a compendium of folkloric stories that didn't make a great deal of sense. But Ambrose made him see that there were hidden meanings to uncover. He began to suspect, he tells God, that "I had accused Your holy ones of seeing things in a way that they didn't actually see them." The problem, after all, had been his own lack of understanding.

Ambrose emphasized in his preaching that too much focus on the superficial meaning of a passage could lead one astray. "He was removing the ritual veil, as it were, from the deeper meaning, to lay open the spiritual meaning of things that, when taken literally, seemed to teach perversity."[29] Here, finally, was a man Augustine felt he could trust to guide his mind as well as his heart.

Now it began to dawn on Augustine that the Christians might actually be more honest than the Manichaeans. He now saw a kind of dignity in their loyalty to the simple fact that their faith involved things that were beyond human understanding. "I saw more modesty and less scope for dishonesty, in believing what hadn't been proved…than in making reckless promises of knowledge and ridiculing a listener's willingness to trust."[30] Now he began to see generosity and humility in the Bible's way of reaching out to simple people, even though it held deeper and more complex ideas as well. That he had not seen this before, Augustine attributed to his own lack of insight, not to any failing of the Bible. "It opened itself to all with straightforward words in the most colloquial style, but also harnessed the mental focus of those inclined to reflection."[31]

Augustine remembered his discovery of Ambrose and his teaching as a moment of the purest relief. A discrepancy between his heart and his intellect, between the faith of his childhood and the philosophical questions of his formal education, had nagged at him for years and years. Now, thanks to Ambrose, he was able to recognize in these artless and familiar ancient stories a tool to integrate the longings of his heart with the capacities of his mind.

We come now to one of the truly puzzling questions of the *Confessions*: Why did things begin to go badly in Milan just as he was beginning to find coherence in his search for understanding? Looking back, Augustine cringes at his younger self's ruthless pursuit of worldly success. "I was obsessed with honor, money, and finding a bride—and You could only laugh."[32] He never quite seems to decide whether to blame Monnica's ambition for him or his own, but he recognizes that worldly ambition was his downfall.

Life in the shadow of the palace was not agreeing with him. As he got closer and closer to the center of power, he began to feel more and more anxious—"How miserable that made me!"—and even the opportunities to put himself forward became a source of distress. A case in point was "that day when I was getting ready to give a speech of praise to the Emperor, telling many lies and in lying winning the approval of an audience that was in the know." The chance to speak at court in praise of the emperor himself was a dizzying opportunity—a shot at becoming a force to contend with at court might genuinely be within reach.

But it was all too much for him: "My heart was gasping and burning with the fever of corrosive thoughts."[33] The harder he pushed, the more he began to notice the pointlessness of the prizes that he was reaching for.

On the day of his speech, Augustine was so jittery that he found himself envying a beggar on a Milanese street corner: "He was already, it seemed to me, a bit tipsy, laughing and enjoying himself."[34] It came to him that he had let ambition draw him into a situation of unbearable enervation. He found himself suddenly seeing things from a new perspective—"all the efforts under which I was laboring, goaded by greed as I strained under the burden of my unhappiness which became ever greater."[35] He was with friends, and he tried to get them to see that despite his poverty, the drunken man had at least managed to not create the kind of trap for himself that they had fallen into: "All we wanted was to reach a state of safe enjoyment; that beggar had got there ahead of us and perhaps we would never get there ourselves."[36] Augustine never tells us how his speech came out; he has come to recognize that such matters have no real importance. Nor does he tell us what happened to the beggar; his enviable state was almost certainly an illusion. But the story captures Augustine's sense that something was terribly wrong with the way he was living his life.

Augustine later remembered that during his time in Milan, the question of marriage came up repeatedly in discussions with his African friends Alypius and Nebridius, as they vacillated over whether to pledge themselves to worldly ambition or the life of the mind.

Marriage was an answer to the question of money: copious funds would be necessary if any of them wanted to convert his potential into real power by securing high office. It was a heady prospect. Augustine describes his reasoning at the time: "What a great thing it is to get a preferment of some kind. What more could one ask for?"[37] Plotting a path toward such an outcome would be difficult but not impossible. "We have lots of important friends; if we push hard and stay focused, it should certainly be possible to come up with a governorship."[38] An office of this kind, he knew, could give him entry into the senatorial class, with the accompanying privileges and immunities—and a ripple effect of opportunity for his friends and family.

Dowry hunting was the essential first step. "Marrying a wife with some money would be necessary, to cover the expenses, and that would be the end of our ambition."[39] Each of them knew that a senatorial dowry was a necessity for the kind of social climbing that they had set their hearts on, but they were not entirely ready to commit themselves.

At the same time, Augustine was aware that philosophers had debated for centuries whether philosophy and the responsibilities of a married *paterfamilias* could be reconciled. He found himself arguing that it was possible. He summarizes his mildly pompous reasoning: "Many great men who are worthy of imitation have pledged themselves to both marriage and the study of wisdom."[40]

His close friend Alypius saw things differently. "Alypius tried to put me off marrying, with the refrain that if I did, there was no way we could live together in carefree leisure dedicated to the love of wisdom as we had long wanted to do."[41] It became a debate, between them, over whether Augustine would be able and willing to renounce the lusts of the flesh for the sake of philosophy. But really it was money, not sexual renunciation, that loomed large at the center of the debate.

Many scholars have assumed that, having fallen under the influence of Alypius and the circle of Ambrose in 385 and 386, Augustine had come to believe that the only true form of Christianity was the ascetic type practiced by Ambrose. But this is not what he tells us. Monnica's ideal of a household presided over by a Christian *materfamilias* was still the guiding principle. So in his debate with Alypius over the respective moral virtues of marriage and continence, Augustine took the side of marriage.

Curiously, Augustine tells us that the loving harmony he enjoyed with the concubine he had brought with him from Africa enabled him to win the debate with Alypius. He writes that Alypius recognized their situation as enviable: "If my way of life had had the honorable name of marriage, he would have had no reason to wonder that I did not want to give up that type of life. He himself began to want to be married."[42]

Later, as he wrote the *Confessions*, Augustine recognized that both he and Alypius had missed the point of the argument. "Neither of us thought more than briefly about how the dignity of marriage is in the obligation to respect its discipline and to raise children."[43] Looking back, he could now see that this *disciplina*—the emotional and material commitment involved in caring for a partner and raising children— was easily a challenge to be respected. In the summer of 386, he and Alypius had been too narrow in their thinking. This failure of the imagination would ultimately cost him dearly.

In 385 and 386, marriage to Una was still technically on the table as a possibility—even if she was a slave or former slave. Only a senator was barred from marrying a freed slave, and Augustine had no hope of gain- ing senatorial status unless he married a rich wife whose dowry could support his political ambitions. There was no legal or moral impediment to marrying Una or continuing in the unmarried relationship. But it would bar his path to the dowry required to put his ambitions on a secure footing, so she had to go. At this stage neither Augustine nor his family had any idea of setting aside the dreams they had nurtured, not when they were so close to realizing them. If Una had to be sacrificed on the altar of these dreams, that was only to be expected.

And so a bride was found. "Energetic pressure was put on me to marry. In no time, I was courting and the bride had been promised."[44] She was a pleasing and aristocratic ten-year-old, and it was in the mat- ter of her age that Monnica made her mistake. The issue was not the age difference itself: Tacita was a year or two younger than Augustine's son Adeodatus, who seems to have been born in 373, but this was not unusual. The problem was the waiting period before Tacita came of age. There would be two years for doubts to take root and grow. For Augustine, this was not good news when it finally sank in. If he was going to sell himself to the highest bidder, he needed to do it quickly.

His first task was to send Una back to Africa. His account of the parting is both heartfelt and disturbingly brief. "In the meantime, my sins were multiplying. The woman I had been sharing a bed with was torn from my side, and my heart, which clung to her, was cut and wounded and bleeding. And she went back to Africa, vowing to You that she would never know another man."[45] This is all we hear of her reaction.

Una must have seen this outcome in the making, when she accompanied Augustine first to Rome and then to Milan and began to witness his brilliance opening doors through which she could not follow. She can only have known that her position was dangerous. Both law and custom would work against her when the time came for Augustine to marry. It was one of the private tragedies that a woman of her status was raised to expect and to accept with dignity if she could. But it would be understandable if she chose to hope things would turn out otherwise. Perhaps she held fast to her ambitions as stubbornly as Augustine pursued his own, willing herself to believe that after coming so far together, their bond would transcend law and custom, travel and time—that after nearly fifteen years and against all odds, their almost-family might become a family after all. And that that would be enough. But it is also possible that she was more realistic and had channeled all her hopes for upward mobility into her son.

We learn next that she left Adeodatus with his father, and this is the hardest thing to accept. In a narrative that bristles with the intensity of the love between sons and mothers, Una's decision to leave the boy behind in Italy goes undiscussed. Augustine simply tells us, "My natural son by her stayed behind with me."[46] Presumably, since Adeodatus was close to maturity, he had something to gain from remaining in the entourage of his brilliant and well-connected father at the center of power. It was perhaps Una's triumph to leave him there, where his future would best be served.

Or it may be that she had no choice in the matter. If Una was a slave or freedwoman and Augustine or his mother was her owner or patron, the decision may have lain with them. Still, whether her hand was forced or she made the choice out of love for the boy, leaving Adeodatus in Milan was a gesture of forbearance on Una's part. Perhaps she felt that commending the boy to Augustine's custody would leave him with a trace of their life together. We later learn that Adeodatus died a few years after his mother was dismissed. It is possible that he visited her before he died, but it is also possible that after she left Milan, she never saw him again.

Chapter Eight

REMEDY FOR A BROKEN HEART

WHILE ENDURING THE DELAY OF HIS MARRIAGE until his fiancée came of age, Augustine did what he could to manage the surprising pain of sending Una away. Somehow, as he had laid the careful plans for his brilliant future, he had failed to anticipate the agony caused by severing the deep emotional bonds of a long life together—a life that he, at least, had found unusually happy. He fell into a serious depression. The fall-out would eventually lead him to renounce his marriage and, with it, the glittering political career that his fiancée's fortune had been meant to fund. But this was all to come. For now, there was the ordeal of waiting.

Whether it was Monnica or Tacita's parents who were ultimately responsible for Una's hasty departure, enforcing this condition of the betrothal so quickly was grossly mistimed. Augustine tells us that

179

having to send Una away nearly two years before his marriage to Tacita left him in an almost unbearably restless and anxious mood. His enervation as he waited turned out to have disastrous consequences. So even if Monnica was right in principle to spare Tacita the misery she might have faced as Augustine's wife with Una nearby, delaying the concubine's departure might have been wiser.

But Monnica was not wrong to think Una could not stay on once he was married. Looking back at herself as a young bride, she knew from experience that a domestic sexual triangle was something to be avoided if possible. She may also have seen a connection between her husband's philandering and his volatile temper, though even affectionate husbands could be prone to domestic violence. In speaking to Augustine, she seems to have downplayed how much the difficulties with Patricius had cost her. Certainly she acted to make sure her son did not follow in his father's footsteps.

What happened next is shocking to a modern sensibility, albeit, within the cultural frame of the fourth century, entirely predictable. Seemingly without much reflection, Augustine replaced his departed concubine with a new woman to occupy his bed on a temporary basis until he could marry. "I wasn't a lover of marriage but a slave of desire, so I found another woman—not a wife, of course. In that way the sickness of my soul could fester, and perhaps even worsen."[1] He is willing to admit that his attitude to women and sex had nothing to do with responsibility or commitment, but still, he was coming to the point of desperation: "The wound made by the earlier excision wasn't healing, but instead, after the acute burning and pain it went septic, and the deeper pain was almost numb."[2] In writing, he is trying to capture the pain of his younger self, of course, but in doing so, he also reproduces his younger self's thoughtlessness—there is no thought for Una or Adeodatus here, only his own suffering.

For Adeodatus, his parents' separation and his mother's departure changed things dramatically. That she could be dismissed from their lives with such expediency and finality may not have occurred to him ahead of time. He may have trusted his father blindly and believed in the strength of their life together. If so, law and custom wouldn't have mattered to him; he had lost his mother and saw his father as the culprit responsible. We have no record of Adeodatus's reaction to the separation, but it is not unlikely that it caused tension between the boy and his father. That his own son might turn against him was a possibility Augustine hadn't prepared for. But given his exposed situation, Adeodatus may well have kept whatever anger he felt to himself.

Once Una had been cast aside, Augustine began to look for a way to put distance between himself and the memory of their happiness. That may have been the point of the second concubine: the relationship surely helped him to erase what he had felt for Una, to put it on the level of a trifling entanglement with a serving maid. The trick was to see the separation as only one more challenge, a task to be performed with precision like any other. But it was not easy to lie to his son—or, in the end, to himself. His feelings for the boy's mother seem to have come to him as an unwelcome surprise.

There are two ways to read Augustine's picture of himself as a slave to lust. On one reading, the scene leads the reader toward Augustine's spiritual crisis in the summer of 386, which turned, as he tells the story, on the question of whether he would go through with the betrothal that had shattered his happiness. His readers already knew, of course, that he did not marry. He wanted them to understand why.

Here we come to one of the great ironies of how Augustine's story has been understood over the centuries. The monks who copied the text for their libraries—and to whom we owe the fact that it has survived—were convinced that Augustine could only fulfill his destiny

181

by tearing himself away from women. This narrowly monkish reading of the narrative has become widely accepted.

Generations of scholars have held the view that the real reason for Augustine's decision not to marry was a sudden call to a vocation as a monk. Augustine's earliest biographer, Possidius—his pupil and a bishop himself—first suggested this logic. Possidius reasoned that when Augustine embraced Christianity, he believed that to be a true Christian, one had to renounce worldly attachments of any kind. On this reading, Augustine had converted not to Christianity but to monasticism, which took shape under the influence of his childhood friend, the famously ascetic monk-bishop Alypius—who was with Augustine in Milan at the time—and Bishop Ambrose, famous for preaching that the most perfect form of Christianity involved sexual renunciation.

But reading the *Confessions* carefully, we encounter a different story. Augustine tells us that he and Alypius had debated whether marriage was a better way of life than asceticism, but he makes clear that he, Augustine, had *won* the debate. Largely by pointing to the example of his own harmonious home life with Una and their small son, Augustine had persuaded his friend that marriage had to be better than the single life. As he saw things in hindsight, the problem he had faced in the summer of 386 was not that sex and marriage were obstacles to communion with God. Rather, it was that his *way* of pursuing them had been immoral.

On this reading, the received view is not wrong that Augustine was recoiling from sin when he decided not to marry. But the sin that repulsed him was not lust; it was greed. What shook him, finally, was his willingness to betray the woman who *ought* to have been his wife—the mother of his child—for a lucrative arranged marriage. The root of his problem was not sexual desire. It was ambition.

Years later, after returning to Africa, Augustine would go on to become first a monk and then a Christian bishop, and his pastoral writings would repeatedly recognize a spiritual value in romantic partnerships outside wedlock. He would argue that a man who had lived with a concubine should not be allowed to marry, since in his day, second marriages were prohibited. Even if Roman law saw concubines as a having no legal standing, he argued, the church should see the union as spiritually equivalent to marriage. In other words, neither one of the pair should move on to marry someone else while the other was still living. This was and remained a minority view. Many Christians shared Monnica's view that divorce was impossible, but this only applied to marriage, while others believed that under the right circumstances, Christians could divorce and remarry. With the exception of Augustine, no one seems to have believed that men should be forever faithful to a concubine whom they had specifically chosen not to marry.

If Bishop Augustine came to argue that a man who takes a concubine has a moral obligation to her, his contemporaries mostly saw a concubine as a person there to be exploited. Whether slave or free, she provided a service, and if she earned genuine affection from her partner, this spoke well of her but did not alter her position. By sleeping with her, the male partner acquired no long-term obligation toward her or her children, even if he was the biological father. Augustine would break with this tradition by arguing that in moral terms an established extramarital relationship carried the same responsibility as the legal bond of marriage.

We can see this in the famous scene in the garden at the climax of Book Eight of the *Confessions*, when Augustine decides to dedicate his life to God. This momentous scene has been persistently misunderstood. Certainly, he was guilty of a terrible sexual sin, but the sin was not sleeping with his concubine. It was casting her away.

Augustine's story of his conversion begins with an admission that he had been a slave to lust and to worldly ambition. But now, God had freed him: "I will tell the story of how You, my help and my salvation, set me free from the chains of sexual desire, which held me so tightly, and from the slavery of my worldly ambition."[3] That Augustine addresses God by the term *dominus*—which means both "lord" and "master"—here is no accident; he wants to underline the helpless subjection he had labored under. "I was going about my usual activities," he says, "with anxiety mounting ever higher, and every day I sighed for You."[4]

His friend Alypius was staying with him during a break between appointments, and the two men were together one day when they received an important visitor who would change how Augustine felt about his relationship with God. That visitor was Ponticianus, who Augustine says "was a countryman of ours, a fellow African, and he held an important position in the palace."[5] Augustine explains that Ponticianus had come on a routine errand, but the encounter became much more meaningful. Upon making small talk, Ponticianus noticed a book of the apostle Paul's letters, which happened "by chance" to be on the table in front of them.[6]

Ponticianus took up the book and discovered what it was, and this led to an unexpected moment of connection between the two men. Augustine writes that Ponticianus "smiled and looked at me with appreciation."[7] Ponticianus, a committed Christian, went on to explain the story of the monk Antony, whose life in the Egyptian desert, retold by Bishop Athanasius of Alexandria, had taken the Christian world by storm and recently been translated into Latin.

All present found themselves in a state of collective amazement and surprise: Ponticianus was shocked that Augustine and Alypius could be unfamiliar with the story of Antony, and for their part,

Alypius and Augustine were mesmerized by the story itself. As a young man, Antony had walked into a church and heard a reading of the passage from the gospel of Matthew in which a rich young man asks Jesus, "What must I do to have eternal life?" Jesus tells him, "If you would be perfect, go, sell what you possess and give to the poor, and you will have treasure in heaven; and come, follow me."[8] Augustine was astonished to discover a whole world that he had been missing, a wider community of people involved in a quest similar to his own—people who had walked away from the demands of their position in society and chosen to live for God alone. "And there was even a monastery in Milan outside the city walls, full of good brothers under Ambrose's care, but we didn't know about it."[9]

Part of the power of Ponticianus's story about the life of Antony lay in how it had changed his own life. He had been in the emperor's service at Trier with three other imperial officials. On a walk one morning while the emperor was at the games, two of them had encountered "a house where some slaves of Yours lived, the poor in the spirit, to whom the kingdom of heaven belongs."[10] In their hut, the monks had a Latin translation of the *Life of Antony*, and one of the men began to read it, whereupon he "began to wonder and caught fire: and while he was reading he started to think about taking up a life like that, and leaving the imperial service, serving You."[11] Just as Antony had imitated the rich young man in the Gospel of Matthew, so he wanted to imitate Antony himself.

So he turned to his friend and said, "Tell me, I ask, where are all of our efforts trying to get us? What are we looking for? For what purpose are we fighting? Could there be any hope greater for us in the palace than to become 'friends of the emperor'? ... [B]ut I can become a friend of God instantly if I want to." After saying this, he returned to reading the book. This was the pivotal point in the transformation of Ponticianus's friend, the "turbulent birth of a new life."[12] He said to his friend, "I've now torn myself away from that hope of ours and decided to serve God, and that is where I am headed from this hour and this place. If you don't want to follow me, don't try to stop me."[13] His companion told him that they had served so long together that he would not abandon him now.

It was only afterward, Ponticianus told Augustine and Alypius, that he and the fourth friend came to the hut where their two friends had experienced their revelation and heard their story. They wept, in part because they were not ready to make the same commitment, and returned to the palace. Their two friends stayed on in the hut with the monks.

Something in the reverence that Ponticianus so obviously felt for his friends spoke to Augustine. "This was the story Ponticianus told us," he concludes. "But while he was talking, You, Lord…set my own face in front of me, so I could see how ugly I was, how dirty and deformed, blotchy and covered with sores."[14] Now, for the first time, he felt able to confront the sense of foreboding he had been feeling. "I saw, and was disgusted—but I could not run away from myself. If I tried to turn away from seeing myself, there he was, telling the story he was telling, and You kept setting me in front of myself and thrusting me before my eyes."[15]

When Ponticianus had finished both his story and the original errand that had prompted his visit, he went away, leaving Augustine "again to what I was."[16] There was no alternative: Augustine had to face himself. "I tore away at myself and a terrible shame spread violently through me."[17] Augustine asks, "What did I not say to myself? With what whips of judgment did I not lash my soul, trying to make it follow me as I struggled to reach You? But it resisted, and refused, even though it had no excuse."[18]

His exasperation, though really aimed at himself, erupted in an outburst directed at Alypius. He yelled, "What is wrong with us? What is this? Did you hear that? The unlearned are rising up and snatching heaven, just look at us with our heartless learning; we are wrapped up in flesh and blood!" It was galling that all their study of philosophy had done them so little good. "Just because they have gone ahead, are we ashamed to follow them, and not ashamed that we aren't following them?"[19]

His inner turmoil drove him out of doors, to the garden of the house where they were staying, with Alypius close behind. Augustine explains, "The tumult in my heart took me to a place where no one could disrupt the flaming row I was waging against myself, until it came to its conclusion—You knew what it would be, but I didn't."[20]

Augustine vividly describes his blistering psychological unrest as he tossed and turned in the garden. And in this moment he has his own revelation: God has been with him the whole time. He is not alone in his pain; the pain is a challenge from God laid out in order for him to find God. "And Lord, You were there in my darkest self, with Your cruel mercy, redoubling the whip of fear and shame so I wouldn't give up."[21]

There is something strangely charming about Augustine's effort to outline the sequence of his thoughts as he wrestled with himself. He knew what he had to do, but he was not quite ready to do it. "I was saying to myself inwardly, 'Look, now, it's happening; right now it's happening.' And even as I spoke, I was making the pact. I was almost taking the step, but I wasn't taking the step just yet."[22] He felt he was on the brink, but he couldn't quite reach his goal—he didn't even know if he would recognize it when he found it. "And I tried again, and I got a little closer, and a little closer again, and I almost—almost—reached it and grasped it. But I didn't reach it and grasp it; I was holding back from dying to death and living in life."[23]

Finally, the emotional and spiritual thrashing brought him to tears. "So I could let it all come out I got up to leave Alypius—it seemed better to be alone if I was going to be wailing—and I moved away, so even his sympathetic presence didn't hold me back."[24] He left Alypius to wait where they had been sitting together; he himself was in "a mood beyond shock."

Now "I threw myself down under a fig tree, I don't know how, and gave my tears free rein."[25] He found himself speaking directly to God, entreating him, "How much further, Lord, how far before your anger reaches its limit?"[26] Again, he uses the language of the slave pleading with a master to stop a punishment. The irony here is that the obstacle was Augustine's own stubbornness: God was waiting with open arms.

Yet Augustine recognized that his tears were a sacrifice to God in and of themselves and that allowing himself to experience and embrace his true emotions in a moment of catharsis marked a step toward the truth that faith would award him. In standing apart from God, he had been betraying not only the truth but himself.

As he wept and raged at God, Augustine heard the voice of a child from the household next door. The child was chanting, "Pick it up! Read it! Pick it up! Read it!"[27] He asked himself whether this could be a child's rhyme or game; it seemed uncannily like a message directed at him. He decided it must be the latter: "I had never heard of anything like it."[28]

The story of Antony was of course still fresh in his mind. "I had heard that Antony had taken his cue from a Gospel reading that he had happened to walk in on; it seemed that what was being read was addressed to him alone: 'Go, sell everything you have, and give it to the poor, and you will have treasure in heaven, and come, follow me.'"[29] So it came naturally to Augustine to return to the book that he had carried with him into the garden. "Shaken, I returned to where

Alypius was sitting; I had put down the book of the Apostle there when I got up. I snatched it and opened it."[30]

Now he felt he was being guided toward the answer to all his questions. "And I read in silence the passage on which my eyes fell first: 'not in reveling and drunkenness, not in promiscuity and shamelessness, not in struggling and rivalry—but put on the Lord, Jesus Christ, and don't make provision for the flesh and its cravings.'"[31] This seemed, to him, to be an answer chosen by God to address his own most intimate doubts about the life he was leading. "I didn't want to read further, nor did I need to. As soon as I finished this passage, it was as if a beacon of freedom from anxiety had flooded my heart. All the shadows of doubt had vanished."[32] Augustine felt that he had been given a sign that God's watchful eye had been present in his struggle. When he closed the book, he had no need for words—his face alone told Alypius what had happened.

Augustine knew instantly that he would call off his marriage. "You turned me to Yourself, and now I neither wanted to pursue marriage nor any other worldly ambition."[33] Yet this also had implications for his other relationships: he felt some dread about how his mother would react, since she expected him to marry. But she surprised him. "She was delighted.... [S]he blessed You, who 'are more powerful than we can hope for or understand.' She saw that you had done far more for me than she had been praying for in her miserable tears and moaning."[34] The watchful eye of God and the passionate prayers of his mother had perhaps been working in unison all along.

The one option Augustine did not consider at this point, at least not publicly, was the obvious one. In principle, the choice not to marry for money and power did not have to involve a vow of sexual continence; it opened the path for him to return to his son's mother. But Augustine never mentions this possibility; we have no way of knowing whether it occurred to him.

In fact, it was the obvious thing to do: Una had vowed never to know another man, but the vow seems to have been motivated by loyalty to their relationship rather than a specific desire for sexual renunciation as a life path. (In any case, the African church did not enroll women as celibates below the age of forty, and at the time their relationship ended, Una was probably in her late twenties.) Of course, the terms of the parting may have been too bitter, or something else could have gone wrong. But it is hard to imagine that the idea was not in play.

Where Monnica figured in all this is difficult to plot. To a modern ear, Augustine's description of his close friendship with Alypius implies shared bachelor lodgings, but his was probably a substantial multigenerational household. Augustine is also ambivalent, throughout the *Confessions*, about his mother's conflicting hopes and ambitions for him. She wanted him to do well and succeed; she wanted him to get baptized; she wanted him to marry a Catholic girl; she wanted him to marry an heiress.

It is hard to tell whether Augustine is shifting the blame for his own conflicted ambitions onto Monnica or her demands on him were fueling his sense of being unfulfilled and at a loss. Patricius was long dead, and Augustine no longer needed to submit his plans to the *paterfamilias* for approval. We do know that his own view was changing, and changing very quickly.

Perhaps Monnica felt that if he were to marry a good Catholic girl, steering him toward baptism would be easier. But the evidence suggests that Una was herself a Catholic, and if this is true, the same spiritual aim—minus the social ambitions—could have been realized by marrying down rather than up. What was most important about the heiress, in Monnica's eyes, was the fact that her wealth could open doors. Or Monnica may truly have felt that among all the dazzling possibilities before him, Augustine really needed only to be at peace with himself. Looking back, he seems uncertain about what she really felt, and of course Monnica herself may not have known. After all, she was human.

We should also consider the possibility that Tacita's family had thought better of the arrangement and Augustine was putting a brave face on things. Perhaps their African connections alerted them to the trouble with Messianus and the fact that in Carthage Augustine was viewed as an outlaw. Possibly they had heard boasts that Monnica had played a starring role in the commotion at Easter and recoiled at being associated with a family whose women called attention to themselves in this way. Or again, if they were loyal to the court, they may have been appalled that Augustine's family supported Ambrose, whose challenge to the emperor they would have viewed as somewhere between unwise and treasonous.

Still, looking back afterward, Augustine viewed his broken engagement through a philosophical lens. He recognized that his fiancée had been, first and foremost, an instrument of ambition rather than an object of desire. (This said, he mentions somewhat sheepishly in the *Confessions* that he found her attractive, almost as if he wants to be sure that no one will blame her for the failed engagement.) In a dialogue written shortly after his broken engagement, Augustine tries to explain why his philosophical studies up to the time of his engagement had made so little progress. "I was detained by the allure of marriage and honor, the result being that I did not dash off quickly to the bosom of philosophy.... [His plan at the time was that] only after I had attained these things would I then set full sail and bend all oars toward the bay of philosophy."[35]

Around the same time, he notes in another imaginary dialogue that he was troubled by lust, but the kind of sex that could be expected within marriage was not what worried him. "If it pertains to the office of a wise man...to devote himself to children," he says, "anyone who for this reason alone sleeps with a woman would seem admirable to me—but there's no way he could be someone that I'd imitate. Indeed, it is more dangerous to try this than it is lucky to be able to do it."[36] After the humiliating scenes he had put himself through in trying to disentangle himself from his beloved, he had come away with a decisively jaundiced view of the power of sexual attraction. "Nothing should be avoided more than sexual relations. I feel that nothing dislodges a male mind from its citadel more than a woman's charms."[37] Augustine's conversion to asceticism seems to have had its beginnings as a way out of a morally untenable position, but he quickly began to look back at his earlier self as an addict who could not be trusted when faced with the delirium he craved.

At the end of the summer of 386, at the age of thirty-one, Augustine announced his retirement as a teacher of rhetoric on grounds of ill health. If the decision not to marry was the beginning of a spiritual awakening, his refusal to be bought by the powerful clans in charge of Milan was a necessary step. In narrative terms, the story of his emotional and sexual torment is there to show the reader how far he had fallen, but the refusal to marry was about money and power rather than sex.

And yet there is a far more disturbing way to read the episode. The very involving story of Augustine's conversion in the late summer of 386 may have been designed to keep his readers' attention focused not only on his conversion but also on a vivid image of his geographical whereabouts—to put it beyond doubt that he was in Milan and not Carthage at the time. In his youth, Augustine was a notorious Manichaean, and for years after his conversion, up to and beyond the time he wrote the *Confessions*, he had enemies who wanted nothing more than to call attention to this fact in order to discredit him. In the 390s, some of these enemies circulated a rumor that he had left

Africa not in 383 but in 386, fleeing Carthage as an outlaw during a crackdown against the Manichaeans that took place in that year.

In 385 and 386 a new proconsul of Africa, Messianus, a religious hard-liner from the inner circle of the Eastern emperor Theodosius, took action against the Manichaean community in Carthage. It quickly became clear that Messianus was out for blood in a way that Eusignius, the religious moderate who had been proconsul when Augustine left in 383, had never approved of. (Eusignius later came to Milan as praetorian prefect for Italy and was one of the members of Valentinian's court who tried to reason with Ambrose during the Conflict of the Basilicas.) In 386, Messianus put into force the law against the Manichaeans that Eusignius had chosen not to act on in 383, and the results were devastating for the Manichaean community. Augustine was safely in Milan, but others were not so lucky. His old idol Bishop Faustus was condemned to death, though his sentence was later commuted to permanent exile. Had Augustine been present, he could have suffered a similar fate, but his enemies suggested that he had taken the coward's option and fled. Indignant, he reminded his enemies that at least some of the speeches he had given in Milan in 385 and 386 were important enough to be preserved and dated as a matter of public record, such as the panegyric he had delivered to celebrate the inauguration of a new consul. What better proof of his whereabouts than speeches given in the presence of the emperor himself?[38] But in the court of public opinion, an argument based on public records had less chance of being widely remembered and repeated than a story of star-crossed lovers.

During the first months after his withdrawal from public life, Augustine joined a philosophical commune at Cassiciacum, in the mountains near Milan. The idea had been brewing for some time: while still planning to marry, he and Alypius had decided to found a philosophical community funded by Romanianus, Augustine's patron from Thagaste, who was in Milan to appeal the ruling in a property dispute, which he hoped to have the emperor review.

Originally, Romanianus had offered to sponsor a group of ten friends who wanted to live together communally on a semipermanent basis. "We decided that two of us, appointed like annual magistrates, should be responsible for all the necessary business, leaving the others free."[39] But the idea foundered on the problem of women. "Yet afterward we began to ask whether the women would accept this, the wives that some already had and that others wanted to have."[40] Women meant responsibility. To a modern reader, the fact that the men's families were only an afterthought is surprising, but in the end the afterthought was decisive. "The whole agreement which we had organized so well fell apart in our hands; it was broken up and thrown away."[41]

But Augustine was able to put a similar idea into practice at least briefly in the autumn of 386, after his crisis, at Cassiciacum in the hills northeast of Milan. There, on the estate of another generous and wealthy friend, Verecundus, Augustine would prepare for baptism, returning to Milan to be baptized by Bishop Ambrose at Easter of 387.

At Cassiciacum, the group seems to have overlapped closely with Augustine's family, augmented by former students: Augustine names his brother Navigius and two cousins, Latidianus and Rusticus, along with his former students Alypius and Trygetius, Romanianus's son Licentius, and his own son Adeodatus. Women, it seems, were welcome: his mother Monnica took a leading role in the discussions, not unlike Diotima in Plato's *Symposium*.[42] Other women are not mentioned, but this does not guarantee that they were not present. (We need only think of how Monnica appears from nowhere after Augustine's conversion in the garden to recognize that women are often invisibly in the background in the stories he tells.)

We know a remarkable amount about what Augustine and his family were thinking during these months thanks to a group of philosophical dialogues he wrote at the time, based on his musings with the group who joined him in his retirement. The Cassiciacum dialogues are Augustine's first surviving writings. They offer a vivid if idealized picture of his postcrisis recovery, when Augustine and his family began to make plans to return to Africa, now that he had turned his back on a future in Italy.

Augustine's dialogue *The Happy Life* records a discussion involving all the friends and family gathered at Cassiciacum, and although stylized—as befits a formal philosophical dialogue—it allows us to glimpse the warmth of the group as they think out loud together. The starting point is an homage to Cicero's *Tusculan Disputations*, which the philosopher had written after the death of his beloved only daughter, Tullia, and like its model, *The Happy Life* is, among other things, a meditation on loss. How can a person find happiness in this fallen world, where so many bitter things happen and we can never keep hold of the things we love? The mother of Adeodatus is never mentioned in the dialogue, but his contribution suggests that she was not far from Augustine's thoughts.

In trying to discover the value that the experience of disaster can have for someone who wants to acquire wisdom, Augustine begins with the metaphor of sailors charting their course across an ocean. He is interested in those who "are deceived by the utterly beguiling appearance of the sea. They have chosen to go out into its midst, and they dare to wander far from their homeland.... [W]hat else should one wish for other than for a thoroughly raging tempest, a headwind that would lead them—even as they weep and mourn—to sure and solid joys?"[43] He then turns the metaphor of the ship on the water to his own life. Obviously, he says, he had been putting off choosing between ambition and wisdom. "What else, therefore, remained than that a tempest, which is *reputed* to be adverse, should come to my aid?" He describes how "I jettisoned everything and steered my ship, battered and worn out, if you will, to the tranquility for which I longed."[44]

Toward the end of the dialogue, the group arrives at the insight that we only know true happiness when we accept that what we love in this world will not be with us forever and try to find the connection between our longing and the greater and more permanent source of Truth. Augustine is reaching toward an idea that will find expression in his later work: that the love we experience in this life is only a part of a deeper love that is more real and full. This love begins and ends with God. In the *Confessions*, he observes that only those who love in God "will never lose those who are dear to them, for they love them in one who is never lost."[45] Augustine's way of handling the reality of human loss was to try to reinvent human relationships in a new dimension, safely beyond the reach of death and time.

By the time Augustine wrote his *Confessions*, his son Adeodatus had been dead for some time. During his short life, the youth had accompanied his father in the long journey from Thagaste to Milan and back again. Augustine's early writings, penned when Adeodatus was still alive, represent him as holding his own in the heady philosophical debates of men twice his age. But the boy disappears from view after *The Teacher*, written two years later in 388, another text in which he appears prominently.

It has always been believed that Adeodatus must have died soon after the return to Africa, but the evidence is elusive. An intriguing possibility is that while Adeodatus still lived, Augustine returned to Thagaste to live as a member of the local gentry without renouncing his wealth or seeking clerical office.[46] On this reading, only after the boy's death did Augustine become involved in the kind of Christian asceticism that involved the renunciation of property. There may be more than a grain of truth in this observation. We will see below that later, as a bishop, Augustine felt strongly that people should not renounce their wealth if they had children, unless the children themselves had shown firm evidence of an ascetic vocation.

The veil of silence that Augustine draws over his son's death reflects the depth of his own grief. Many have noticed how quietly Augustine acknowledges his son's death in the *Confessions*, the only place where he mentions it at all. We hear of the loss in the midst of a layered scene—one of the most important in the book—describing his own baptism in April 387.

Augustine begins by indicating that his friend Alypius, who had been with him on the day of his conversion in a Milanese garden late the previous summer, had also enrolled himself for baptism. After praising Alypius's virtues, he adds, "We joined with us [in baptism] the boy Adeodatus, born from me in the flesh from my sin."[47]

Augustine then turns to expand upon the boy's many merits, recalling with pride his contribution, not long after the baptism, to a philosophical dialogue that Augustine later published. He addresses God: "There is a book I wrote called *The Teacher*. Adeodatus is in it, talking with me. You know that all the ideas that my dialogue partner there expresses are actually his, even though he was only sixteen.... [H]is intelligence made me tremble."[48] His next words follow so swiftly that the reader almost fails to register their meaning: "And who but You could be the maker of such wonders? Too soon you took his life away from this earth."⁴⁹ Before the reader has quite taken in that Adeodatus is dead, Augustine moves ahead. "I can remember him without worry, not fearing anything in his boyhood or adolescence or even his manhood."

Perhaps to spare himself the pain of dwelling on the loss, he turns swiftly to speak of his gratitude for the fact that they had been baptized together: "We shared our baptism with him, of the same age in Your grace, learning your system together. We were baptized, and anxiety about the past fled away."⁵⁰ Like Monnica, Augustine could only be grateful that in baptism, his beloved son had gained *salus*; the Latin word is often translated as "salvation," but it actually means "safety."

And with that, the death of the boy passes so quickly as to be almost unnoticeable. Augustine turns back to describing the baptismal liturgy, and the boy slips out of the narrative. There is no way of knowing whether Augustine was present at his death. But one feels, here, that Augustine has found in the bond of shared baptism a way to claim honest kinship with the boy. We will encounter Adeodatus one last time, at the end of Book Nine, during Augustine's account of the death of Monnica, his beloved mother.

We don't know what happened to Tacita after Augustine jilted her. I like to think that after the plan for her marriage fell through, she defied her parents and joined a community of Christian virgins. But the likelihood is that her parents found a way to absorb the insult of the broken engagement and place her with another husband, probably another man whom her father thought could be useful to the family. Of course, Maximus's invasion of Italy in 387 and the chaos of the civil war may have disrupted the family's plans for their daughter. If Tacita's family joined the mass migration of elite families away from Milan at that time, many following Valentinian and his court to the East, the broken engagement may have been forgotten in the wake of the crisis.

If she survived the birth of her children, Tacita may have lived to be fifty or older, well into the new century. One wonders whether she lived to see the Gothic invasion of Italy and the resulting sack of Rome in 410, which was the beginning of the end for the Roman Empire in western Europe. Just as the imperial court had fled Milan in 387, many aristocrats living in Italy again fled in 409 and 410, this time to Africa, where many of them had estates.[51] Tacita could well have been among them. If she did spend those difficult years in Africa, she may have encountered Augustine, who by then was bishop of one of Africa's principal ports and a sought-after advisor to many of the visiting Italian families. Augustine maintained a correspondence in later years with several women of these families. It is pleasant to imagine that one of the stiff, solicitous letters that survive from this correspondence could have been addressed to Tacita herself.

FIGURE 5. Hippo Regius, where Augustine would eventually serve as bishop for thirty-five years from 395 to 430, was a prosperous port city on the Mediterranean coast of Numidia. This second-century mosaic from the Museum of Hippo Regius (Annaba, Algeria) captures the splendor of the villas of the wealthy landowners of the region. By the time he returned to Africa, Augustine had given up his dream of joining the ranks of the super-wealthy. *Photo courtesy of the author.*

~ CHAPTER NINE ~

THE LONG WAY HOME

*So then we were baptized, and anxiety over our past
life vanished. In those days of marvelous sweetness,
I couldn't get enough of contemplating the profundity
of Your plan for the salvation of humankind.*[1]

AUGUSTINE'S ACCOUNT OF THE TIME DIRECTLY BEFORE
and after his baptism, in the spring of 387, is remarkably
tender. In the months leading up to the crisis, he had wound
himself into a terrifying pitch of distress, and now he felt boundless
gratitude and relief.

He was delighted, too, by the channels the church laid open for
expressing these new emotions. "How much I wept at Your hymns
and songs, fiercely shaken as I was by the voices of Your sweetly sono-
rous church! Those voices filled my ears, and the truth flowed into my
heart."[2] Even though he tended to be self-conscious about expressing
emotion, "a feeling of reverence bubbled up, and my tears flowed, and
it did me good to cry this way."[3] There was something in the ritual
that set him at ease.

Underneath the surface, he felt the very structure of his self-understanding beginning to shift: "You reached into the depth of my death and You emptied the abyss of my corruption from the depth of my heart. What this meant was that I stopped wanting what I wanted; now I wanted what You wanted."[4]

But even as Augustine was changing, things all around him were changing. Milan in the spring of 387 was a noticeably different place than it had been in the summer of 386. The stand-off between the child emperor Valentinian and the usurper to the north was reaching a new stage. That Maximus would invade Italy was clear; the question was when, and whether he would succeed.

During the spring and summer of 387, many of those who were in Milan for professional reasons looked for chances to move elsewhere and even to leave Italy if possible. Augustine was part of this group. Since returning to Milan in January of that year, he had been gathering a group of like-minded Africans, some of whom were baptized along with him at Easter, while others had been baptized previously. Their intention was to return to Africa: "We were looking for a place where as slaves of Yours we could be more useful; we were returning to Africa together."[5] After the long winter in Cassiciacum and Milan, Augustine and his family were headed home to make a new life. There was nothing left for them in Italy once Augustine had decided, after his change of heart, to renounce his professorship in the capital.

They had gotten as far as Ostia, the main port of Rome, in August, where they were waiting to see whether they could find passage on a boat sailing across the Mediterranean to the coast of Africa. Because of the war, this turned out to be impossible, and most of the group would return to Rome for several months before attempting the journey again. They did not return to Africa until the summer of 388.

But Monnica would not be with them. In August 387, "When we were at Ostia, at the mouth of the River Tiber,"[6] Monnica fell ill. "The day was approaching when she would depart this life, a day which You knew, and we did not."[7]

Augustine's story of her illness and death focuses on a single scene in which the two of them talk at a window together. "It happened—and surely You made this happen in your hidden way—that she and I were standing alone together, leaning on a windowsill looking out into the garden of the house where we were staying." It is a spare, evocative setting for a moment he wants to mark as set apart from the practical business of their return to Africa. "We were away from the crowds after the effort of a long journey and resting up for our voyage."[8] Augustine is marking how far they had come in their homeward journey, but he also wants to evoke, with the window and the garden, the *locus amoenus*, the "pleasant setting" where a Roman reader would expect philosophical musing to take place.

Monnica appears often in Augustine's early philosophical dialogues as an alter ego who sums up the substance of what the others are trying to say, occasionally catching his eye and asking a useful question that will help someone who is struggling to understand. At Cassiciacum, the complicity between the two is evident but understated. But at Ostia, Monnica is the center of the story. "We talked very sweetly together, just the two of us.... [W]e asked ourselves what the eternal life to come of the saints will be like, 'which neither eye has seen nor ear heard, nor has it entered into the heart of man.'"[9]

United in their musing they found themselves able to reach beyond the limits of reason and into a deeper kind of contemplation. "Our minds were drawn up by an ardent feeling toward Being itself....

[I]n it there is no past and future, but only Being, which is eternal." Augustine is conscious that in that moment, the two of them understood something of the nature of eternity, the fuller life beyond that here on earth. "And while we spoke and considered it with longing, we touched it—just barely—for a single beat of the heart."[10]

Augustine implies that he did not yet understand that his mother was dying, but Monnica herself almost certainly knew. The conversation was about coming closer to God, but it also very specifically concerned moving out of bodily existence and into direct contact with the plan of eternity. "So we said, 'If it happened to someone that the uproar of the body should go quiet, and the illusions of land and water and air'"[11]—this, they said, would be the moment when God would reveal himself. "And He himself speaks, alone, not through them but through Himself, so that we hear His word not through the tongue of flesh or through the voice of an angel or the thunder of a cloud, or the obscurity of a likeness." There is an almost unbearable excitement in the idea of experiencing directly the Being who is perceptible only indirectly by the human senses. "Instead we hear Him whom we love in these things, but we hear Him without them."[12]

Augustine remembers this moment as a vision of heaven: "If this continued, and other visions of a much lesser kind were taken away, and this single thing would ravish and swallow and bury the viewer in its inward joys, and the life without end would be like this moment of understanding."[13] As Monnica neared death, she and Augustine began to glimpse a revelation of union with God. By now the reader is ready, emotionally, for what comes next.

Now Monnica gently turns the conversation to her death. "Then she said, 'Son, as far as I am concerned, I no longer wish for anything in this life. What I have yet to do here and why I am here, I don't know; I have nothing more to hope for in this world.'"[14] Augustine does not say so, but if he is remembering the conversation as it really happened, it was Monnica herself who steered the conversation toward thoughts of eternity and the life beyond the body. "There was one reason why I wanted to linger in this life, to see you a Catholic Christian (*christianum catholicum*) before I die. My God has granted this. . . . [W]hat have I left to do here?"[15] She may well have known that in her fragile condition the long sea journey from Ostia back to Africa was impossible and, ever the mother guiding her beloved son, wanted to prepare Augustine for the likelihood that he would have to make the voyage without her.

Before the week was out, Monnica had fallen into a fever. "While she was ill, one day she lost consciousness and for a while she was taken away from us. We rushed to her side, but she swiftly came to her senses and looked at my brother and me standing next to her, and she said, in a questioning manner, 'Where was I?'"[16]

Shortly afterward, she told Augustine and Navigius to begin making plans to bury her in Ostia. "I was quiet and tried to control my tears, while my brother said something about hoping that she would complete her life in her homeland and not abroad."[17]

But Monnica would have none of it. "Having heard this she made an anxious face and fixed him with her eyes for thinking that way. Then she turned to me and said, 'Listen to what he's saying.'"[18] Augustine seems to be relishing the idea that he and his mother could still enjoy a moment of complicity, this time at Navigius's expense.

Ever practical, she turned to giving instructions about her burial. "And soon, to both of us: 'Bury this body wherever. Don't make a fuss about it. What I do want is for you to remember me at the altar of my Lord, wherever you are.'"[19] Augustine was relieved, as he knew that she had been hoping to be buried in a shared tomb with his father Patricius back in Thagaste. It seemed a minor miracle that she had relinquished her desire for her final resting place in favor of the ritual of praying for her during Mass wherever they might find themselves. Whether she was truly at peace with being buried far from her homeland or simply wanted to ease the anxiety of her sons upon her death is impossible to know. Perhaps both were true. In any case, she was not with them for much longer. "On the ninth day of her illness, when she was in the fifty-sixth year of her life and I in the thirty-third of mine, that holy and devout soul was set free from her body."[20] The next few paragraphs record the efforts of Augustine and the men around him to channel their grief into a confident expectation of the afterlife.

Despite the uplifting moments before her death, letting her go wasn't easy. "I closed her eyes, and into my heart an immense sadness flowed, which led to tears." Augustine seems to have tied himself up in knots trying to keep control of himself: "By a forceful effort from my brain my eyes held back the fountain and dried it up, but wrestling in this way put me in a terrible state."[21]

So much of Book Nine concentrates on the intimate bond between Augustine and Monnica, but the final scene shifts focus to take in the crowd of friends and family keeping vigil as she neared death. The boy Adeodatus gave outward expression to their grief, a wailing that the older men were quick to silence. "And then when she breathed her last breath, the boy Adeodatus cried out in grief; then he was hushed by us all and fell quiet. In the same way, even in me something childish was flowing into weeping, and it was hushed by a fierce voice in my heart and fell silent."[22] Yet Augustine tells us he felt it desperately. "What was it that caused me such deep inner pain, if it wasn't the recent wound, of our sweet and loving daily life together that had suddenly been torn apart?"[23]

Augustine begins to muse on his last days with his mother, grateful for her kindness in telling him, as he tended to her, how much she valued his devotion to her as a son. "In the very last part of her illness she said sweet things to me while I was caring for her; she said I was a loving son and with great affection told me that from my mouth she had never heard anything hard or contentious directed at her."[24] Yet somehow he seems to feel that their lovely last days together ought to have lessened the pain of losing her.

Augustine seems honestly puzzled by how much her death affected him. "And yet, my God who made us, what was there to compare in the respect I offered her with her slavery to me?"[25] A theme of Augustine's later writings is the idea that human loss is too powerful to bear with dignity, unless one can remember that we are connected to those we love through God, even when they are physically absent. Here, he manages to bring the pain to the surface: "My soul was wounded deeply, and my life was torn apart, because her life and mine had become one."[26]

As the chanting of psalms and the preparations for the burial of the body began, Augustine went to a place apart, to struggle with his feelings. When his friends followed him, he found himself able—just barely—to maintain his composure. "Those listening without understanding believed I did not feel the pain."[27] This performance—of command over what he felt—was of paramount importance in the culture of the Roman male, a culture that Augustine did not question, although he often strayed beyond its boundaries.

Later, however, alone with his thoughts and with God, he found an opportunity to weep freely. "And now I let the tears I had been holding back flow, so that they poured out as freely as they wanted, and my heart surrendered to them. And I took solace in them, because Your ears were listening, not those of some person insolently interpreting my weeping."[28] Although Augustine shared the view of his contemporaries that for a man to grieve openly was somehow to lose honor, he understood, at the same time, that in the sight of God it had not been wrong to confess how deeply his life had been connected to that of another one of his creatures and how painful he had found the prospect of going forward without her.

He ends his account of Monnica's death with a prayer. "My praise and my life, God of my heart, for a moment setting aside my mother's good works, for which I rejoice to thank You, I now beg You to forgive her sins." He wants God—and his readers—to know how tenaciously she clung to her faith: "No one could tear her away from Your protection; neither the lion nor the serpent could get in her way, whether by force or by tricks." Drawing on the Lord's Prayer, he asks God to forgive her as she forgave others. "I know she did works of mercy, and from her heart she forgave the debts of her debtors. You, too, forgive her any debts she incurred in all those years after her baptism." In the end, what matters is God's mercy: "May Your mercy reach beyond judgement, since Your words are true, and You promised mercy to the merciful."[29]

As Augustine wrestles with his mother's hopes and ambitions for him in the *Confessions*, we should recognize that he too had cherished hopes and ambitions for his own son. And after losing Adeodatus, Augustine had a far clearer understanding of the uncertainty and yearning his own mother had felt. But there was also a painful difference between the two stories. Monnica had given everything for Augustine, and he was able to tell himself—and to believe—that whatever the petty deceptions and betrayals of their long relationship, he had in the end been true to her as well. But he could not say the same, regrettably, where Adeodatus was concerned. The loss was far harder; it was unnatural for a father to survive his son.

Among Augustine's many losses, Monnica's death was the one on which he could most comfortably permit himself to dwell. There are a number of reasons for this. First, perhaps, for a Roman son—or a Christian—to reflect on what he owed his parents could never be wrong: the value of filial piety ran as a deep current in both traditions. Second, Augustine's intervening years as a priest and then a bishop had taught him that others might learn from his mother's story: from her fortitude in working for her son's salvation even when the prospect was at its bleakest or from her tenacity in finding a way to mediate the peculiar difficulties of her lot as a wife and mother.

In reflecting on her life, Augustine returns again and again to her virtues—as is only natural—but he tries to angle his praise so that it becomes a form of praise to God. "I won't speak of her gifts, but instead of Your gifts in her, since she didn't create herself or raise herself. It was You who made her, and neither her father nor her mother knew what she would become."[30]

Having faced so many troubles during her own marriage, Monnica had acquired an uncanny ability to smooth things over when others fell out. "Whenever she could, she interposed herself as a peacemaker between souls who were in discord and disagreement. Even when she had heard bitter comments from both sides...she never told one person what the other had said unless she thought it would help them to reconcile."[31] In trying to explain how rare this is, he cannot resist the temptation to comment on how other women took pleasure in stirring up trouble: "This might seem a small thing to me if I didn't, sadly, know countless people...who not only pass on the comments from one agitated enemy to another, but even add things that weren't said."[32]

Augustine could tell this story in detail because he could make sense of the loss. It was right and natural that a grown man should lose his parents, he knew, and he could say, in all honesty, that Monnica's life on earth had ended well. "Let her be in peace, then, with her husband, for she was married to no one before or after him."[33] Augustine's long meditation on Monnica has neglected Patricius, and now he is invoked to help Augustine's readers appreciate her devotion and dedication as a wife. But also, more importantly, Augustine now sees an ulterior motive—to win her family for Christ—visible in her every action. "She served him as a slave would, bringing fruit to You through her patience, because she won him for You as a prize."[34]

The final passage of Augustine's prayer returns to the idea that as she prayed for others during this life, so now others will pray for her. "And breathe Your spirit, my Lord, my God—breathe it into...those whom I serve with my heart and my voice and my writing, so that as many who read this will remember Your slave Monnica, with Patricius, at Your altar."[35] Almost as an afterthought, Patricius returns to the picture. As he closes, Augustine brings together the themes of God and eternity and also of human interdependence: "Through their flesh You brought me into this life—how, I don't know. Let them remember with reverent affection those who were my parents in this passing light."[36]

PART 3

∞

THE AFTERMATH

MAP 4. After five years in Italy, Augustine returned to his native Africa in 388. He would spend over thirty years as bishop of the port city of Hippo Regius on the north coast of Numidia. He lived to see the end of the Roman Empire in Africa, dying in 430 as the Vandal armies were besieging Hippo. After his death, his biographer tells us, the city was abandoned by its inhabitants and destroyed by enemy armies (Possidius, *Life of Augustine*, chap. 28). *Credit: Kate Blackmer.*

~CHAPTER TEN~

TROUBLE IN PARADISE

S OMETIME IN THE EARLY FIFTH CENTURY, THE HEIRESS
Ecdicia wrote a plangent letter to the bishop of Hippo, a bus-
tling port city on the coast of Roman Africa.[1] She had recently
experienced a dazzling religious conversion, but it had led to problems
in her marriage. Not only had her husband failed to follow her in her
spiritual ambitions, but he had staged a series of protests. Worse, he
had started an indiscreet sexual relationship with another woman, a
gesture only too clearly aimed at humiliating Ecdicia herself.

Naturally she was devastated. But what could she do? As far as
she could tell, her conduct had been blameless. She had been living
peaceably with her husband and son when she experienced her religious conversion. They were already Christian—many families had
left paganism for Christianity decades ago—but the spiritual conversion she had experienced changed her life. Someone had told her
that the most serious Christians became monks and nuns, but as a
married person she could not hope to take that path in the faith. So

213

she told her husband that she was no longer going to sleep with him and made him take a vow not to approach her for sex; this seemed the best she could do to emulate pious virgins and widows. Around the same time, she had a visit from some traveling holy men—whether they were the ones who had suggested she should stop sleeping with her husband isn't clear—and they reminded her of Jesus's saying that it is easier for a camel to pass through the eye of a needle than for a rich person to enter the Kingdom of Heaven.[2] Accordingly, she made over a large part of her personal wealth to them, so they could distribute it to the poor. Furthermore, in an effort to set herself apart from worldly women who thought only about their clothes, hair, and jewelry, she decided to adopt the sober attire worn by widows and nuns. She found it strangely satisfying to make so many changes in her lifestyle, to mark the change that had taken place in her worldview.

But her husband's reaction was not at all what she expected. At first, he supported her, even taking the vow not to sleep with her, but then he came home from a trip and discovered that she had given a large donation to the traveling holy men. Furious, he pointed out that they couldn't know whether the men would in fact use it for good works; in those days, monks often lived in informal groups and were not required to report their doings to an abbot or bishop. Now that the recipients of her largesse had moved on, there was no way to be sure they were even real men of faith rather than canny beggars or charlatans. That they had not encouraged her to wait until her husband returned was not a promising sign. Even though she had the legal right to do what she pleased with her own property, there was something predatory about their behavior.

Ecdicia's husband was so angry that he turned against her—and worse, he turned against God. Even if he now hated his wife, giving up on his vow of sexual renunciation put him in mortal danger, and she did not want him to burn in hell. So Ecdicia now faced a choice: Should she give up on him?

Sadly, her correspondent did not keep the letter. But we can reconstruct its contents from his reply, because he did keep a register with copies of his own letters. So we have at least one point of view on Ecdicia's situation. As it happens, the case would have a remarkable influence on the future of Latin Christendom, because it captured the thinking of an important early bishop on key aspects of Christian marriage. Centuries later, medieval monasteries made manuscript copies of this bishop's letters, and the divines of the medieval church studied them closely in their search for rulings on points of ethical conduct, many of which passed into canon law.

The letter to Ecdicia caught the eye of these later divines for it contained many distinctive ideas about the spiritual value of the marriage bond. It argued that marriage was not, as the Romans had always believed, simply a contract between families to organize the transmission of property. Instead, it was a spiritual fellowship that could be undertaken between individuals who had no intention of having children or even sleeping together, and it involved a vow before God that would last into eternity.

No one would have been more surprised than Ecdicia to learn that something good had come of her troubles. But in the eyes of the medieval church, her predicament was nothing less than providential; it was the grain of sand around which the pearl of the medieval Christian sacrament of marriage later grew.

Reading through modern eyes, the thing that strikes one most strongly about the bishop's letter to Ecdicia is how interested he is in her thought process and how open he is about his own. He tells her quite frankly that, not entirely believing her story, he questioned the man who had brought the letter—most letters in those days were hand-delivered by an acquaintance who happened to be traveling in the right direction—and this man produced some details about the husband's side of the story that Ecdicia had tried to bury. The bishop then tells her in detail what his mother—who had been one of those women to whom other women unburdened themselves—would have said about the situation, had she been alive to give advice. He also notes, shrewdly, that the problems between Ecdicia and her husband seem to have been caused, at least in part, by his being too eager to please her. He hazards that if she can bring herself to turn on the charm, the poor man will repent of the error of his ways before long. If Ecdicia expected the bishop to place all the blame on her husband, she will have been disappointed, but the response is not unsympathetic. The writer clearly knows women and likes them.

It should come as no surprise that the bishop to whom Ecdicia addressed her troubles was none other than Augustine, bishop of Hippo, for it is well known that a year after his mother's death in 387, Augustine returned to Africa, and within a few years he had founded a monastic community there with his old friend Alypius. It was not long before both men were consecrated as Christian bishops, influential in their lifetimes and, in Augustine's case, long afterward.

In the early 390s Augustine visited the port city of Hippo. Its bishop, Valerius, encouraged him to become a priest there and gave him permission to found a monastery in the garden next to the episcopal residence. Alypius joined him there for a few years, until he was called to become bishop of their hometown, Thagaste, in 394. When Augustine himself became bishop of Hippo the following year, he left the garden monastery but made sure to surround himself with men living a monastic life—although it was, in theory, permissible for a professed celibate to live with his own female kin.

Even Augustine's widowed sister, who lived in Hippo as the head of a community of widows and virgins, was excluded. Augustine's biographer Possidius later boasted, "No woman ever lived or stayed in Augustine's house, not even his own widowed sister, though she had long served God and lived as superior of His handmaids even to the day of her death."[3] Possidius is fierce and specific about the line Augustine took on the presence of women in his episcopal household: "He also refused his brother's daughters who were also serving God, although they were considered exceptions to this law by the councils of bishops."[4]

In Augustine's view, the problem was not the relatives themselves but the other female traffic that would be generated once there were women on site. "Augustine used to say that, even if no evil suspicion could arise from the fact that his sister and nieces lived with him, yet they could not exist without servants and other women being with them, and still others would come in from outside to visit them."[5] In their sociable world, a pyramid of service tended to follow people of means. (To us it might seem strange to think of nuns having servants, but this was common in medieval monasteries, if the nun herself was a person of standing. Families did not want to be accused of demoting their daughters too far from their original status.)

And of course, the real problem was the men: once the female entourage had breached the sanctuary, the self-control of the male celibates might begin to weaken. "Because of these [female visitors] a stumbling-block or an occasion to fall might arise for the weak."[6] It was far easier to keep women out than to ensure that the men would pass the test set by their presence. So in one sense Augustine left the company of women from this point forward. But he remained close to his sister, and his work as a Christian pastor meant that women were never far from his thoughts.

In his years as a bishop, Augustine would discover a gift for friendship with women, corresponding with a network of influential heiresses from powerful Christian families across the empire, especially in the Italian circles surrounding the court and the Senate. These women played an important role in carrying his writings to a wider readership and ultimately in ensuring the preservation of his legacy after his death.

Becoming a bishop in 395 changed Augustine's life dramatically. It meant that he could no longer spend his days with the other monks or even with the members of his episcopal household; a bishop was constantly on the move. However deep his commitment to the common life of the monastery, in the years after 395, Augustine's principal sphere of accountability was not to the community of his fellow monks or priests but rather to his city, Hippo, along with its vast hinterland. It was also to the other bishops of North Africa, whom he regularly visited both in their own cities and at Carthage. Although he continued as an ascetic, his consecration as a bishop removed him from the company of monks. His became a life of nonstop circulation—whether visiting the smaller settlements of his own see or traveling to consult with other bishops. The number of days he spent in motion annually would have been daunting enough under modern conditions but was all the more so in the heat of the Maghreb on the back of a donkey.[7]

Writing after Augustine's death in 430, Possidius sought to cast the bishop's relentless activity in his diocese and beyond as the fruit of a life firmly rooted in the common practice of what has come to be known as the "garden monastery" at Hippo.[8] But in the late 390s, Augustine himself was relating a different story. As he told it around the time of his elevation to the episcopate, his was by no means a tale of serene belonging. Rather, it was one of expulsion from various relationships where he had found human warmth and solidarity and a meditation on the frail and provisional quality of all such constellations in this life.

As a theological writer, Augustine stood out from his fellow monks as a critic of their complacency and self-importance. The late-fourth-century churches were shaken by upheaval on the question (among so many others) of whether serious Christians ought to marry, and many ascetics argued that they should not. This position challenged an ancient consensus, built up over the centuries, that only men who had managed a household successfully could be trusted to lead a community.[9]

From a traditional Roman point of view, the ascetic argument that married people lacked self-control must have seemed absurd and perhaps even unsavory. In the past, the pagan philosophers had disagreed about marriage: while Seneca advised that the wise man avoid or downplay the folly that came with love, Musonius had warned that a philosopher who did not marry might be ridiculed as unable to cope with responsibilities borne by the average man.

Augustine now found himself taking the side of the critics who thought that the monks and nuns were going overboard with their self-important enthusiasms, even though he himself had by this time become a monk. Some years later, the emperors Honorius and Theodosius II would publish a law addressing the awkward repercussions that reasoning like Jerome's could have for the married clergy. Their law stipulated that the wives of men newly ordained to the Christian priesthood "must not be separated from their husbands; surely those women who have rendered their husbands worthy for the priesthood, are suitable companions for the priests whom they have fostered."[10]

One Christian bishop, Paulinus of Nola in southern Italy, found his happy marriage the topic of debate among his friends. Around 396, Augustine himself congratulated Paulinus on the fact that his wife, Therasia, had so clearly encouraged his pursuit of Christian virtue, while at roughly the same time, the irritable Jerome warned that Therasia's company must surely be an obstacle to spiritual progress. Paulinus's later correspondence makes clear that he prized Augustine's encouragement, and in perhaps the sincerest form of flattery, he borrowed from it when giving advice himself. In a letter written shortly after 396 to a young senator and his wife, Aper and Amanda, Paulinus spoke of Amanda's chaste influence on her husband in words borrowed directly from Augustine's praise of Therasia.[11]

For civic-minded bishops such as Augustine and Paulinus, the outsized craving that was most spiritually dangerous was not lust but the love of money. Rallying a crowd around the condemnation of sexual license was easy—sensationalists such as Jerome had left no doubt about that—but it was greed that was tearing apart families and communities.

The older Augustine is widely assumed to have regarded sexual desire as excessive and dangerous. This is simply not the case. Let us look at how he posed the problem of lust in his most influential mature work, *The City of God*. Ancient writers had for millennia discussed male desire as the limit case for imagining uncontrolled self-indulgence. But Augustine set out to explain, in his discussion of grace and free will in Book Fourteen of his magnum opus, that the real problem lay not in desire itself but in the unstable quality of the human spirit. Lust was only a symptom of a deeper problem.

Sex, he argued, was certainly an area where men's inability to control their own minds and bodies was obvious. (Like most writers of his day, he often wrote about "men" with some ambiguity as to whether the term included women as well, though in this case, where sex was in play, he acknowledged that there were differences.) The most profound challenge for men, as he saw it, was not to bridle their lust but to face the humiliation of impotence. Lust required mobilization and, when summoned, might not appear, with no explanation for its absence. Astonishingly, impotence captured Augustine's imagination as a symbol of the human condition. More emphatically even than the involuntary erection, sexual failure spoke to the true state of humanity after the Fall.

The truly astounding aspect of Augustine's *The City of God* is his detailed and fascinating discussion of sexual impotence. One of the most troubling unresolved problems of ancient biology, impotence fascinated Augustine as an instance in which the imperfect yoking between the body and the will could be closely examined.

Most ancient authors who opined on the subject of impotence regarded it as an embarrassment, to be sure, but also as a relatively minor medical condition for which there were several tried-and-tested remedies. Unlike excess, impotence was certainly not a problem for which philosophers had established a tradition. Augustine, however, departed from conventional wisdom by introducing impotence as a counterexample in the philosophical discourse of excess and self-control.

Augustine pointed out that men were at the mercy of not only the strength but also the hollowness of their desires. "Sometimes, the [sexual] impulse is an unwanted intruder," he admits. But, he continued, what makes desire so disturbing is not desire itself but the fact that one can't control it. The lack of desire can be just as disturbing. "Thus strangely does lust refuse to be a servant not only to the will to procreate, but even also to the lust for lascivious indulgence; and although on the whole it is totally opposed to the mind's control, it is quite often divided against itself." Particularly disturbing was the fact that lust could speak to the mind and the body in opposite ways: "It arouses the mind but does not follow its own lead by arousing the body."[12] This was not a temporary embarrassment. Impotence pointed to the fundamental and humiliating inability of the mind to control the body, a rift deep in the psyche itself between will and desire or even within desire itself.

And male subordination to lust—for here Augustine was thinking of men, exclusively—did not only, or even primarily, involve passion-crazed transgression. It was a sign of a systemic dysfunction. "The genital organs have become as it were the private property of lust, which has brought them so completely under its sway that they have no power of movement if this passion fails." This in turn gave rise to an almost unbearable fear of failure. "It is this that arouses shame; it is this that makes us shun the eyes of beholders in embarrassment." To exhibit one's own lack of self-control is always humiliating, but in the sexual arena, the pain of exposure is unusually sharp. "A man would be less put out by a crowd of spectators watching him visiting his anger unjustly upon another man than by one person observing him when he is having lawful intercourse with his wife." All of this was a sign that the original perfection of Paradise had been lost and that humans suffered under dire punishment.

Although many commentators would have it otherwise, Augustine was adamant that the body and its desires were not to blame for the expulsion from Paradise. The original sin had nothing to do with sex: it was the sin of pride. Adam and Eve took the apple not out of gluttony or due to a series of sexual seductions—the serpent of Eve, Eve of Adam. The problem was that they had thought they might live independently of God who had created them. Sex in Paradise, Augustine believed, would have been unimaginably exquisite. Humans would have known no frustration or interruption of desire:

men would have been spared the embarrassment of impotence, women the pain of the breaking of the hymen (and later, of labor). The body was a site of punishment, but it was not the cause of the problem.

Sex was, however, where men came face-to-face with Original Sin—that is to say, with the disjunction of the human will, the fact that outside Paradise even desire could only be, irredeemably, "divided against itself." To the degree that he acknowledged sex as a central site for the human experience of this dislocation, Augustine was attempting to situate his theory of the will in terms of the ancient discourse that had linked masculine authority to sexual morality. But Augustine was not, after his ascetic conversion, himself deeply interested in sex. Instead, his mind returned again and again to the problem of human weakness. When he watched babies (most likely his own son, Adeodatus, born before he had reached the age of twenty), he saw their vulnerability to their own needs and desires, their powerlessness to control, or even to understand, the currents of volition pulsing through them. This profound human helplessness was visible in sex, but only because its signs were visible everywhere.

Augustine wants his readers to understand that not only are the preening lotharios of the Roman cities ridiculous, but so are the monks who pride themselves on how they have turned away from sex altogether. It is Monnica's old point again: it is not a person's social location or status that can tell you whether he or she has wisdom to offer.

In an age when learned monks were writing self-congratulatory treatises claiming to have found a way to rise above the urgings of the body altogether, Augustine turned the powerful weapon of his irony to suggest that such advice only showed that the writer had entirely missed the point.

Some lines below the passage on Adam and Eve mentioned above, Augustine turns his critique of ascetic triumphalism into parody. The only humans capable of exerting serene control over themselves, he suggests, are the circus artists who do tricks in the town squares: "Some can swallow an incredible number of various articles and then with a slight contraction of the diaphragm, can produce, as if out of a bag, any article they please, in perfect condition."[13] Building momentum now, he considers the street performers who blur the line between humanity and the animal kingdom. "There are others who imitate the cries of birds and beasts and the voices of any other people, reproducing them so accurately as to be quite indistinguishable from the originals, unless they are seen."[14] Finally, he escalates to the point of absurdity: "A few people produce at will such musical sounds from their behind (without any stink) that they seem to be singing in that region."[15] The scatological *chutzpah* of this argument has gone largely unremarked, but it captures something very important about his way of thinking.

In his survey of ancient attitudes toward the body, Augustine parades a solemn regiment of world philosophers—Cicero, the Platonists, the Cynics, the gymnosophists of India—only to bring before his readers the street performers of provincial North Africa. He reasons, with impeccable tabloid logic, "I know from my own experience of a man who used to sweat whenever he chose; and it is a well-known fact that some people can weep at will and shed floods of tears"[16]—but such is not the case with the flow of semen. Book Fourteen of *The City of God* may be "a story of human bondage," but it is also a remarkable satire of the pretensions of ancient men.

In the end, Bishop Augustine would make a significant contribution to the Christian theology of marriage, and the core of his contribution was built on Monnica's idea that worldly status cannot be the basis for evaluating a person's voice or worth.[17] Somehow, Augustine was starting to see, this insight had to find purchase in relations between men and women.

Fourth-century Christian preachers were beginning to address the hypocrisy of the double standard in sexual ethics and to suggest that a Christian ideal of equal standing in the sight of God ought to temper the exploitative conduct of the male householder, which Roman law had always upheld as within his right. Where did marriage fit into this landscape for a fourth-century Christian writer? Augustine's writings form part of a wider critique by Christian ascetics directed against the lay householders, who included most government officials and other men in power at the time. But his position is less self-righteous than that of some of his contemporaries. He is genuinely concerned to establish an ethical standard for the men's partnerships with women, both in and outside marriage.

In his treatise *On the Good of Marriage*, Augustine makes an unprecedented argument for an element of fair play between the sexes. The *Confessions* and *On the Good of Marriage* have traditionally been dated to the same period, the years directly after Augustine's consecration as a bishop in 395, but in fact the date of both is uncertain. Yet the two texts need not have been written at the same time for us to see what they have in common. Both develop an impulse of self-criticism and offer an implicit critique of male privilege in relations with women.

Marriage is about trust, Augustine argues—the Latin term is *fides*, often translated as "faith" or "fidelity." This means that each partner should be accountable to the other in the same way. A husband and wife enter the bond on the same terms: "They owe equal fidelity to each other."[18] So far, Augustine might not have ruffled too many Roman feathers—but only if he held back from spelling out in detail what his words actually meant.

But Augustine did not hold back: "Betrayal of this fidelity," he says, "is called adultery, when through the prompting of one's own lust, or through acceding to the lust of another, sexual intercourse takes place with another man or woman contrary to the marriage-pact."[19] With a stroke, he makes a radical departure from the Roman understanding of marital fidelity, which deemed the relationship exclusive only for the wife.

By suggesting that for a man to sleep with a woman other than his wife constitutes adultery simply because he himself is married, even if she is single, Augustine steers definitively away from the Roman legal definition of adultery as a crime that turned exclusively on the violation of a married woman's chastity. That definition was still in force at the time he was writing.

With the distinction between marriage and concubinage, Augustine will again diverge from long-established cultural lore and legal principle, the idea that marriage is defined by the father's intent to produce heirs. This was by no means a matter of ignorance. In the *Confessions*, although the account of his long relationship to the mother of his son is tantalizingly brief and elusive, Augustine makes clear that he is well aware of the difference between concubinage and marriage: he explicitly discusses "how wide a difference there is between the discipline of a marriage partnership for the sake of having children and . . . an arrangement based on lust, in which children are born *despite* the parents' intent, even if they force one to love them once they are born."[20] It is no accident that he refers here to the same criterion—the intent to have children—that is central to the Roman legal definition of marriage. Augustine was certainly aware of the importance of this distinction in Roman law. Across the centuries, the intent to conceive legitimate heirs had been the indispensable defining characteristic of the married estate—and indeed, the capacity to bequeath property to heirs was one of the defining characteristics of citizenship itself.

This makes Augustine's departure in *On the Good of Marriage* from the long-accepted terms encapsulated in the Roman legal tradition all the more remarkable. He encourages his readers to see marriage principally as a forum for cultivating the virtues, and in particular the virtue of *fides*. In framing the question of what can be called a marriage, he begins from the starting point not of begetting heirs but of lust. Is it a marriage, he asks, "when a man and a woman, neither of them married to anyone, have sex with each other"—so far, he is describing something his Roman contemporaries might recognize as a marriage, but now he makes a sharp turn—"not to have children, but merely to indulge in intercourse because they cannot control their lust[?]"[21] Next, he turns back in the direction of marriage again: "But they show fidelity to each other in that the man does not have sex with another woman, nor the woman with another man."[22]

To most of his contemporaries, the answer would be a firm and definitive no: the intent to produce legal heirs was the defining element of marriage. But Augustine pushes ahead. His only concession is a curious, backhanded compromise. "Doubtless without absurdity it can indeed be labeled a marriage (*potest quidem fortasse non absurde hoc appellari conubium*), provided that they agree to maintain the relationship until one of them dies,"[23] though birth control, which was widely practiced in the Roman period, would be a deal breaker: "provided, too, that they do not avoid having children, even if they did not cohabit for this purpose."[24]

Augustine's principal concern here seems to be understanding whether lust can give way to a more ethical bond. Yet he blurs as many questions as he addresses. From the perspective of the female partner, for example, his suggestion that such a relationship arises from lust on both sides seems unlikely. Cross-cultural evidence suggests that in strongly patriarchal societies, women's involvement in nonmarital relationships tends to be motivated by material rather than psychosexual needs. But Augustine shows little interest in the female subject position.

It is here that Augustine makes his most unprecedented move. Even in the absence of marital intent, he suggests, a marital ethos may evolve between a couple as the result of shared experience. The idea that human beings can establish a relationship on one basis and suddenly find themselves crossing an invisible line is one of several elements here that push against the legal and moral tradition Augustine inherited.

Another is the suggestion that concubinage involved a binding agreement of exclusivity. But what defined concubinage was not a contract or agreement; rather, it was its habitual quality—the sense of the female partner having been chosen for a long-term role—although without marital intent. If in some cases an agreement did exist—for example, an offer of material support for the female partner—it was not required. To be sure, the modest respectability a concubine might acquire involved a perception that she had been singled out for special treatment, and custom required that no rival be given equivalent status. But, as with marriage, there was no expectation that her male partner should avoid incidental sexual partners or reciprocate the sexual fidelity that he demanded.

In other words, the idealized vision of concubinage that Augustine puts forward here allows him to muddle the social difference between the two estates. Yet he shifts the frame in an important way. In his version of concubinage, there is a consensus between the two partners. It is not the *consensus maritalis*—the intent to produce heirs—but rather a consensus of sexual exclusivity. This view of concubinage as conferring sexual parity between the partners is perhaps overly idealistic, since concubinage by definition involved a female partner who had been judged unsuitable as a marriage partner. But he is reaching here to say that the mutual loyalty (*fides*) characteristic of marriage can also exist in at least some relationships that are not aimed at producing children.

Coming at the problem from the other direction, we have seen in his letter to Ecdicia that Augustine had broken with the legal tradition that defined marriage on the basis of the intent to produce children. The letter makes clear that, in Augustine's eyes, Ecdicia's having taken a vow of continence without consulting her husband and even the husband's taking up with another woman did not, in and of themselves, dissolve the marriage. In *On the Good of Marriage* Augustine drives the point home. When a couple remains together in a sexually exclusive relationship for life, he suggests, even though they do so "not to have children, but merely to indulge in intercourse because they cannot control their lust,"[25] the relationship should be understood as a marriage, even if not in name.

Augustine's reading here has a remarkably naive and self-involved quality. From the point of view of a low-status woman such as Una, who was being used for sex by a higher-status man, such a shadow marriage would in fact withhold from the female partner exactly the recognition, protection, and status that she might hope for as an acknowledged wife. Any concern on the mother's part that the father has refused to commit to supporting the children is waved away as insignificant.

But in his admittedly self-involved way, Augustine seems to be steering in the direction of making men more accountable. The original choice of a father (like his younger self) not to allow a legal relationship to spring up that makes him accountable for any children is not material. Rather, what is important, Augustine suggests, is that the man eventually has a moral awakening. By staying in the relationship, the male partner eventually learns that the relationship had actually been a marriage all along. The unnecessary anxiety he has caused to his sexual partner for years or even decades is waved away, perhaps not surprisingly in a society that saw low-status women as essentially disposable.

To be fair to Augustine, he almost certainly was not condoning this type of game playing; in fact, he was trying to call men to account. But his attempt to name the hypocrisy of the Roman male can only go so far. Perhaps realistically, he doesn't try to argue that men should treat low-status women as people whose well-being should be a matter of priority; in that male-dominated society, making the case that it matters at all is difficult enough.

He does, however, have some inkling of how self-serving the male partner's perspective in these cases is. The passage continues, "For if a man takes on some woman on a temporary basis (*si aliquam sibi vir ad tempus adhibuerit*), until such a time as he find another whom he can marry as his equal, worthy either of his rank or means"[26]—in this second scenario he is thinking much more realistically about social class and the power balance—"he is an adulterer at heart, not with respect to the one whom he is looking for, but toward the one with whom he has sexual intercourse without intending to marry her."[27] The fluidity here has become quite remarkable.

Indeed, Augustine has abandoned altogether the unstable line between marital intent and his idealized version of concubinage. The man who takes a concubine in the traditional way—in other words, offering her nothing except the opportunity to be exploited—has fallen into a trap. He is now expected to be sexually faithful in the way that is usually imposed only on women. Adultery is no longer defined by the involvement of a married woman; it takes place in a moral reality that has broken free from Roman law and custom altogether. It is now defined by the state of the male partner's heart.

The problem with this scenario, of course, is that it has no basis in reality. Neither the male partner nor Roman law recognizes the relation to a concubine as involving any kind of moral obligation.

When Augustine speaks in his second scenario of the man who "takes on some woman on a temporary basis, until such a time as he find another whom he can marry as his equal," he is almost certainly thinking of his own relationship with Una. In line with the custom of the time, Augustine's own arrangement was understood to be temporary (and did indeed end).

On the face of things, that relationship is not so different from the idealized *concubinatus* of which he says, "Without absurdity it can indeed be labeled a marriage."[28] But for Augustine, there is a crucial moral difference. Summarizing the intent of the male partner, he says, "He is an adulterer at heart."[29] As Augustine saw things looking back, he had engaged in the moral equivalent of adultery by living with Una while planning for a future with Tacita.

But Una had not responded in kind; she had shown a loyalty to Augustine that was characteristic of a wife. His discussion of the moral situation of the woman in this second, more despicable kind of union fits what he writes elsewhere about Una: "However, should she maintain sexual fidelity with him, and after he takes a wife she gives no thought to marriage herself and steels herself to refrain utterly from such sexual intercourse, I should not perhaps readily presume to call her an adulterer."[30]

He is not quite willing to absolve her completely from blame, however: "But would anyone claim that she does not sin when he knows that she is having intercourse with one not her husband?"[31] Yet his powers of reason are exhausted by the effort to assess the moral accountability of a person whose scope to control her situation is extremely limited. Finally, he lands with a conclusion that may well describe Una, as he understood her. "But if for her part all that she seeks from that intercourse is children, and she undergoes unwillingly such sexual activity as is not aimed at procreation, she is to be ranked higher than many matrons."[32]

Augustine's attempt to think out the situation from the woman's point of view is limited in scope, but he does capture a sense that a woman may have her own motivations and concerns. And he brings in a Monnica-like appreciation for the fact that the person with lower social status—the concubine—might be morally more admirable than her social superior, her male partner.

Augustine's thinking here is noticeably out of line with the traditional values of Roman marriage. To begin with, the idea that a married man is liable to a charge of adultery based on his own married state is a radical departure. Similarly, the idea that a man could be held responsible for treating someone who was not his wife as if they were married would have been seen as an absurdity, since the presence or absence of intent to recognize a woman as a wife was the criterion defining whether the union was a marriage or something else. By focusing on the fact that the male and female partners in the same union might have different motivations, Augustine has taken the ambiguity of marital intent as defined by the jurists to its outer limit.

The full significance of Augustine's exploration becomes visible when we remember that under Roman law, who was married and who was not was not always clear. Roman law did not require a document to prove marriage except where there were legal arrangements regarding the dowry; as a result, the Code of Justinian preserves cases from the third and fourth centuries showing that citizens who had no marriage contract were worried about whether their heirs' status was secure. (In theory, the answer was yes.) In other cases, men of property took up concubines for the sake of pleasure and later sought—retrospectively—to confer rights of heirship on the resulting children; we know this because a lost law of Constantine shows that the first Christian emperor tried to close the loophole.[33]

We are left, then, with a small but significant episode in a wider transformation. Augustine's sense that the male and female sexual partners ought to be held to the same standards—and that the female partner might experience needs and motivations different from those of the male—was a departure.

It would be centuries before Augustine's idea of marriage as a partnership between two individuals who owed each other sexual fidelity—and might or might not intend to have children—was widely accepted. In this sense he was ahead of his time. But experience had taught him that the asymmetry of Roman sexual relations had a cost. Where women of low status were concerned, to be sure, Augustine shared many of the blind spots common to the men of his day. Yet he had at least learned that the heart has its own sense of justice and that, in matters of the heart, even the best-laid plans may come undone.

EPILOGUE

BEFORE TAKING OUR LEAVE OF AUGUSTINE AND THE women of his *Confessions*, it is worth asking how things could have turned out differently. In order to understand the impact of Augustine's decision not to marry on his own future and indeed on history, we need to consider what difference it made to him and the people around him. So there is value in imagining what would have become of them all if Augustine had recognized in time what he owed Una, or if he had held his nerve and married Tacita.

We can begin with Monnica, since in that other future she might never have made her fateful visit to Ostia or have fallen ill and died there. She might still have had to say good-bye to her beloved Ambrose, however. If Augustine had married Tacita, she would in all likelihood have followed the newlyweds when he took up his next post in a new province, the next step on his path toward the hoped-for senatorial career.

Monnica might have grown old surrounded by grandchildren, dispensing her hard-worn wisdom to all and sundry. But that wisdom would never have found its way into the moral fabric of medieval Christianity, because as a married layman, her son would have become a minor Roman senator who dabbled in philosophy, not an indispensable pillar of Latin Christendom. The homespun wisdom of his mother would have been of little interest to anyone. Is this what she would have wanted, had she been given the choice? From what we know of Monnica, the answer is almost certainly no.

Even if Augustine's way of talking about Monnica's piety is sometimes cloying, he conveys her genuinely thoughtful way of looking at the world and her desire to make her mark on it. She would have loved nothing more than to know that the moral kernels at the heart of the stories she told her children—for example, the idea that seemingly important people sometimes have less to offer than others whom you might overlook—became, through her son's writings, an influential part of the Christian spiritual tradition.

For Una, it is hard to know whether Augustine's marriage to Tacita would have made a difference. History does not record whether she returned to Carthage or to Thagaste after being sent away from Milan. It is reasonable to imagine that she lived out her years on one of the properties in Augustine and Monnica's family portfolio. If she intended her parting words to Augustine as a vow never to sleep with a man other than him, she would have needed to stay close to her patron's household for economic support because there she stood the best chance of having her sexually unavailable status respected. Alternatively, she may have found that her best option was to join a nunnery.

For Tacita, marriage to Augustine would have been a mixed blessing. It is unlikely she was looking forward to it at the time of their betrothal. She almost certainly did not want to leave her family and probably tried to keep the prospect out of her mind. Still, she would have tried to make the best of things and play her part with dignity.

If the marriage had gone ahead, she would have looked for a way to make a success of it, as Monnica had done before her. Monnica herself might have been on hand to give advice, to coax her daughter-in-law into treating her husband with the kind of gentle deference that might make him want to wear his authority lightly. In the end, Augustine may have found himself following her lead, sometimes without quite noticing that she was leading. Or—if he did notice—he might have felt pleased at how well she had turned out.

For Justina, the marriage of two minor figures in the wider circle around her son Valentinian might not have been of tremendous importance had it taken place; she would have seen it as one of those welcome but minor signs that the world is rolling forward in the way that it ought to. Sometimes it is only when steady progression of these signs is disrupted that one notices them at all. But the fact that it did not happen may have been more noticeable: the kind of small sign that an alert viewer notices, as one point in a larger pattern of disruption. She may have read it as a sign that the tide was turning against her son.

And how would things have played out if Augustine had not lost his nerve? At some point in 387 or possibly 388, Tacita would have turned twelve and been able to marry. With luck, the birthday and the resulting wedding would have taken place before the invasion of Magnus Maximus in the summer of 387.

If it did not, when war came and the court left Milan, Tacita's parents would have had to make a difficult decision. Should they send their as yet unmarried daughter with Augustine and Monnica to wait out her betrothal until she could marry—or to keep her at home and accept the risk that the war might part her permanently from Augustine? Their choice would have depended on why they had been so keen on the engagement in the first place. What had made them willing to promise her to Augustine so long before she was ready to marry? Did they see something unique in him, or were they simply eager to settle her?

If they had indeed married, Augustine and Tacita might have ended up in the Eastern capital. After the death of Maximus, that was where the ambitious men were heading—at least those with no gift for commanding an army. Tacita might have become a political wife in an unfamiliar city, perhaps with a lovely villa overlooking the Bosporus. Her main business would have been to steer her husband into behaving like a man of standing—someone with a bit less fire, perhaps, and a bit more wit and grace. He would almost certainly have turned out well enough. And perhaps Augustine would have gained the series of postings in the provincial administration he hoped for, eventually capturing the longed-for appointment as governor of a province and, with it, the prize of entry into the Senate.

Though we can't be sure how, the events of 387 would have altered his prospects. The favor he had earned at court with his beautiful speech in praise of the consul Bauto would not have counted as much as he might have wanted, because Bauto died not long after the usurper Maximus, probably in 388. Perhaps he might have received help from Bishop Ambrose, if they were still in touch, or Ambrose's old pagan sparring partner, Quintus Aurelius Symmachus, who had been so useful to Augustine during his first year in Rome. But Symmachus had some troubles in the late 380s because, like many senators, he had made the mistake of backing Maximus, and this may have muted his ability to offer assistance. Still, Augustine had already come such a long way. There is no reason to think he could not have gone farther.

Augustine and Tacita would almost certainly have had children, and in that different life, Adeodatus might have grown to adulthood as the benevolent older brother of his well-born younger siblings. He might even have been something like an older brother to his stepmother, Tacita, two or three years his junior. Slowly, his African accent would have faded, to be replaced by a more cosmopolitan sound. He would have found himself slowly forgetting his childhood in Carthage. One imagines they could have got along well together, Adeodatus and his father and his little stepmother, a complicated cosmopolitan family like so many others. Whether Adeodatus would have died so young in that other life we can never know.

None of this means that there would not have been other joys and other tragedies if Augustine had held his nerve and married Tacita. But the central wound of his life, the loss of the woman he loved as a result of unthinking ambition, would have remained unhealed. Fulfilling expectations would have become a way to bury the pain.

What happened instead, of course, is that Augustine did lose his nerve, and the wound grew to become a touchstone. Whether he initially broke his engagement to become a monk, as some believe, or because he could not stomach playing the game of social advancement and only later joined a monastery, the end result is the same. Instead of having a family, Augustine dedicated himself to the ascetic life, and Una held her place as the one woman he had loved.

And instead of slowly fading, the wisdom of his mother and grandmother, the losses and lessons of his youth, the bold and heartfelt declaration of Una and the silences of Tacita would linger and grow in memory. What he learned from them would become the well of experience from which he drew during his long years as a pastor, preacher, and writer. In his writings, which became so indispensable to the later church, their voices can still be heard.

Much of what modern people take for granted has its roots in Augustine's contribution to Christianity: for example, the idea that marriage should be a trustful partnership—a *fida societas*—between two people who are equal in the sight of God and who may or may not intend to have children together.

In one of his sermons, Augustine's hero Ambrose suggested that when Adam and Eve ate of the fruit of the Tree of Knowledge, it was a "lucky mistake"—*felix culpa*—because their disobedience spurred God to send Jesus to save the world. Had they remained innocent, he suggested, something more precious than their innocence would have been lost. It was an idea Augustine returned to again and again in his own writings, and it is not hard to see why. Perhaps he felt that his own regrettable failings had led him to find a path that allowed him to contribute something to the human conversation that might otherwise have been missed. One hopes he did feel this. It is a consoling thought, and it is almost certainly true.

Before taking our leave of Augustine and his women, we should pause to imagine one last version of the future for them. It involves sending Augustine on a different path in the summer of 386, after he had discovered that he could not go through with a marriage that was so obviously about money and so clearly a betrayal of the woman who was his wife in all but name. It involves accepting the premise that his disgust with the idea of marrying Tacita was not a rejection of sex but a revelation about money and loyalty—a refusal to sell himself, a desire to live up to the implicit if unspoken promise that he now saw he had made to Una. What would have happened if, instead of withdrawing with his friends and family to the villa at Cassiciacum, Augustine had followed Una back to Africa?

If Una was now in Thagaste, the swiftest route for Augustine to follow her involved a journey of between two and three weeks, first by wagon down the Po Valley to Placentia and then across the Ligurian Apennines to Oppidum Genua (modern Genoa) on the coast. He would then have sailed along the south coast of Gaul to Massilia (Marseilles) and boarded a larger ship to make the four-day sea journey southward to Chullu on the north coast of Numidia. From there, a smaller boat eastward along the Numidian coast to Hippo Regius, and then two to three days' journey up into the highlands by donkey. If he left as soon as he decided that the marriage was off, he could have reached Thagaste by mid-September, well ahead of the olive harvest.

Perhaps this is what Una hoped for. What would it have meant for her if her powerful parting words to Augustine—that despite his betrayal she would remain loyal for the rest of her life—had worked their magic and he had followed her? Of course, we cannot know whether her words were heartfelt or an operatic gesture by someone who has lost not the love of her life but a more pragmatic hope of economic security.

But even if Una's need for Augustine was practical rather than romantic, his choice to put her ahead of the opportunities laid before him in Milan might have touched her heart. How would she have felt about him if suddenly the undertow of fear for the future—that unwelcome third partner in their relationship—were suddenly to ebb away? If he were to propose, would she want to say yes? She may have wondered this herself in the autumn of 386, imagining but not expecting that he might suddenly appear and explain that it had all been a mistake.

And what of Augustine? In this very different version of his life, Augustine returns to Thagaste and takes up the mantle of the local landowner and town councilor, like his father, Patricius, before him. It takes very little to persuade Una to take him back—properly this time. He recognizes that he had been churlish not to marry her long ago and is suitably grateful when she forgives him. Una is still young enough to want more children, and soon the two of them join forces as the captains of a small army.

Every now and then Augustine achieves something in their little world that stirs his sense that he could have made his mark on a wider stage. He manages to settle a dispute or broker a compromise in the town council, and life becomes that little bit easier for his neighbors. He is gentle with Una and the children. He avoids becoming his father. His life is a good one.

Sometimes Augustine wonders how he could have lived with himself if he hadn't found his way back to Una. On late summer evenings, sitting with her in the garden and looking out over the hills, he recognizes his own contentment. He shudders to think how close he came to losing all this. Since the time of Creation, men have been tempted to give up what they love for a hollow promise of glory; it still makes him shiver to think how close he came to falling into that trap. He pauses to give thanks that he did not, that he understood the value of what he has, here in this garden. Here is everything he loves, everything he would have lost.

Acknowledgments

Justina, Tacita, Monnica, Una, and Illa have been my constant companions for a decade, and I have got to know them well enough to recognize that they might be scandalized by my effort to unravel their secrets. I would like to record my gratitude for the traces they left of their struggles, and the lessons they have taught me about their world and about my own. It has been a privilege to spend time in their company.

And I am grateful to the friends, teachers, colleagues, and family who have offered insight and inspiration along the way. Margaret Miles first introduced me to the *Confessions*, and I will always be grateful to her and to Clarissa Atkinson for their role in kick-starting what has become an ongoing scholarly conversation about the role of women in the text. Peter Brown and Robert Markus have proved to be incomparable friends and mentors in addition to their wider role as indispensable interpreters of Augustine and his world.

To Rebecca Carter I owe thanks for the early conversations that gave the book its initial shape, and thanks are due to friends and colleagues for their thoughts on the book or its subject: Stephanie Cobb, Jen Ebbeler, Judith Evans Grubbs, Lisa Fentress, Barbara Gold, Kyle Harper, Thomas Heffernan, Erica Hermanowicz, David Hunter, Henrietta Leyser, Markus Mindrebø, Neil McLynn, Candida Moss, Tina Sessa, Kenneth Steinhauser, and Jo Sadgrove—and to Julia Hillner for countless useful and inspiring discussions over the years.

The gifts of the extraordinary George Lucas at Inkwell Management and the editorial team at Basic Books—Sarah Caro, Marissa Koors, and Claire Potter—are well known to all who have worked with them. I cannot say enough to thank them and the wonderful production staff at Basic Books, especially Shena Redmond and Jen Kelland, whose careful work and good cheer made such a difference in the final stages. Working with Kate Blackmer, mapmaker extraordinaire, has been an inspiration. I am grateful to Angela C. Davies for permission to include her marvelous photograph of the Djemila Lion Hunt mosaic.

Finally, three communities have been a source of ongoing help and inspiration. To my colleagues and students at Royal Holloway, University of London, I owe a special debt of gratitude for creating a community where talking about ideas is an unparalleled pleasure. Caroline Leavitt, Susan Lee, and Andrew Starcher kept me from veering farther off course than I did by reading parts of this work in a way that radically changed my thinking—in Susan and Andrew's case over and over again; their insights and companionship have made an incomparable difference to my spirits and to my sense that the task I had set for myself was mad, but not impossible. Lastly but most importantly, the debt I owe Conrad, Hester, and Hildelith Leyser is beyond describing—even if, or perhaps because, they are

Acknowledgments

so good at finding the weak points in what I have to say. Hildie in particular showed boundless patience reading and re-reading the manuscript, and I could not imagine a more imaginative critic or a more sparkling conversation partner. It is to her that the book is dedicated.

A Note on Sources
and Further Reading

FURTHER READING

For the reader who would like to know more about Augustine and his world, a bewildering variety of books await you. Of the biographies, the most insightful and by far the most beautifully written is Peter Brown, *Augustine of Hippo* (London: Faber & Faber, 1967). A thoughtful and pleasingly plainspoken recent treatment is Gary Wills, *Saint Augustine: A Life* (Harmondsworth, UK: Penguin, 1999). More iconoclastic, and marvelous in a very different way, is James J. O'Donnell, *Augustine: A New Biography* (New York: Ecco/HarperCollins, 2005). And future scholars will forever be grateful to Jim for giving us something we really couldn't do without: a name for "Una."

Where Augustine's women are concerned, there is less to choose from but much to celebrate. Clarissa W. Atkinson, " 'Your Servant, My Mother': The Figure of St. Monica in the Ideology of Christian Motherhood," in *Immaculate and Powerful: The Female in Sacred Image and Social Reality*, ed. Clarissa W. Atkinson, Constance H. Buchanan, and Margaret R. Miles (Boston: Beacon Press, 1985), 139–172, has been widely influential and is still well worth reading. Two articles that captured my imagination as a young scholar take similar questions about the power balance in Augustine's household and find interestingly different answers: Patricia Clark, "Women, Slaves, and the Hierarchies of Domestic Violence: The Family of St. Augustine," in *Women and Slaves in Greco-Roman Culture: Differential Equations*, ed. Sandra R. Joshel and Sheila Murnaghan (New York: Routledge, 1998), 109–129, and Brent D. Shaw, "The Family in Late Antiquity: The Experience of Augustine," *Past & Present* 115 (1987): 3–51. Kim Power's *Veiled Desire: Augustine's Writing on Women* (London: Darton, Longman & Todd, 1995) focuses more on theology than social history but contains many illuminating observations and a valuable discussion of Augustine's relationship with Una. Gillian Clark's *Monica: An Ordinary Saint* (Oxford: Oxford University Press, 2015) is well-informed and wide-ranging.

Danuta Shanzer, "Avulsa a Latere Meo: Augustine's Spare Rib— Confessions 6.15.25," *Journal of Roman Studies* 92 (2002): 157–176, is immensely learned and thought-provoking, although Shanzer's sense of Una differs widely from my own. Judith Chelius Stark, ed., *Feminist Interpretations of Augustine: Re-reading the Canon* (University Park: Pennsylvania State University Press, 2007), contains valuable studies of Augustine and women from a fascinating variety of viewpoints, among them a thoughtful study of Una by Margaret R. Miles ("Not Nameless but Unnamed: The Woman Torn from Augustine's Side," at 167–188). Finally, the late Maureen A. Tilley's "No Friendly Letters: Augustine's Correspondence with Women," in *The Cultural Turn in Late Ancient Studies: Gender, Asceticism, and Historiography*, ed. Dale B. Martin and Patricia Cox Miller (Durham, NC: Duke University Press, 2005): 40–62, considers the wide variety of women Augustine corresponded with in his years as a bishop.

A NOTE ON TRANSLATIONS

In the case of Augustine's *Confessions*, I have worked directly from O'Donnell's Latin edition (Augustine, *Confessions*, ed. James J. O'Donnell [Oxford: Clarendon Press, 1992]) and made my own translations, occasionally borrowing phrases from the many excellent English translations available. For those who want to read (or reread) the text itself, there are many possibilities. Sarah Ruden, *Augustine, Confessions: A New Translation* (New York: Modern Library, 2017), and Garry Wills, *Saint Augustine: Confessions* (New York: Penguin, 2006), both have a fresh and modern tone, while F. J. Sheed, *The Confessions of Augustine* (New York: Sheed and Ward, 1943), strikes a vintage, almost biblical note. Pleasingly clean and close to the Latin in its phrasings is Henry Chadwick, *Saint Augustine: Confessions* (Oxford: Oxford University Press, 1991). The warhorse of translations is R. S. Pine-Coffin, *Confessions* (London: Penguin, 1961), which, despite its somewhat Victorian diction, often captures the perfect phrase. For all other sources, I have cited a modern English translation, occasionally with modest revision.

TRANSLATIONS CITED

Ambrose of Milan, *Letters*: J. H. W. G. Liebeschuetz, *Ambrose of Milan: Political Letters and Speeches* (Liverpool, UK: Liverpool University Press, 2005).

Ambrose of Milan, *On Widows*: Trans. H. De Romestin in Philip A. Schaff and Henry Wace, eds., *A Select Library of the Nicene and Post-Nicene Fathers of the Christian Church*. Series 2, vol. 10 (Grand Rapids, MI: W. B. Eerdmans, 1890–1900), 389–407.

Augustine, *The City of God: Concerning the City of God Against the Pagans*, trans. Henry Bettenson and John O'Meara (London: Penguin, 1984).

Augustine, *On the Good of Marriage*: Augustine, *De bono coniugali and De sancta virginitate*, ed. and trans. P. G. Walsh (Oxford: Oxford University Press, 2001).

Augustine, *The Happy Life*: Trans. Ludwig Schopp in Augustine, *The Happy Life; Answer to Sceptics; Divine Providence and the Problem of Evil; Soliloquies*, ed. Ludwig Schopp. Fathers of the Church 5 (Washington, DC: Catholic University of America Press, 1948), 27–84.

Augustine, *Soliloquies*: Trans. Thomas F. Gilligan in Augustine, *The Happy Life; Answer to Sceptics; Divine Providence and the Problem of Evil;*

A Note on Sources and Further Reading

Soliloquies, ed. Ludwig Schopp. Fathers of the Church 5 (Washington, DC: Catholic University of America Press, 1948), 333–426.

Ausonius, *The Order of Famous Cities* 7—Milan: *Ausonius, Volume 1: Books 1–17*, ed. and trans. Hugh G. Evelyn-White. Loeb Classical Library 96 (London: Heinemann and Cambridge, MA: Harvard University Press, 1919), 272–273.

Codex Theodosianus: Clyde Pharr, *The Theodosian Code and Novels, and the Sirmondian Constitutions* (Princeton, NJ: Princeton University Press, 1952).

Gregory Nazianzen, *Panegyric on Flaccilla*: To my knowledge, no published translation exists in English. I have therefore drawn from the translations given in Kenneth G. Holum, *Theodosian Empresses: Women and Imperial Dominion in Late Antiquity* (Berkeley: University of California Press, 1989), 22–31.

Jerome, *Letter 22 to Eustochium*: Translation in *Jerome: Select Letters*, trans. F. A. Wright. Loeb Classical Library 262 (London: Heinemann 1933), 52–158.

John Chrysostom, *Homily on Ephesians 15*: I have drawn from the extracts translated in Blake Leyerle, "Sermons on City Life," in *Religions of Late Antiquity in Practice*, ed. Richard Valantasis (Princeton, NJ: Princeton University Press, 2000), 247–260.

John Chrysostom, *On Virginity*: I have drawn from the extracts translated in Joy A. Schroeder, "John Chrysostom's Critique of Spousal Violence," *Journal of Early Christian Studies* 12 (2004): 413–442.

John of Nikiû, *Chronicle*: *The Chronicle of John, Bishop of Nikiu, Translated from Zotenberg's Ethiopic Text*, trans. R. H. Charles (London: Williams & Norgate, 1916; rpt. Merchantville, NJ: Evolution Publishing, 2007), 83.

Paulinus of Milan, *Life of Ambrose*: An English translation by Sister Mary Magdeleine Muller, OSF, and Roy J. Deferrari is included in Roy J. Deferrari, ed., *Pontius, Paulinus, Possidius, St. Athanasius, St. Jerome, Ennodius, St. Hilary, et al.: Early Christian Biographies* (Washington, DC: Catholic University of America Press, 1952), 33–66.

Possidius, *Life of Augustine*: An English translation by Sister Mary Magdeleine Muller, OSF, and Roy J. Deferrari is included in Roy J. Deferrari, ed., *Pontius, Paulinus, Possidius, St. Athanasius, St. Jerome, Ennodius, St. Hilary, et al.: Early Christian Biographies* (Washington, DC: Catholic University of America Press, 1952), 69–124.

Rufinus of Aquileia: *The Church History of Rufinus of Aquileia: Books 10 and 11*, trans. P. Amidon (Oxford: Oxford University Press, 1997).

Socrates Scholasticus, *Ecclesiastical History*: Trans. A. C. Zenos in *Socrates and Sozomenus Ecclesiastical Histories*, ed. Philip Schaff and Henry Wace. A Select Library of Nicene and Post-Nicene Fathers, Series 2, vol. 2 (Oxford, UK: Parker, 1891).

Symmachus, *Third Relation*: R. H. Barrow, ed. and trans., *Prefect and Emperor: The Relationes of Symmachus* (Oxford: Clarendon Press, 1973), 34–47.

Theodoret of Cyrrhus, *Ecclesiastical History*: Trans. Blomfield Jackson in *Theodoret, Jerome, Gennadius, Rufinus: Historical Writings, Etc.*, ed. Philip Schaff and Henry Wace. Nicene and Post-Nicene Fathers, Series 2, Vol. 3 (Buffalo, NY: Christian Literature Publishing Co., 1892).

Zosimus, *New History*: *Zosimus: Historia Nova; The Decline of Rome*, trans. James J. Buchanan and Harold T. Davis (San Antonio: Trinity University Press, 1967).

Notes

CHAPTER ONE: JUSTINA

1. Ausonius, *The Order of Famous Cities*, 7—Milan, trans. Evelyn-White (revised).

2. Socrates, *Ecclesiastical History*, 14.31, trans. Zenos.

3. Socrates, *Ecclesiastical History*, 14.31, trans. Zenos.

4. Socrates, *Ecclesiastical History*, 14.31, trans. Zenos.

5. Socrates, *Ecclesiastical History*, 14.31, trans. Zenos.

6. Socrates, *Ecclesiastical History*, 14.31, trans. Zenos.

7. John of Nikiû, *Chronicle*, 82.11, trans. Charles.

8. John of Nikiû, *Chronicle*, 82.13, trans. Charles.

9. Ammianus calls it a *villa* (*History*, 30.10.4).

10. Ammianus, *History*, 29.6.7.

11. The inscription from Regium Iulium (modern Reggio di Calabria) dedicating a bath to Justina and Constantia appears in *L'Annee épigraphique* of 1913 (1914), item 227.

12. Ammianus, *History*, 30.10.5, trans. Rolfe [revised].

13. Ammianus, *History*, 30.10.5, trans. Rolfe.

14. Ammianus, *History*, 30.10.5, trans. Rolfe.

15. Rufinus of Aquileia, *Ecclesiastical History*, 11.12. A useful discussion of the sources for the episode can be found in Gavin Kelly, "The Political Crisis of AD 375–376," *Chiron* 43 (2013): 357–409, at 362.

16. J. H. W. G. Liebeschuetz, *Ambrose of Milan: Political Letters and Speeches* (Liverpool, UK: Liverpool University Press, 2005), 11.

CHAPTER TWO: TACITA

1. Augustine, *Confessions*, 6.13.23.

2. On dolls as "miniature adult bodies" that girls could practice comportment with, see Eve D'Ambra, *Roman Women* (Cambridge: Cambridge University Press, 2007), 62.

3. Fanny Dolansky, "Playing with Gender: Girls, Dolls, and Adult Ideals in the Roman World," *Classical Antiquity* 31 (2012): 256–292.

4. Rodolfo Lanciani, *Pagan and Christian Rome* (London: Macmillan, 1895), 301–305.

5. Christian Laes contrasts Pascoli's romantic vision of the young bride's death with a more bleak and perhaps historically accurate scenario: "One could also envision the bride becoming ill some weeks before the wedding, the ensuing contention between the two families due to the wedding possibly being called off, and the potential financial consequences of such a scenario, especially with regards to the wedding dowry." Christian Laes, "Close Encounters? Giovanni Pascoli's Crepereia Tryphaena (1893): Accessing Roman Childhood Through the Lens of a Romantic Neo-Latin Poem," *Classical World* 112 (2019): 335–355, at 349.

6. On the Roman wedding ceremony, see Susan Treggiari, *Roman Marriage: Iusti Coniuges from the Time of Cicero to the Time of Ulpian* (Oxford: Oxford University Press, 1991), particularly chap. 5, "*Nova Nupta* and *Novus Coniunx*," 161–180.

7. Treggiari, *Roman Marriage*, 164.

8. Arnold Van Gennep, *The Rites of Passage*, trans. Monika Vizedom and Gabrielle L. Caffee (London: Routledge & Kegan Paul, 1960), from the original French (*Les rites de passage* [Paris: Émile Nourry, 1909]).

9. Evidence for the survival of *flamines* up to the sixth century in Christian Africa is discussed in Maria Silvia Bassignano, *Il Flaminato nelle province romane dell'Africa* (Rome: Bretschneider, 1974).

10. The Projecta casket is discussed in Kathleen J. Shelton, *The Esquiline Treasure* (London: British Museum Publications, 1981), 72–75, with plates 1–11.

11. Lauren E. Caldwell, *Roman Girlhood and the Fashioning of Femininity* (Cambridge: Cambridge University Press, 2015), examines the bride's fear of her new role in chap. 5, "The Wedding and the End of Girlhood," 134–165.

12. Treggiari, *Roman Marriage*, 39–43. Still immensely valuable are M. K. Hopkins, "The Age of Roman Girls at Marriage," *Population Studies* 18 (1965): 309–327, and Brent D. Shaw, "The Age of Roman Girls at Marriage: Some Reconsiderations," *Journal of Roman Studies* 77 (1987): 28–46.

13. Sarah B. Pomeroy, *The Murder of Regilla: A Case of Domestic Violence in Antiquity* (Cambridge, MA: Harvard University Press, 2007).

14. Lanciani, *Pagan and Christian Rome*, 289–293, discusses the monuments Herodes erected to Regilla after her death on the vast tract of land she owned near the via Appia and the dedication of her jewels to the mother-and-daughter goddesses Ceres and Proserpina (Persephone).

15. An excellent translation of the *Passion of Anastasia, Chrysogonus, and Companions* is now available in Michael Lapidge, ed. and trans., *The Roman Martyrs: Introduction, Translations, and Commentary* (Oxford: Oxford University Press, 2018), 54–87.

16. Chrysostom, *On Virginity*, 52, trans. Schroeder. (I have cited Joy A. Schroeder's translation, drawn from her illuminating discussion of the passage: Joy A. Schroeder, "John Chrysostom's Critique of Spousal Violence," *Journal of Early Christian Studies* 12 [2004], 413–442.)

17. Chrysostom, *On Virginity*, 52, trans. Schroeder.

18. For an introduction and translation of the *Passion of Eugenia, Protus, and Hyacinthus*, see Lapidge, *The Roman Martyrs*, 228–249.

19. The anonymous homily by an author known only as Pseudo-Athanasius has been translated by Teresa M. Shaw, "Homily: On

Virginity," in Vincent Wimbush, ed., *Ascetic Behavior in Greco-Roman Antiquity* (Minneapolis: Fortress Press, 1990), 29–44.

20. Still fundamental is Peter Brown, *The Body and Society: Men, Women, and Sexual Renunciation in Early Christianity* (New York: Columbia University Press, 1988), esp. chap. 17, "Aula Pudoris: Ambrose," 341–365, and chap. 18, "'Learn of Me a Holy Arrogance': Jerome," 366–386.

21. Jerome, Letter 22 to Eustochium, 16, trans. Wright.

22. Jerome, Letter 22 to Eustochium, 16, trans. Wright.

23. Matthews, *Western Aristocracies*, 43, notes that, at this period, "for those willing to devote their talents and industry to the emperor's service…the court was a busy channel of social mobility." Worth attention is Matthews's discussion of the meteoric rise of Ausonius, the tutor to the young Gratian, at 51–100.

24. Augustine, *Confessions*, 6.11.19.

25. On Eudoxia, Kenneth G. Holum, "Aelia Eudoxia Augusta," in *Theodosian Empresses: Women and Imperial Dominion in Late Antiquity*, 48–78 (Berkeley: University of California Press, 1989), remains indispensable.

26. Holum, *Theodosian Empresses*, 52–53.

27. Most of what we know about Savina comes from the letter written to her by Jerome after her husband's death (Jerome, Letter 79), and from Jerome's later letter to the widow Agruchia (Jerome, Letter 123). For discussion of the milieu Savina joined in Constantinople by marrying Nebridius, see Wendy Mayer, "Constantinopolitan Women in Chrysostom's Circle," *Vigiliae Christianae* 53 (1999): 264–288, at 270–272.

28. Stewart Irwin Oost's short 1962 article on Gildo, "Count Gildo and Theodosius the Great," remains a valuable introductory overview on Gildo and his connections to the Theodosian court (*Classical Philology* 57 [1962]: 27–30).

CHAPTER THREE: MONNICA

1. On Monnica's epitaph, see now the illuminating discussion of Douglas Boin, *Ostia in Late Antiquity* (Cambridge: Cambridge University

Press, 2013), 228–231, arguing that the surviving gravestone derives from a seventh-century restoration of Monnica's grave.

2. Augustine, *Confessions*, 9.8.17.

3. Augustine, *Confessions*, 9.8.17.

4. Augustine, *Confessions*, 9.8.17.

5. Augustine, *Confessions*, 9.8.17.

6. Augustine, *Confessions*, 9.8.17.

7. Numerous names preserved on inscriptions in Roman Africa have this root: Monna, Monnina, Monnis, Monnula. See Gabriel Camps, "Qui sont les Dii Mauri?," *Antiquités Africaines* 26 (1990): 131–153, at 143.

8. Annette Gordon-Reed, *The Hemingses of Monticello: An American Family* (New York: W. W. Norton, 2008), chap. 5, "The First Monticello," 111–130.

9. Augustine, *Confessions*, 9.8.18.

10. Augustine, *Confessions*, 9.8.18.

11. Augustine, *Confessions*, 9.8.18.

12. Kyle Harper, *Slavery in the Late Roman World, AD 275–425* (Cambridge: Cambridge University Press, 2011).

13. Petronius, *Satyricon*, 119, 14–18.

14. A. H. M. Jones, *The Decline of the Ancient World* (London: Longman, 1966), 208.

15. Augustine, *Confessions*, 9.8.17.

16. Judith Evans Grubbs, *Women and the Law in the Roman Empire: A Sourcebook on Marriage, Divorce and Widowhood* (London: Routledge, 2002).

17. In late antiquity, the law of three children became less important, and guardianship of women seems to have weakened and eventually disappeared, while guardianship of minors (males and females under twenty-five) remained in force, although men aged twenty and women aged eighteen could apply for *venia aetatis*, a personally granted majority. See Antti Arjava, *Women and Law in Late Antiquity* (Oxford: Oxford University Press, 1996), 112–116.

18. Augustine, *Confessions*, 9.9.20.

19. Augustine, *Confessions*, 9.9.20.

20. Augustine, *Confessions*, 9.9.20.

21. Augustine, *Confessions*, 9.9.20.

22. John Chrysostom, *Homily on Ephesians 15*, 3, trans. Leyerle.

23. John Chrysostom, *Homily on Ephesians 15*, 3, trans. Leyerle.

24. On Canon 5 of the Council of Elvira, see Bartosz Zalewski, "If a Maidservant 'Dies a Horrible Death': Canon 5 of the Synod of Elvira," *Studia Iuridica Lublinensia* 30 (2021): 385–400.

25. Augustine, *Confessions*, 9.9.19.

26. Augustine, *Confessions*, 9.9.19.

27. Augustine, *Confessions*, 9.9.19.

28. Augustine, *Confessions*, 9.9.19.

29. Augustine, *Confessions*, 9.9.19.

30. Augustine, *Confessions*, 9.9.19.

31. Augustine, *Confessions*, 9.9.19.

CHAPTER FOUR: UNA

1. Augustine, *Confessions*, 4.2.2.

2. Augustine, *Confessions*, 6.12.22.

3. Augustine, *Confessions*, 6.15.25.

4. Augustine, *Confessions*, 6.12.22.

5. Tatjana Sandon and Luca Scalco, "More Than Mistresses, Less Than Wives: The Role of Roman Concubinae in Light of Their Funerary Monuments," *Papers of the British School at Rome* 88 (2020): 151–184.

6. Augustine, *Confessions*, 4.2.2.

7. Augustine, *Confessions*, 4.2.2.

8. Augustine, *Confessions*, 4.2.2.

9. Katharine P. D. Huemoeller, "Freedom in Marriage? Manumission for Marriage in the Roman World," *Journal of Roman Studies* 110 (2020): 123–139, discusses the inscription (*C.I.L.* 6.20905) at 126.

CHAPTER FIVE: A SON OF AFRICA

1. E. R. Dodds, *Pagan and Christian in an Age of Anxiety: Some Aspects of Religious Experience from Marcus Aurelius to Constantine* (Cambridge: Cambridge University Press, 1963).

2. Published over a half century ago but still invaluable is W. H. C. Frend, *The Donatist Church: A Movement of Protest in Roman North Africa* (Oxford, UK: Clarendon Press, 1952).

3. Augustine, *Confessions*, 1.6.7.

4. Augustine, *Confessions*, 1.6.8.

5. Augustine, *Confessions*, 1.6.8.

6. Augustine, *Confessions*, 1.6.8.

7. Augustine, *Confessions*, 1.6.8.

8. Augustine, *Confessions*, 1.7.11.

9. Augustine, *Confessions*, 1.7.11.

10. Augustine, *Confessions*, 1.9.14.

11. Augustine, *Confessions*, 1.9.15.

12. Augustine, *Confessions*, 1.9.15.

13. Augustine, *Confessions*, 1.17.27.

14. Augustine, *Confessions*, 1.17.27.

15. Augustine, *Confessions*, 1.17.27.

16. Augustine, *Confessions*, 1.13.21.

17. Augustine, *Confessions*, 1.11.17.

18. Augustine, *Confessions*, 2.1.1.

19. Augustine, *Confessions*, 2.2.2.

20. Augustine, *Confessions*, 2.2.2.

21. Augustine, *Confessions*, 2.3.5.

22. Augustine, *Confessions*, 2.3.6.

23. Augustine, *Confessions*, 2.3.6.

24. Augustine, *Confessions*, 2.3.7.

25. Augustine, *Confessions*, 2.2.4.

26. Augustine, *Confessions*, 2.3.8.

27. Augustine, *Confessions*, 2.3.8.

28. Augustine, *Confessions*, 2.2.4.

29. Augustine, *Confessions*, 3.3.6.

30. Augustine, *Confessions*, 2.3.7.

31. Augustine, *Confessions*, 2.3.7.

32. Augustine, *Confessions*, 2.4.9.

33. Augustine, *Confessions*, 2.4.9.

34. Augustine, *Confessions*, 2.6.12.

35. Augustine, *Confessions*, 2.5.11.

36. Augustine, *Confessions*, 2.5.11.

37. Augustine, *Confessions*, 2.5.11.

38. Augustine, *Confessions*, 2.8.16.

39. Augustine, *Confessions*, 2.8.16.

40. Augustine, *Confessions*, 2.9.17.

41. Augustine, *Confessions*, 3.4.7.

42. Augustine, *Confessions*, 3.4.7.

43. Augustine, *Confessions*, 3.4.7.

44. Augustine, *Confessions*, 3.4.7.

45. Augustine, *Confessions*, 3.4.7.

46. Augustine, *Confessions*, 3.5.9.

47. Augustine, *Confessions*, 3.5.9.

48. Augustine, *Confessions*, 3.11.19.

49. Augustine, *Confessions*, 3.11.19.

50. Augustine, *Confessions*, 3.11.19.

51. Augustine, *Confessions*, 3.11.19.

52. Augustine, *Confessions*, 3.11.20.

53. Augustine, *Confessions*, 3.11.20.

54. Augustine, *Confessions*, 3.11.20.

55. Augustine, *Confessions*, 3.12.21.

56. Augustine, *Confessions*, 3.12.21.

57. Augustine, *Confessions*, 5.9.17.

58. Augustine, *Confessions*, 5.9.17.

59. Augustine, *Confessions*, 4.4.7.

60. Augustine, *Confessions*, 4.4.7.

61. Augustine, *Confessions*, 4.4.8.

62. Augustine, *Confessions*, 4.4.8.

63. Augustine, *Confessions*, 4.4.8.

64. Augustine, *Confessions*, 4.4.9.

65. Augustine, *Confessions*, 4.4.9.

66. Augustine, *Confessions*, 4.4.9.

67. Jason David BeDuhn, "Augustine Accused: Megalius, Manichaeism, and the Inception of the *Confessions*," *Journal of Early Christian Studies* 17 (2009): 85–124, at 99.

68. Augustine, *Confessions*, 5.8.15.

69. Augustine, *Confessions*, 5.8.15.

70. Augustine, *Confessions*, 5.8.15.

71. Augustine, *Confessions*, 5.8.15.

72. Augustine, *Confessions*, 5.8.15.

73. Augustine, *Confessions*, 5.8.14.

74. Augustine, *Confessions*, 2.3.7.

CHAPTER SIX: THE EMPRESS AND THE BISHOP

1. On populist rhetoric in fourth-century Christianity, see Kate Cooper, "Constantine the Populist," *Journal of Early Christian Studies* 27 (2019): 241–270.

2. Much remains to be done to develop a nonbiased analysis of the theological developments of the fourth century. Two invaluable studies, which between them introduce the crucial issues—though they don't always agree with one another—are David M. Gwynn, *The Eusebians: The Polemic of Athanasius of Alexandria and the Construction of the "Arian" Controversy* (Oxford: Oxford University Press, 2006), and Carlos R. Galvão-Sobrinho, *Doctrine and Power: Theological Controversy and Christian Leadership in the Later Roman Empire* (Berkeley: University of California Press, 2013). Still immensely valuable is R. P. C. Hanson, *The Search for the Christian Doctrine of God: The Arian Controversy, 318–381 A.D.* (Edinburgh: T & T Clark, 1988).

3. On Probus, see John Matthews, *Western Aristocracies and Imperial Court, AD 365–425* (Oxford, UK: Clarendon Press, 1975), 195–196.

4. An early version of the story appears in Rufinus of Aquileia, *Ecclesiastical History*, 11.11, written in 402 or 403; it was later taken up by Ambrose's biographer Paulinus of Milan (*Life of Ambrose*, 3.6).

5. Paulinus of Milan, *Life of Ambrose*, 3.6.

6. Paulinus of Milan, *Life of Ambrose*, 2.4.

7. On the politics surrounding the writing of Ambrose's *De fide*, see Neil B. McLynn, *Ambrose of Milan: Church and Culture in a Christian Capital* (Berkeley: University of California Press, 1994), 102–119.

8. Belinda Washington, "The Roles of Imperial Women in the Later Roman Empire (AD 306–455)" (PhD diss., University of Edinburgh, 2015), 117–118, offers a useful assessment of the conflicting sources on Justina's whereabouts in these years.

9. Ambrose, *On Widows*, 44, trans. De Romestin.

10. For discussion of the social logic behind early Christian misogyny, see Kate Cooper, *Band of Angels: The Forgotten World of Early Christian Women* (New York: Overlook Press), 33–36.

11. On the events leading up to the Battle of Hadrianople, see Matthews, *Western Aristocracies*, 88–93, along with the insightful discussion in Peter J. Heather, "Refugees and the Roman Empire," *Journal of Refugee Studies* 30 (2017): 220–242.

12. Brian Croke, "Reinventing Constantinople: Theodosius I's Imprint on the Imperial City," chap. 12 in *From the Tetrarchs to the Theodosians: Later Roman History and Culture, 284–450 CE*, ed. Scott McGill, Cristiana Sogno, and Edward Jay Watts (Cambridge: Cambridge University Press, 2010), 241–264.

13. On Gregory's funerary oration for Flaccilla, see Kenneth G. Holum, *Theodosian Empresses: Women and Imperial Dominion in Late Antiquity* (Berkeley: University of California Press, 1989), 22–31.

14. Gregory Nazianzen, *Panegyric on Flaccilla*, trans. Holum.

15. Theodoret of Cyrrhus, *Ecclesiastical History*, 5.18.2–3, trans. Jackson (revised).

16. Gregory Nazianzen, *Panegyric on Flaccilla*, trans. Holum.

17. On the death and burial of Constantia, see Meaghan McEvoy, "Constantia: The Last Constantinian," *Antichthon* 50 (2016): 154–179, at 167–169.

18. A valuable collection edited by Brian Croke and Jill Harries has gathered the primary source material for the controversies between pagan and Christian senators and imperial officials over religious policy in the later fourth century, with useful introductions: Brian Croke and Jill

Harries, *Religious Conflict in Fourth-Century Rome: A Documentary Study* (Sydney: Sydney University Press, 1982).

19. On Gratian's repudiation of the robe of the *pontifex maximus*, see Alan Cameron, "Gratian's Repudiation of the Pontifical Robe," *Journal of Roman Studies* 58 (1968): 96–102.

20. For an overview of Theodosius's religious legislation, see Stephen Mitchell, *A History of the Later Roman Empire, AD 284–641*, 2nd ed. (Oxford, UK: Blackwell, 2015), 265–267.

21. David M. Gwynn, *The Eusebians*, traces how the Nicene party established a misleading and rhetorically effective characterization of their opponents.

22. McLynn, *Ambrose of Milan*, 63–69, explores the working relationship between Ambrose and Symmachus, arguing that a family relationship is unlikely.

23. For a useful introduction to the Altar of Victory controversy, see Matthews, *Western Aristocracies*, 205–209; Alan Cameron, *The Last Pagans of Rome* (Oxford: Oxford University Press, 2011), offers an illuminating discussion of the "cultural politics" of the controversy.

24. Symmachus, *Third Relation*, 4, trans. Barrow.

25. Symmachus, *Third Relation*, 6, trans. Barrow.

26. Symmachus, *Third Relation*, 10, trans. Barrow.

27. Symmachus, *Third Relation*, 10, trans. Barrow (revised).

28. Ambrose, Letter 72 to Valentinian. Translations of Ambrose's letters relating to this conflict, with useful introductions and notes, can be found in J. H. W. G. Liebeschuetz, *Ambrose of Milan: Political Letters and Speeches* (Liverpool, UK: Liverpool University Press, 2005), 61–94.

29. Augustine, *Confessions*, 5.13.23.

30. A persuasive argument that it was only in the second half of the fourth century that emperors began to attend public liturgies rather than private services held in the palace is put forward by Neil McLynn, "The Transformation of Imperial Churchgoing in the Fourth Century," in *Approaching Late Antiquity: The Transformation from Early to Late Empire*, ed. Simon Swain and Mark Edwards (Oxford: Oxford University Press,

2006), 235–270. On the political value of imperial liturgies in Theodosius's Constantinople, see Croke, "Reinventing Constantinople."

31. For an illuminating construction of Ambrose's program of church building during his episcopacy, see Richard Krautheimer, *Three Christian Capitals: Topography and Politics* (Berkeley: University of California Press, 1983), 77–81.

32. Here I follow the dating of the most recent sustained study: Michael Stuart Williams, *The Politics of Heresy in Ambrose of Milan: Community and Consensus in Late-Antique Christianity* (Cambridge: Cambridge University Press, 2017), 226–228. Building on the arguments of Timothy D. Barnes, "Ambrose and the Basilicas of Milan in 385 and 386: The Primary Documents and Their Implications," *Zeitschrift für antikes Christentum* 4 (2000): 282–299, Williams makes a persuasive case for two flash points in the controversy, at successive Easters (first in 385 and then in 386). Augustine, whose *Confessions* (9.7.15) is one of the earliest sources for the conflict, refers to his mother's involvement in the standoff of 386 but leaves it open whether it was the second of two incidents. An insightful and detailed overview arguing a different reading (assigning the majority of evidence to a single crisis in 386) can be found in McLynn, *Ambrose of Milan*, chap. 4, "Persecution," 158–219. A useful collection of the principal sources for the conflict can be found in Liebeschuetz, *Ambrose of Milan: Political Letters and Speeches*.

33. On the date of San Lorenzo, see Krautheimer, *Three Christian Capitals*, 81–86, and W. Eugene Kleinbauer, "Toward a Dating of San Lorenzo in Milan: Masonry and Building Methods of Milanese Roman and Early Christian Architecture," *Arte Lombarda* 13 (1968): 1–22, at 12. However, some recent studies favor a later date in the early fifth century for the building in its present form, so the identification must remain a hypothesis; see Elisabetta Neri, Roberto Bugini, and Silvia Gazzoli, "Marble Wall Decorations from the Imperial Mausoleum (4th C.) and the Basilica of San Lorenzo (5th C.) in Milan: An Update on Colored Marbles in Late Antique Milan," in *ASMOSIA XI: Proceedings of the Eleventh International Conference of ASMOSIA, Split, 18–22 May 2015*, ed. Daniela Matetić Poljak and Katja Marasović (Split, Croatia: University of Split, 2018), 79–88, at 82.

34. This is the ninth-century bishop Benzo of Alba; see Neri, Bugini, and Gazzoli, "Marble Wall Decorations," 82.

35. Krautheimer, *Three Christian Capitals*, 82.

36. The date of Letter 76 to Marcellina is disputed; here I follow Williams's suggestion that it describes a first phase of the crisis in 385. For a useful overview of the dispute over the letter's date, arguing that it describes a first conflict, at Easter of 385, followed a year later by a second crisis at Easter of 386, see Williams, *The Politics of Heresy*, 226–235.

37. Ambrose, Letter 76.1, trans. Liebeschuetz.

38. Ambrose, Letter 76.2, trans. Liebeschuetz.

39. Ambrose, Letter 76.2, trans. Liebeschuetz (revised).

40. Ambrose, Letter 76.3, trans. Liebeschuetz.

41. Ambrose, Letter 76.3, trans. Liebeschuetz.

42. Kleinbauer, "Toward a Dating of San Lorenzo," 8n12.

43. Ambrose, Letter 76.5, trans. Liebeschuetz.

44. Ambrose, Letter 76.6, trans. Liebeschuetz.

45. Ambrose, Letter 76.7, trans. Liebeschuetz.

46. Ambrose, Letter 76.8, trans. Liebeschuetz.

47. Ambrose, Letter 76.8, trans. Liebeschuetz.

48. Ambrose, Letter 76.8, trans. Liebeschuetz (revised).

49. Ambrose, Letter 76.9, trans. Liebeschuetz.

50. Ambrose, Letter 76.13.

51. Ambrose, Letter 76.17, trans. Liebeschuetz.

52. Ambrose, Letter 76.18, trans. Liebeschuetz.

53. Ambrose, Letter 76.18, trans. Liebeschuetz.

54. Ambrose, Letter 76.18, trans. Liebeschuetz.

55. Ambrose, Letter 76.3.

56. On the letter from Maximus to Valentinian preserved in the *Collectio Avellana*, a sixth-century collection of letters and legal documents related to the relationship between the emperors and the bishops of Rome, see Barnes, "Ambrose and the Basilicas of Milan in 385 and 386," 296–298.

57. For analysis of Symmachus's effort to rehabilitate himself after the death of Maximus, see Matthews, *Western Aristocracies*, 228.

58. On Ambrose's second embassy to Maximus, see Matthews, *Western Aristocracies*, 180; on the burial of Gratian, see McEvoy, "Constantia," 170.

59. Williams, *The Politics of Heresy*, 239–243.

60. Ambrose accused Justina and her entourage of being followers of the Arian heresy, but this was untrue; they subscribed to the Council of Rimini, which was the benchmark of orthodoxy under Constantius (d. 361); after Constantius's death, neither the Creed of Nicaea nor that of Rimini had gained a consensus, and legally each had the imprimatur of both church and state. See Williams, *The Politics of Heresy*, 221.

61. In Letter 75a.21, Ambrose insinuates that Auxentius of Durostorum had originally been named Mercurinus but adopted the name of Ambrose's predecessor, Auxentius, in order to claim the mantle of the earlier bishop.

62. Alessandro Portelli, "The Death of Luigi Trastulli: Memory and the Event," in *The Death of Luigi Trastulli and Other Stories: Form and Meaning in Oral History* (Albany: State University of New York Press, 1991), 1–26.

63. Augustine, *Confessions*, 9.7.15.

64. Augustine, *Confessions*, 9.7.15.

65. For discussion, see Cooper, "Constantine the Populist," 248, with Bart Bonikowski and Noam Gidron, "The Populist Style in American Politics: Presidential Campaign Rhetoric, 1952–1996," *Social Forces* 94 (2016): 1593–1621.

66. Augustine, *Confessions*, 9.7.15. There is some ambiguity here, but there is reason to think that he has the episode of 386 in mind, since he refers to it as taking place a little more than a year before Monnica's death in August 387.

67. Augustine, *Confessions*, 9.7.16.

68. On Theodosius in the Rhineland in the summer of 384, see Matthews, *Western Aristocracies*, 178, with discussion of evidence from Themistius, *Oration* 18; however, Barnes argues that the expedition did not in fact take place ("Ambrose and the Basilicas of Milan in 385 and 386," 295–296).

69. Zosimus, *New History*, 4.44.

70. Donald G. Dutton and Arthur P. Aron, "Some Evidence for Heightened Sexual Attraction Under Conditions of High Anxiety," *Journal of Personality and Social Psychology* 30 (1974): 510–517.

71. Zosimus, *New History*, 4.45.

72. Zosimus, *New History*, 4.46.

73. Sozomen, *Ecclesiastical History*, 7.14.

74. On Theodosius's entry to Rome, see Matthews, *Western Aristocracies*, 228.

75. Accounts of Valentinian's death are found in Rufinus, Sozomen, and Zosimus. For discussion, see Matthews, *Western Aristocracies*, 238–239.

76. Hagith Sivan, *Galla Placidia: The Last Roman Empress* (Oxford: Oxford University Press, 2011).

CHAPTER SEVEN: THE HEIRESS

1. Augustine, *Confessions*, 9.7.15.

2. Augustine, *Confessions*, 5.15.23.

3. Augustine, *Confessions*, 6.10.1.

4. Oddly, this detail has come down to us not because Augustine treasured the memory but because it established an alibi for him when he was accused of being somewhere else. Years later, Augustine's enemies suggested that he had first left Africa under criminal charges in 386 when the Manichaeans were persecuted by the proconsul Messianus, but Augustine replied (*Against Petillian*, 3.25.30) that the fact that he was already in Italy in 385 was a matter of public record since he had given the panegyric to the new consul Flavius Bauto in January of that year. (I owe this observation to Jason David BeDuhn, "Augustine Accused: Megalius, Manichaeism, and the Inception of the *Confessions*," *Journal of Early Christian Studies* 17 [2009]: 85–124, at 99.)

5. Augustine, *Confessions*, 2.3.5.

6. Possidius, *Life of Augustine*, 1.1.

7. Olympiodoros on dowries: *Fragment* 41.2, with discussion in Edward J. Watts, *The Final Pagan Generation: Rome's Unexpected Path to Christianity* (Berkeley: University of California Press, 2015), 95.

8. Augustine, *Confessions*, 6.13.23.

9. Augustine, *Confessions*, 2.3.8.

10. Augustine, *Confessions*, 2.3.8.

11. Augustine, *Confessions*, 2.3.8.

12. Augustine, *Confessions*, 5.23.

13. Augustine, *Confessions*, 6.1.1.

14. Augustine, *Confessions*, 6.2.2.

15. Augustine, *Confessions*, 6.2.2.

16. Augustine, *Confessions*, 6.1.1.

17. Augustine, *Confessions*, 6.2.2.

18. Augustine, *Confessions*, 5.13.23; "man of God": 2 Kings 1:9.

19. Augustine, *Confessions*, 6.3.3.

20. Augustine, *Confessions*, 6.3.3.

21. Augustine, *Confessions*, 6.3.3.

22. Augustine, *Confessions*, 6.3.3.

23. Augustine, *Confessions*, 6.3.3.

24. Augustine, *Confessions*, 6.3.3.

25. Augustine, *Confessions*, 6.3.4.

26. Augustine, *Confessions*, 6.3.4.

27. Augustine, *Confessions*, 6.3.4.

28. Augustine, *Confessions*, 6.4.5.

29. Augustine, *Confessions*, 6.4.6.

30. Augustine, *Confessions*, 6.5.7.

31. Augustine, *Confessions*, 6.5.8.

32. Augustine, *Confessions*, 6.6.9.

33. Augustine, *Confessions*, 6.6.9.

34. Augustine, *Confessions*, 6.6.9.

35. Augustine, *Confessions*, 6.6.9.

36. Augustine, *Confessions*, 6.6.9.

37. Augustine, *Confessions*, 6.11.19.

38. Augustine, *Confessions*, 6.11.19.

39. Augustine, *Confessions*, 6.11.19.

40. Augustine, *Confessions*, 6.11.19.

41. Augustine, *Confessions*, 6.12.21.

42. Augustine, *Confessions*, 6.12.22.
43. Augustine, *Confessions*, 6.12.22.
44. Augustine, *Confessions*, 6.13.23.
45. Augustine, *Confessions*, 6.15.25.
46. Augustine, *Confessions*, 6.15.25.

CHAPTER EIGHT: REMEDY FOR A BROKEN HEART

1. Augustine, *Confessions*, 6.15.25.
2. Augustine, *Confessions*, 6.15.25.
3. Augustine, *Confessions*, 8.6.13.
4. Augustine, *Confessions*, 8.6.13.
5. Augustine, *Confessions*, 8.6.14.
6. Augustine, *Confessions*, 8.6.14.
7. Augustine, *Confessions*, 8.6.14.
8. Matthew 18:16 and 21.
9. Augustine, *Confessions*, 8.6.15.
10. Augustine, *Confessions*, 8.6.15.
11. Augustine, *Confessions*, 8.6.15.
12. Augustine, *Confessions*, 8.6.15.
13. Augustine, *Confessions*, 8.6.15.
14. Augustine, *Confessions*, 8.7.16.
15. Augustine, *Confessions*, 8.7.16.
16. Augustine, *Confessions*, 8.7.18.
17. Augustine, *Confessions*, 8.7.18.
18. Augustine, *Confessions*, 8.7.18.
19. Augustine, *Confessions*, 8.8.19.
20. Augustine, *Confessions*, 8.8.19.
21. Augustine, *Confessions*, 8.11.25.
22. Augustine, *Confessions*, 8.11.25.
23. Augustine, *Confessions*, 8.11.25.
24. Augustine, *Confessions*, 8.11.25.
25. Augustine, *Confessions*, 8.12.28.
26. Augustine, *Confessions*, 8.12.28.

27. Augustine, *Confessions*, 8.12.28.

28. Augustine, *Confessions*, 8.12.28.

29. Augustine, *Confessions*, 8.12.28.

30. Augustine, *Confessions*, 8.12.28.

31. Romans 13:13–14; Augustine, *Confessions*, 8.12.28.

32. Augustine, *Confessions*, 8.12.28.

33. Augustine, *Confessions*, 8.12.30.

34. Augustine, *Confessions*, 8.12.30. He is quoting here from the New Testament: Ephesians 3:20.

35. Augustine, *The Happy Life*, 1.4, trans. Schopp.

36. Augustine, *Soliloquies*, 1.10.17, trans. Gilligan.

37. Augustine, *Soliloquies*, 1.10.17, trans. Gilligan.

38. Jason David BeDuhn, "Augustine Accused: Megalius, Manichaeism, and the Inception of the *Confessions*," *Journal of Early Christian Studies* 17 (2009): 85–124, at 99.

39. Augustine, *Confessions*, 6.14.24.

40. Augustine, *Confessions*, 6.14.24.

41. Augustine, *Confessions*, 6.14.24.

42. Catherine Conybeare, *The Irrational Augustine* (Oxford: Oxford University Press, 2006), argues (at pp. 64–69) that Monnica's role in Augustine's dialogues is very like Diotima's in Plato's *Symposium*, and for this reason we can know very little about her actual role at the time. Conybeare's argument builds on a view of male appropriation of femininity developed by David M. Halperin, "Why Is Diotima a Woman? Platonic Eros and the Figuration of Gender," in *Before Sexuality: The Construction of Erotic Experience in the Ancient Greek World*, ed. Froma I. Zeitlin, John J. Winkler, and David M. Halperin (Princeton, NJ: Princeton University Press, 1990), 257–308.

43. Augustine, *The Happy Life*, 1.2, trans. Schopp.

44. Augustine, *The Happy Life*, 1.4, trans. Schopp.

45. Augustine, *Confessions*, 4.9.14.

46. James J. O'Donnell, *Augustine: A New Biography* (New York: Ecco/HarperCollins, 2005), 11.

47. Augustine, *Confessions*, 9.6.14.

48. Augustine, *Confessions*, 9.6.14.

49. Augustine, *Confessions*, 9.6.14.

50. Augustine, *Confessions*, 9.6.14.

51. Peter Brown, *Through the Eye of a Needle: Wealth, the Fall of Rome, and the Making of Christianity in the West, 350–550 AD* (Princeton, NJ: Princeton University Press, 2012), 359–360.

CHAPTER NINE: THE LONG WAY HOME

1. Augustine, *Confessions*, 9.7.15.

2. Augustine, *Confessions*, 9.7.15.

3. Augustine, *Confessions*, 9.7.15.

4. Augustine, *Confessions*, 9.1.1.

5. Augustine, *Confessions*, 9.8.17.

6. Augustine, *Confessions*, 9.8.17.

7. Augustine, *Confessions*, 9.10.23.

8. Augustine, *Confessions*, 9.10.23.

9. 1 Corinthians 2:9; Augustine, *Confessions*, 9.10.23.

10. Augustine, *Confessions*, 9.10.24.

11. Augustine, *Confessions*, 9.10.25.

12. Augustine, *Confessions*, 9.10.25.

13. Augustine, *Confessions*, 9.10.25.

14. Augustine, *Confessions*, 9.10.26.

15. Augustine, *Confessions*, 9.10.26.

16. Augustine, *Confessions*, 9.11.27.

17. Augustine, *Confessions*, 9.11.27.

18. Augustine, *Confessions*, 9.11.27.

19. Augustine, *Confessions*, 9.11.27.

20. Augustine, *Confessions*, 9.11.28.

21. Augustine, *Confessions*, 9.12.29.

22. Augustine, *Confessions*, 9.12.29.

23. Augustine, *Confessions*, 9.12.30.

24. Augustine, *Confessions*, 9.12.30.

25. Augustine, *Confessions*, 9.12.30.

26. Augustine, *Confessions*, 9.12.30.
27. Augustine, *Confessions*, 9.12.31.
28. Augustine, *Confessions*, 9.12.33.
29. Augustine, *Confessions*, 9.13.35.
30. Augustine, *Confessions*, 9.8.17.
31. Augustine, *Confessions*, 9.9.21.
32. Augustine, *Confessions*, 9.9.21.
33. Augustine, *Confessions*, 9.13.37.
34. Augustine, *Confessions*, 9.13.37.
35. Augustine, *Confessions*, 9.13.37.
36. Augustine, *Confessions*, 9.13.37.

CHAPTER TEN: TROUBLE IN PARADISE

1. The letter itself is lost, but Augustine's reply survives as his Letter 262 to Ecdicia.

2. Matthew 19:24.

3. Possidius, *Life of Augustine*, 26, trans. Muller and Deferrari.

4. Possidius, *Life of Augustine*, 26, trans. Muller and Deferrari.

5. Possidius, *Life of Augustine*, 26, trans. Muller and Deferrari (revised).

6. Possidius, *Life of Augustine*, 26, trans. Muller and Deferrari (revised).

7. Othmar Perler, *Les voyages de Saint Augustin* (Paris: Études Augustiniennes, 1969).

8. Possidius, *Life of Augustine*, 5.

9. Kate Cooper, "Closely Watched Households: Visibility, Exposure, and Private Power in the Roman *Domus*," *Past & Present* 197 (2007): 3–33.

10. Codex Theodosianus 16.2.44, Honorius and Theodosius to Palladius, Praetorian Prefect, May 8, 420, English translation in Clyde Pharr, *The Theodosian Code and Novels, and the Sirmondian Constitutions* (Princeton, NJ: Princeton University Press, 1952), 448.

11. Paulinus of Nola, Letter 44.3.

12. Augustine, *The City of God*, Book 14.6, trans. Bettenson. The discussion here develops an argument first made in Kate Cooper and Conrad

Leyser, "The Gender of Grace: Impotence, Servitude and Manliness in the Fifth-Century West," *Gender & History* 12 (2000): 536–551.

13. Augustine, *The City of God*, Book 14.24, trans. Bettenson.

14. Augustine, *The City of God*, Book 14.24, trans. Bettenson.

15. Augustine, *The City of God*, Book 14.24, trans. Bettenson.

16. Augustine, *The City of God*, Book 14.24, trans. Bettenson.

17. On Monnica's role in Augustine's search for the voice of God, see Janet Martin Soskice, "Monica's Tears: Augustine on Words and Speech," *New Blackfriars* 83 (2002): 448–458. An earlier version of the discussion here appears in Kate Cooper, "A Predator and a Gentleman: Augustine, Autobiography, and the Ethics of Christian Marriage," in Kate Cooper and Jamie Wood, eds., *Social Control in Late Antiquity: The Violence of Small Worlds* (Cambridge: Cambridge University Press, 2020), 76–101.

18. Augustine, *On the Good of Marriage*, 4.4, trans. Walsh.

19. Augustine, *On the Good of Marriage*, 4.4, trans. Walsh.

20. Augustine, *Confessions*, 4.2.2.

21. Augustine, *On the Good of Marriage*, 5.5, trans. Walsh.

22. Augustine, *On the Good of Marriage*, 5.5, trans. Walsh.

23. Augustine, *On the Good of Marriage*, 5.5, trans. Walsh.

24. Augustine, *On the Good of Marriage*, 5.5, trans. Walsh.

25. Augustine, *On the Good of Marriage*, 5.5, trans. Walsh.

26. Augustine, *On the Good of Marriage*, 5.5, trans. Walsh (revised).

27. Augustine, *On the Good of Marriage*, 5.5, trans. Walsh (revised).

28. Augustine, *On the Good of Marriage*, 5.5, trans. Walsh.

29. Augustine, *On the Good of Marriage*, 5.5, trans. Walsh.

30. Augustine, *On the Good of Marriage*, 5.5, trans. Walsh.

31. Augustine, *On the Good of Marriage*, 5.5, trans. Walsh.

32. Augustine, *On the Good of Marriage*, 5.5, trans. Walsh.

33. Judith Evans Grubbs, *Law and Family in Late Antiquity: the Emperor Constantine's Marriage Legislation* (Oxford: Oxford University Press, 1994), 298.

Index

Index

Augustine, Bishop of Hippo—and
women *(continued)*
imagined futures of the four
women in his life, 235–242
writings on, 7, 11–12
See also Justina; Monnica of
Thagaste; Tacita; Una
Augustus (emperor), 135
Aurelius Ambrosius. *See* Ambrose
(bishop of Milan)
Ausonius (poet), description of
Milan, 21
Auxentius (bishop), 128–129, 149

babies and infants, 37–38, 39
baptism
of Augustine, 108, 194, 197, 198,
201
in Christianity, 104, 105
barbarian invasions, 5, 6, 132
barbary lions and leopards, 67–68
Basilica Martyrum, 124
Basilica Nova, 124, 143
Basilica Portiana
as center of conflict in Easter of
385, 141, 144–145, 146, 148
description, 124, 144
Basilica Vetus, in events of conflict,
124, 144, 145, 146–147
baths (public), 24, 109
Baths of Hercules, 21
Bauto, Flavius, 54, 161, 238
beauty in Roman Empire, 9, 26, 44
betrothal
vs. marriage, 22
and sending away of Una, 47–48,
177–180
Tacita to Augustine, 9, 11, 35, 37,
56–57, 236

Bible, 171–172
bishop, Augustine as, 216, 218–219
Bishop of Hippo. *See* Augustine,
Bishop of Hippo
bishops (Christian), 21, 126–127, 130
boys, training in schools, 106–107
bride(s)
and casket of Projecta, 44–45
marriage consent, 42, 51–53,
56, 71
and mothers-in-law, 46–47
in Roman Empire, 41, 42–44,
45–46
Tacita as, 176, 190
bureaucracy, 68, 69
Byzantium, 132
See also Constantinople

Carthage
education of Augustine, 113–114
Manichaeans as enemy of the
state, 120–121, 192–193
Monnica with Augustine in,
115–116
casket of Projecta, 44–45
Cassiciacum, philosophical
commune at, 193–196
Cassiciacum dialogues, 195
Castulus (priest), 144–145
Cerealis (brother of Justina), 23, 28
ceremonial speech of January 385 by
Augustine, 158, 161
children
as babies and infants, 37–38, 39
born out of wedlock, 86
custody issues, 93–94
and fatherhood, 90–91, 94
importance in Roman
Empire, 26

278

Index

Index

Index

Index

Theodosius, Flavius (Spanish general)
  Constantinople and imperial Christianity, 132–133, 139–140
  as emperor, 30–31, 132
  in Italy and Rome, 154
  and Justina, 33–34, 152–155
  marriage with Galla, 153–154
  and Maximus, 33, 152
  and pagans, 136
  and rebels in Numidia, 102
Theodosius II, 219
Theodosius the Younger (Theodosius the Great; AD 347–395), 102, 120
Therasia (wife of Paulinus), 220
Third Relation, 137–138
Trier (Rhineland/Gaul)
  Gratian in, 26–27, 31
  Maximus in, 31–32, 33
  Severa and Justina, 24
  Valentinian II and Justina, 30
Trinitarian controversy, 17, 130
  See also conflict Ambrose-Justina
Tusculan Disputations (Cicero), 195

una, meaning of, 81
Una (concubine and mother of Augustine's son)
  and Adeodatus, 82, 160, 181
  brokering of relationship, 110–111
  concubinage viewed by Bishop of Hippo, 231–232
  consequences of breakup, 163, 179–180, 236
  description and life of, 10, 81, 83, 85, 89
  and future of Augustine, 161, 163
  imagined future, 236, 240–242

  love of Augustine for, 81–82, 87, 88, 163, 175
  marriage, 11, 176
  in Milan, 160, 163, 177
  name, 81
  overview in *Confessions*, 8, 10–11, 81
  own views in relationship, 81, 85, 88–89, 96
  pain of separation for Augustine, 10–11, 179, 180, 181
  in relationship with Augustine, 82–83, 84–85, 86–89, 98
  return of Augustine to, 189–190, 240–242
  sending away by Augustine, 47–48, 177–180
  and sex, 97–98
  as slave or freedwoman, 82, 83, 84, 85, 89, 97–98, 178

Valens, 28, 30, 132
Valentinian I (AD 321–375)
  appeal of Justina and claim on, 23, 24–26
  campaign against Quadi, 26, 128
  death, 18, 28
  as emperor, 24, 25–26
  as husband of Justina, 18, 23, 25, 26
Valentinian II (AD 375–392)
  actions against pagans, 137–139
  armies, 33
  authority of church vs. emperor's, 141, 147, 148, 149
  birth, 26
  as co-emperor, 28–29, 30, 128
  death, 155
  Easter celebrations in 385, 142–148

289

Index

Valentinian II *(continued)*
  invasion of Italy by Maximus,
    152, 153, 154, 202
  Maximus's move on, 31–33
  protection and safety of, 19,
    33–34, 139, 152, 154
Valentinian III, 155
Valerius (bishop), 216
Varro (antiquarian), 41
veil in marriage (*flammeum*), 43
Venus (goddess), 44
Verecundus (friend of Augustine),
  194
Victor (count), 31, 32
Victory's altar in Rome, 135,
  137–138, 139
Virgil's *Aeneid*, 107, 122

wedding. *See* marriage in Roman
  Empire
Western Empire, 8, 21, 22
wheatfields and grain, 68
widows, 53, 56, 132
women
  in baths, 24
  Christian rhetoric on, 21
  as enemies, 132, 147
  free and enslaved women, 72–73
  law and rights for, 70–71, 76–77
  and lust, 228
  and male privilege, 225, 226, 230,
    232
  in marriage ritual, 42, 43

  and new bishop in Sirmium, 131
  as pawns for men, 11–12, 55, 90,
    225
  refusal of marriage, 42, 51–53,
    56, 71
  social mobility, 9, 54–56, 88
  and sons, 12
  traces of their lives, 3, 4–5, 7, 59
  undermining of male
    righteousness, 147
  virginity vs. marriage, 52–53, 71
  virtue, 46, 134
  as wet nurses, 37–38
women and Augustine
  in bishop's role, 216, 217–218
  in communal life, 194, 217
  four women in his life (as group),
    4, 5, 6, 7–8, 11–12
  imagined futures of the four
    women in his life, 235–242
  writings on, 7, 11–12
  See also Justina; Monnica of
    Thagaste; Tacita; Una
women of imperial family
  death and burial, 28
  and dolls for girls, 39
  life and travels, 16, 27
  treatment of, 18, 21
  virtues of, 133–134
worth of person and status (birth or
  social), 66, 79, 223, 224–225

Zosimus (historian), 152, 153

290

HESTER LEYSER

Kate Cooper is professor of history at Royal Holloway, University of London. She writes for many publications, including the *Times of London*, the *Guardian*, and *History Today*. Her books include *Band of Angels*, *The Fall of the Roman Household*, and *The Virgin and the Bride*. She and her husband have two grown daughters, who have taught them most of what they know about bold and spirited women. They live in Buckinghamshire with the magnificent Niko, a border collie.